Dear Mart
Thanks fo
and prayers. May
God bless you always.
Your friend
Ira Lane

THE GOSPEL!

A layperson's guide to Christ-centered living for the end times

by Ira M. Lane, Jr.

Christian Education Forum, Publisher
Nashville, Tennessee

ISBN: 0-966-2647-0-3
Library of Congress Catalog Number: 98-92390
Printed in the United States of America

Christian Education Forum
938 Downey Drive
Nashville, Tennessee 37205
(615) 352-0267

Dedication

I dedicate this book to . . .

JESUS CHRIST who made our salvation possible by shedding His blood and dying on the cross for our sins;

the memories and ministries of Christian servants like John and Charles Wesley, John Calvin, Dwight L. Moody, and currently Billy Graham, who have spread the Gospel around the world in the past;

all the ministers, teachers, and workers who have enabled me to learn about Jesus Christ and accept Him as my Lord and Savior.

Acknowledgments

I thank God for the patience and love shown me by my wife, Jan, my son and his wife, and my daughter and grandson. The several years of research and writing time during these last few months caused me to spend less time with my family.

I am grateful to an immense number of people for their evangelism and teaching, including Billy Graham, Charles Stanley, Adrian Rogers, and many others who have written Christ-exalting books. Dr. David Cooper from Bible Research Society and my pastor, Dr. Carrier, have influenced me greatly.

I wish to thank Evelyn C. Walker from Administrative Services of Tennessee for her patience in typing all the copy. I thank my prayer partners who have read the manuscript and offered suggested changes. This included four ministers, a school administrator, lay leaders, students of God's Word, and young college students.

Thanks to Joseph (Joe) S. Johnson, Jr., longtime author and editor, for his editorial counsel and expertise.

I am profoundly appreciative to the Board of the Christian Education Forum for letting the Foundation finance this work.

Most of all, I thank God for calling me to write this book. It has challenged me, giving me a far deeper understanding of God—His grace, love, righteousness, mercy, power and sovereignty.

The Gospel!

The Gospel! by Ira M. Lane, Jr., is a compelling, powerful book. It is an exhaustive treatment of major Christian doctrines. In this era of moral and spiritual declension it is a laser beam of light, right, and truth. I wish it were possible for every layperson and clergyman to read and study this book, along with a copy of The Book, the Bible, God's inspired Scriptures.

In my career as an editor, author, and editorial consultant, I have had the privilege of being the editor for authors like President Jimmy Carter, astronaut Jim Irwin, and numerous personalities in religion , entertainment, sports, and politics. I have never encountered a book that glorifies and magnifies Jesus Christ more—and I have now read over 25,000 manuscripts and thousands of published books in my half-century as a minister and professional writer. As I read the manuscript and offered my consultation, I must confess that the book caused me to study God's Word more deeply and to intensify my walk with our Lord and Savior. Although Mr. Lane refers to it as "a layperson's guide," it would also benefit ministers, church-staff persons, professors, collegians, and seminarians.

We are living in an era when sticky, sweet, "feel-good" religion predominates. Lane runs the entire gamut of the Gospel, the Good News of Jesus Christ, accentuating not only the positives but also the necessary negatives. In depth, he deals with grace, love, joy and heaven—but also with the opposite side of the coin, which includes holiness, righteousness, condemnation, judgment, hell, the end times, and the fate of those who reject God's offer of redeeming love. No doubt many non-Christians who read the book will accept Christ. *The Gospel!* gives evidence of Lane's deep commitment to the Lord and His lengthy labor of loving research. Read it with an open mind. If you are a believer, it will buoy your faith and cause you to rejoice more than ever over God's saving grace. If you are not a Christian, it will make you wish you were . . . and you may well trust Christ.

You're probably tired of hype, but this evaluation frankly is . . . *The Gospel!* truth.

In Christ,
Joe Johnson
Author-Editor-Editorial Consultant
Editor of Inspirational/Trade Books, Broadman Press (Retired)

Preface

You may ask, "What qualifies Ira Lane to write a book entitled *The Gospel!*?" Admittedly, I am not a "professional" theologian or pastor, but I have ardently explored God's Word, the Bible, since I opened my life to Christ fifty-four years ago. Like billions in the last two millennia, Jesus Christ, the living Word, and the Bible, the written Word, have transformed me.

In my thorough investigation of Christian literature I have discovered that the majority of books on doctrine (I hesitate to use the scholarly-sounding term, "theology) are geared to clergy, professors, collegians, and seminarians. So, God laid on my heart the vision of writing a book that will deal with a cross-section of Christian doctrines. Although I believe the book will also appeal to ministers, church-staff persons, and college and/or seminary professors and students, its main purpose is hopefully to provide "a layperson's guide to Christ-centered living for the end times."

My modus operandi (there, I've used a high-sounding term) is to make this guidebook available to help its readers "grow in grace and knowledge of our Lord and Savior Jesus Christ" (2 Peter 3:18). In extended seasons of meditation, prayer, and digging into God's Word I have prepared *The Gospel!* My desire is to share God's spiritual truths in a manner that will edify and encourage believers in Christ.

In spite of our nation's multi-culturalism, polls indicate that over 95 percent of the populace believe in the existence of God. However, it seems that genuine knowledge of biblical truth is perhaps at its lowest point in our century . . . and the majority of Americans face the pivotal year 2000 with scant knowledge of what the Bible actually teaches. My goal is to spur followers of Christ into a deeper life with God—first, with a renewed interest in the Scriptures. From that base believers may move forward spiritually "unto the measure of the stature of the fulness of Christ" (see Ephesians 4:13, KJV).

Then, fortified with the Word believers will become more Christ-centered and Christ-like. As they do the Church will become the salt and light for which that Body was founded and exists (see Matthew 5:13-14). Living by the precepts and foundation truths of the Word, Christians will experience individual and corporate revival that will result in intensified evangelism. It is my prayer that non-Christians, who are seeking the truth, will avail themselves of this book—and allow Christ to reveal Himself to them. They will discover that He, the living, incarnate Word, is "the way, and the truth, and the life" (see John 14:6, KJV).

May *The Gospel!* prepare believers for life here and hereafter. It may well assist churches, Christian schools, and families in challenging the young, interested minds of our generation. I fervently believe that Jesus will snatch away His followers in the "rapture" soon. The signs of the times point in that direction. Further, I fondly hope that non-believers will search this book, along with a Bible, and accept Jesus Christ as Savior and Lord.

—Ira M. Lane, Jr., Nashville

Introduction

In August 1977, my family and I rented a beach house in Daytona Beach for vacation. All of my family was out on the beach as I was sitting on the porch. Suddenly, the radio announced the death of Elvis Presley. The announcer reported that people all over the world were crying as millions were marching in the streets and mourning. I remember remarking to myself, *How wonderful for Elvis to have touched the lives of so many people.*

An inner feeling asked my spirit, "Why don't you write a book about God's spiritual truths to help believers grow in Christ." My immediate response was, "I'm certainly not qualified to do that." Yet, that calling or feeling remained with me without a letup. Within a couple of years I began avidly reading books, especially God's Word, researching and assembling spiritual material. I rationalized by musing to myself, *God just wants me to learn the Bible.*

In August 1993, I retired as a business executive and soon after I asked God to become **absolute Lord of my life.** Only then did I realize that God really wanted me to write a book that would assist believers in their spiritual journeys. It has proved difficult and expensive, yet it has been tremendously fulfilling for me.

I grew up in a Christian home and accepted Christ as my Savior at age fifteen. After college and then becoming an executive in business, I drifted away from God for awhile and had ups and downs in my fellowship with Him. Yet, I never lost my love for God, and He never left me without His love.

The God we read about in the Bible is alive and active, loving and forgiving. I had accepted Jesus as Savior but was not allowing Him to be Lord of my life. I had His Spirit in my life, but I quenched the power of the Holy Spirit. For me the Holy Spirit was *resident* but not *president*. He was *residing* but not *presiding*. I still wanted to run my life—in the words of one of Elvis's songs—*My Way*. When I surrendered myself totally to God, He began to give supernatural confirmation of His will for my life.

During the research for this book, I learned plenty about walking by faith. I discovered that God does not call us to service without spiritually gifting us to fulfill the assignments He sets before us. Growth in the Lord comes after hours of Bible study and prayer, fellowship with believers, and obedient service to God. A flashlight is a lifesaver when the power goes off, and the house is plunged into darkness. That flashlight illuminates the scene. I hope and pray that this book can become a flashlight—if only a penlight—on God's truths and encourage the reader to in-depth Bible study.

The rights to this book have been donated to the Christian Education Forum—a non-profit foundation. I will receive no pay for sales of this book but hope to receive spiritual satisfaction from helping others understand *The Gospel!* of Jesus Christ. Certain books are designed merely to entertain and perhaps to help one think. My prayer for this book is: it will help you get to know God better. To really get to know a person, we must learn about his/her character and interests.

Through *The Gospel!* may you study God's truths and experience a more profound fellowship with Him. May this offering serve to proffer both information and invitation. Trusting His Word, living by faith, standing on God's promises are essentially the same realities for us today as they were in the Old and New testaments. God has promised: "My grace shall be yours to *pardon* you, and My *power* shall be yours to *protect* you, and My *wisdom* shall be yours to *direct* you, and My *goodness* shall be yours to *relieve* you, and My *mercy* shall be yours to *supply* you, and My *glory* shall be yours to *crown* you."

God willed this book and motivated it. He will direct its use to His glory and honor.

Contents

Part I

CHRIST'S MESSAGES TO US

Born to poverty and loss,
Destined to hang upon a cross,
To borrow a boat, share a home,
Left to weep and pray alone.
Forsaken by friends, by a kiss betrayed,
A fish supplied the tax He paid;
Glad to fill a lowly place,
Ordained to die in deep disgrace.
Was it for this that Jesus came,
Forsaking Heaven, wealth, and fame?
Or was His coming prophesied?
Was it for others that He died?
Ah, yes! For dying He was born,
Suffered the cross and cruel thorn;
Conquered death, hell, and the grave,
Our most unworthy souls to save.
From eternity past the plan was laid;
No accident this, no error made;
But love, forsaking all, came down.
To take our sins and give a crown.
In eons past God planned it all
Because of Adam's awful fall;
Love sought the sinner, lost, forlorn . . .
To save the dying He was born.

—Author Unknown

Jesus Christ, the Lord and Savior, assures His followers, "And surely I am with you always, to the very end of the age" (Matthew 28:20). The apostle Paul declared that the gifts and fruit of the Spirit were set in the church "for the perfecting of the saints, for the work of the ministry, for the edifying of the body of Christ: till we all come in the unity of the faith, and of the knowledge of the Son of God, unto a perfect man, unto the measure of the stature of the fullness of Christ" (Ephesians 4:12-13).

The Twenty-third Psalm

Lord is my shepherd; I shall not want.
He maketh me to lie down in green pastures;
He leadeth me beside the still waters.
He restoreth my soul;
He leadeth me in the paths of righteousness
for His name's sake.
Yea, though I walk through the valley
of the shadow of death, I will fear no evil:
for Thou art with me;
Thy rod and Thy staff they comfort me.
Thou preparest a table before me
in the presence of mine enemies;
Thou anointest my head with oil; My cup runneth over,
Surely goodness and mercy shall
follow me all the days of my life:
And I will dwell in the house of the Lord forever.

1
Christ's Ministry

For God so loved the world, that he gave his only begotten Son, that whosoever believeth in him should not perish, but have everlasting life. For God sent not his Son into the world to condemn the world; but that the world through him might be saved. He that believeth on him is not condemned: but he that believeth not is condemned already, because he hath not believed in the name of the only begotten Son of God (John 3:16-18, KJV).

Jesus Christ traveled throughout Palestine to fulfill His purpose for entering the world. "I am come that they might have life, and that they might have it more abundantly," He explained (John 10:10, KJV), pointing out, "For the Son of man is come to seek and to save that which was lost" (Luke 19:10, KJV). He identified Himself with the people He purposed to save. He even called them "friends" and "brethren," though He is the God-man, "Emmanuel," meaning "God with us" (see Matthew 1:23, KJV).

Jesus Christ is for all classes and cultures

Years ago Bruce Barton penned a best-seller, *The Man Nobody Knows*. That title is only partially true. We humans, even in eternity, will never be able to fathom all there is about Jesus. Yet, by His grace we can have a personal relationship with Him. When He launched His ministry at age thirty, He was well aware of the classes of people He would encounter as He preached, taught, performed miracles, and mingled with the motley crowds.

Even as today, there were class distinctions in Palestine and discrimination based on social standing and race. The Sadducees belonged chiefly to the upper wealthy classes. The Pharisees and scribes (sometimes called "lawyers," for they were copyists of scrolls and "legal" interpreters) comprised what we would call the middle class, and also included many from the so-called "upper crust." The lower classes and the country folk were separated by a chasm between them and the wealthy. However, many of those simple people attached themselves by admiration to the Pharisees.

Down below all of those was a subculture of drifters who had lost all connection with religion and well-ordered social life—the publicans (tax collectors), prostitutes, and other "sinners" for whose souls most people, either rich or poor, did not care. Such were the pitiable, tragic features of the society Jesus was about to influence profoundly. The upper classes devoted themselves to selfishness, courtiership, and skepticism; teachers and chief professors of religion were submerged in mere shows of rites and liturgies, boasting that they were the favorites of God.

Christ invited all classes into the kingdom: the rich by showing, as in the parable of the rich man and Lazarus (Luke 16:19-31), the vanity and danger of seeking blessedness in wealth; and the poor by imbuing in them a sense of their dignity. He persuaded them with *agapé* (God's love) and positive words that the only genuine wealth is in character, assuring them that if they would put God's kingdom first, their Heavenly Father would not allow them to want (see Matthew 6:33).

The fame of His name

Almost immediately His name was echoing throughout the province. He was the subject of conversation in every boat on the lake, in every marketplace, and every dwelling in the region. The people's hearts and minds were stirred with ecstatic excitement, and almost everyone desired to see Him. Crowds began to gather, multiplying to thousands and tens of thousands. The throngs, often called "the press" in the *King James Version*, followed Him wherever He went. The news spread far and wide beyond Galilee. Hosts poured in from Jerusalem, Judea, Perea, and even from Idumea in the far south and Tyre and Sidon in the far north. Sometimes He could not remain in a town, because the multitudes blocked the streets and trampled one another.

He often led them out to the fields, deserts, and waterways. The country was stirred from end to end, and Galilee was ablaze with excitement over Him. How did He generate such a burgeoning and widespread movement? It was not by declaring Himself the Messiah. That assuredly would have caused every Jewish heart to beat in wild anticipation. But although Jesus now and then—as at Nazareth—revealed Himself, in general He rather concealed His true character. Perhaps the reason was that among the excitable crowds of rough Galilee, with their grossly materialistic hopes, the declaration would have stirred a revolutionary uprising against the Roman government.

The only perfect person in history

Jesus lived by the highest ethical and moral standards. Of course, it seems that most, even His apostles, were not onto the fact of His Deity and sinlessness. "For we do not have a high priest who is unable to sympathize with our weaknesses, but we have one who has been tempted in every way, just as we are—yet was without sin (Hebrews 4:15). He had compassion on people (see Matthew 9:35-38) and taught as no other man had ever done (see John 7:46). The masses loved Him, but the religious and political leaders were jealous of Him and determined to snuff Him out.

Christ did not set up an office in the Temple and wait for people to approach Him for counseling. Instead, He went to them—to the habitats of the most notorious sinners, to the areas where He would most likely encounter the handicapped, the sick, the needy, and the outcasts of society. He demonstrated that one's presence in a deprived place is more powerful than a dozen sermons. Being there is our witness.

Jesus' method of conveying God's truth

Jesus was successful in preaching and teaching because He spoke in parables. A parable is a short story or narrative drawn from life or nature by which an important lesson is taught or a moral precept is drawn. His scenarios were from nature or everyday experiences. His parables are known for their clarity, purity, chasteness, intelligibility, and simplicity. Young and old like to hear a story. Storytelling is one of the most eminent means of piquing interest, securing attention, and putting across vital truths. By connecting His teaching to the scenes of life, experience, or nature, He grabbed their attention and stirred their hearts. Each parable was designed to teach one overriding, pivotal truth.

Jesus recognized that the Pharisees—with all their synagogues and Temple going and their scrupulous keeping of the minutiae of their law—were inwardly lovers of money and were living for prestige and possessions and not for the praise of God. He related a story about a rich man who suddenly became poor, and a poor man who instantly became rich.

"There was a rich man," Jesus noted, "who dressed in purple robes, like a king, and lived in a splendid house. Many servants waited on him, and he feasted every day on the most sumptuous foods. Every morning outside the door of the rich man's house was laid a poor beggar named Lazarus, who was covered with sores. The poor man was only too happy to eat the crumbs and broken pieces from the rich man's table. The dogs of the street used to come and lick the sores.

"After a time, the poor man died, and his soul was carried by the angels to be in heaven with Abraham, the father of the Hebrews. Doubtlessly, in all of his poverty, Lazarus had lived for God, trying always to do His will. The rich man died, too, and was buried. But no angels transported him to the land where Abraham was living in happiness. His soul was consigned to a place of woe, sorrow, and suffering; not because of his riches, but because in his riches he had never thought of God.

"The rich man, being in torment, looked up, and far away saw Abraham, with Lazarus in his arms.'O Father Abraham,' he called out, 'take pity on me, and send Lazarus to dip the tip of his finger in water and cool my tongue, for I am burning in this flame!' 'My son,' answered Abraham, 'Remember that when you were alive on the earth, you had all your enjoyment, while Lazarus in his life had poverty and pain. Now

Lazarus has comfort for all his trouble, and you are in misery. Besides all that, between us in heaven and you in the dwelling place of the wicked, there is a mammoth cavern, a gulf which no one can cross, either to go from us to you or to come from you to us.' 'If that be so,' begged the once-rich man, now poor, 'and Lazarus cannot come to me, I beg of you, Father Abraham, send Lazarus to my father's house, for I have five brothers. Let him speak to them in time, so they may not come to this place of terrible suffering.'

"'They have the writings of Moses and the words of all the prophets,' answered Abraham; 'let them listen to these.' 'But, Father Abraham,' he pled. 'if someone from the dead should go to them, they would turn from sin to God.' 'If they will not listen to Moses and the prophets,' Abraham concluded, 'they will not believe, even if someone should rise from the dead.'"

As the twelve apostles of Jesus heard this plaintive story, they requested, "Lord, make our faith stronger!" "If you had faith like a grain of mustard seed," said Jesus, "you could say to this mulberry tree, 'be uprooted and planted in the sea,' and it would obey you. Which one of you, if he had a servant plowing in the field or tending sheep, when he comes in from the field will say to him, 'Come at once and take your place at the table for your supper'? No, he will say to his servant, 'Get my supper ready; then make yourself ready to wait on me while I am eating and drinking; and after that you may have your supper.' "Does a master thank his servant for doing what he has been told? Well, it is the same with you; when you have done all that you have been told, say, 'We are only servants; we have done no more than we ought to have done.'"

Jesus' forceful lessons taught through parables

- Good and evil in life and judgment
- Value of the Gospel
- Salvation through Him
- The visible church of Christ
- Truths—new and old
- Building a good foundation
- The love of the Father
- His love for children
- The value of lost sheep

The qualities of Christ's lifestyle:

• **Authority**—The people were astonished at His doctrine for He taught them as one having authority and not as the scribes who nitpicked on such matters as correct postures for prayers, proper length of a fast, distance one could walk on the Sabbath, etc. Jesus taught justice, mercy, love, and God's qualities.

• **Boldness**—"Lo, he speaketh boldly" (John 7:26, KJV). He displayed His boldness chiefly in attacking the abuses and twisted ideas of the time.

• **Power—**Christ was filled with the Spirit without measure. The Holy Spirit descended on Him at His baptism and empowered Him throughout His ministry. "As soon as Jesus was baptized, he went up out of the water. At that moment heaven was opened, and he saw the Spirit of God descending like a dove and lighting on him" (Matthew 3:16). He has all power in heaven and on earth (see Matthew 28:18).

• **Graciousness—**He reflected a glow of grace and love in all He did. The scribes and Pharisees were hard, proud, and loveless. To Jesus every soul was precious. He spoke to His hearers of every class with the same respect. Some of Christ's most concentrated teachings were to His disciples.

Unlikely prospects for apostleship

Christ in picking His apostles did not choose the learned "doctors" of the Sanhedrin or the self-righteous religious teachers. The Master selected "diamonds in the rough" to proclaim the truths that would revolutionize the world. He chose the most unlikely candidates for apostleship who were considered "dumb and dumber" by the religious leaders (see Acts 4:13). Yet, He would train and educate them as the leaders of the church, His body. They, in turn, were to disciple (evangelize, teach, and train) others and send them out with the Gospel message.

The twelve chosen were: Simon called Peter; Simon's brother Andrew; James, the son of Zebedee, and his brother John; Phillip; Bartholomew; Thomas; Matthew, the tax collector; James, the son of Alphaeus; Thaddeus; Simon the Zealot; and Judas Iscariot, who betrayed

Christ. After Christ's ascension, the apostles picked Matthias to replace Judas Iscariot as the twelfth apostle.

Christ, upon leaving earth for heaven, sent the Holy Spirit to remind them of all He had taught them and to empower them for service. For three-and-a-half years the apostles were under the instruction of the greatest teacher the world has ever known. He revealed the mysteries of the kingdom of God; He unfolded the truths of salvation to those whose hearts were receptive to accept Him.

"And he ordained twelve, that they should be with him, and that he might send them forth to preach" (Mark 3:14; see also 15-20). This group became the first who worked to organize the church that would carry out their Lord's "Great Commission" on earth (see Matthew 28:18-20). Before His ascension from the Mount of Olives He promised them, "But you will receive power when the Holy Spirit comes on you; and you will be my witnesses in Jerusalem, and in all Judea and Samaria, and to the ends of the earth" (Acts 1:8). They would become His bellwethers who would set the pace for the evangelization of the world. Every Christian is to follow in their footsteps.

The 'Good News' for all mankind

During Christ's early ministry He began to break down the partition wall between Jews and Gentiles and to preach salvation to all mankind. God unfolded the truth that "the Gentiles should be fellow heirs" with the Jews and "partakers of His promise in Christ by the gospel" (Ephesians 2:14; 3:6). Christ anticipated that His followers would suffer persecution, be ejected from the synagogues, and be thrown into prison. According to historians all of the apostles but John (who died of old age either in Ephesus or on the Isle of Patmos, where he was exiled) would suffer horrendous deaths for bearing the message of their Lord. They were the first to admit that they could do nothing of themselves. Their dynamic preaching and teaching, their New Testament writings, and their words of courage and trust were empowered by the "Comforter" ("The Paraclete" from the Greek *parakletos*, meaning one who walks alongside; see John chapters 13—16). In establishing the Christian Church through them, God achieved a work of eternal, immeasurable significance.

During His last six months on earth, Jesus abandoned to a large extent His preaching and miracle working and devoted Himself to preparing the apostles for the monumental work ahead of them—carrying the gospel (Greek: *evangellion*—good news, good tidings). While at Caesarea Philippi, Jesus asked His disciples, "Whom do men say that I the Son of man am?" (Matthew 16:13b, KJV). They replied Elias (Elijah) or John the Baptist. Christ then put them on the spot, inquiring, "But whom say ye that I am?" (v. 15b). Gung-ho, impetuous Peter blurted out, "Thou art the Christ, the Son of the living God" (v. 16). Jesus joyfully received Peter's confession and commended him for his insight.

The Sermon on the Mount (Matthew 5–7)

I love the practicality and simplicity of Jesus' teaching. It was clear, relevant, and applicable. The Sermon on the Mount was the greatest sermon ever preached. Jesus began the sermon by sharing secrets of genuine happiness:

- Living an exemplary lifestyle
- Controlling anger
- Restoring relationships
- Avoiding adultery and divorce
- Keeping promises
- Returning good for evil
- Giving with the right attitude
- Practicing prayer
- Storing up treasures in heaven

The Beatitudes: Formulae for happiness (Matthew 5:3-11)

■ *Blessed are the poor in spirit for theirs is the kingdom of heaven.*

Here the "poor in spirit" are actually rich because they are submissive to God. They will inherit the kingdom of heaven, reigning and ruling with Christ throughout eternity. The person who is "puffed up" and proud within the inner life will never live in the kingdom of God. You are living in spiritual poverty if you have refused to receive Christ as the Lord of your life.

■ *Blessed are they that mourn: for they shall be comforted.*

Above all else, Jesus refers to mourning over sin in one's life—experiencing godly sorrow for one's transgressions—and in the lives of others. The believer is to mourn over the conditions of a lost world.

■ *Blessed are the meek: for they shall inherit the earth.*

Human nature touts selfishness. Certain modern psychologists dwell on self-esteem and "proper" self-image, claiming that we must be assertive and look out for "number one," namely oneself. Even Christians struggle with meekness, because it is often associated with gentleness, or even weakness (being a "wimp"). God expects our obedience, so we must yield ourselves to His control. It is a joy to the Lord when we follow His directives.

■ *Blessed are they who hunger and thirst after righteousness: for they shall be filled.*

The only genuine righteousness (rightness, holiness) is from God as revealed in Christ. When Christ died on the cross and rose from the dead, He purchased a "robe of righteousness" for you. When you repent of your sin and receive Him into your heart, He clothes you with His righteousness. Paul wrote about the source of righteousness, faith: "Abraham believed God, and it was counted ["credited," NIV) unto him for righteousness" (Romans 4:3b, KJV). When God looks at you *after* your conversion, He no longer sees your sins. He views only the righteousness of Jesus Christ.

■ *Blessed are the merciful for they shall be shown mercy.*

Although forgiving and merciful, Jesus came down hard on those who were unforgiving and unmerciful. His love extends grace to us, which provides for the forgiveness of our sins. Maybe you have heard about the criminal who stood before the judge, and the judge asked, "Mister, do you want justice?" The defendant instantly replied, "No Sir, I want mercy!"

■ *Blessed are the pure in heart for they will see God.*

Have you ever eaten tainted food with impurities of salmonella that caused botulism? Even though you didn't die (you're reading this, so you must be alive), you probably felt like it. Lately there is extensive concern over impurities in food and medications. We have become acquainted with deadly E-coli and Ebola germs that have sometimes infested meat. As I write this a huge meat company is going out of business because it accidentally sent out vast shipments of ground beef rendered inedible because of E-coli which has killed several people since 1994. Yet, purity is far more vital in the spiritual life. Paul insisted that we are to think on certain things, among them, "whatever is pure" (see Philippians 4:8). Purity of heart and spirit go hand in hand with righteousness. Only those who are authentically pure in heart will be privileged to see God.

■ *Blessed are the peacemakers for they will be called sons of God.*

Christ is the Prince of peace (Isaiah 9:6). He has made peace through His atoning sacrifice on the Cross (Colossians 1:20; also see Ephesians 1:7). He promised all of His disciples, including us, "Peace I leave with you, my peace I give unto you: not as the world giveth, give I unto you. Let not your heart be troubled, neither let it be afraid" (John 14:27, KJV), and, "These things I have spoken unto you, that in me ye might have peace. In the world ye shall have tribulation: but be of good cheer; I have overcome the world" (John 16:33, KJV). We are to promote and seek peace as we further His gospel of peace. "For God is not a God of disorder but of peace. As in all the congregations of the saints" (1 Corinthians 14:33).

■ *Blessed are those who are persecuted because of righteousness, for theirs is the kingdom of heaven.*

No believer should deliberately seek persecution, but he might as well expect it—that is, if he lives a devoted life of righteousness and witnessing for the Lord. Jesus predicted that because the unsaved world would hate Him, it would also hate us. Note, though, we are blessed (abundantly enriched and joyful) if we are persecuted because of righteousness. Certain people are discriminated against and persecuted because of being obnoxious and offensive as they allegedly represent the Lord. Paul reminds us, "In fact, everyone who wants to live a godly life in Christ Jesus will be persecuted" (2 Timothy 3:12). Have you ever heard this about a minister? "Why, Doctor (or Reverend or Brother) So and So doesn't have an enemy in the world. Everybody just adores him." If they were telling the truth, Doctor So and So was not preaching "the whole counsel of God," for the devil and his crowd will despise a bona fide servant of Christ.

■ *Blessed are you when people insult you, persecute you and falsely say all kinds of evil against you because of me.*

Rejoice and be glad, because great is your reward in heaven; for in the same way they persecuted the prophets who were before you.

We learn from the Sermon on the Mount

- Do not swear;
- Do not retaliate;
- Do give more than asked for;
- Do not refuse to give or to lend;
- Do not hate your enemy;
- Do pray for him who wrongs you;
- Do not give for selfish gain or for show;
- Do not be pretentious in prayer;
- Do pray in secret;
- Do not lay up treasures as a miser;
- Do not attempt to serve the world system and God;
- Do not be overly anxious about provisions;
- Do not judge, lest you be judged by the same judgement;
- Do not condemn another in the things you yourself do;
- Do have the humility of a child;
- Do not be called by titles of honor;
- It is better not to promise than to promise and not honor the promise;
- If we want to be forgiven, we must be forgiving;
- Do follow the Golden Rule—do unto others as you would have them do unto you;
- The easy way is not usually the good way;
- We are not judged by words, but by deeds.

— *Anonymous*

Christ's love for children (Matthew 19:13-15; Mark 10:13-16; Luke 18:15-17)

Jesus loves the entire world. What revealed His joy and good nature perhaps best of all was His love of children and the fact that they adored Him. Children have never responded well to "grumpy old (or young) men" (or women). Sometimes children still sing, "Jesus loves the little children, all the children of the world. Red and yellow, black and white, they are precious in His sight. Jesus loves the little children of the world." Their giggles and lightheartedness from innocent lips were music in His ears.

At one town, Perea, en route to Jerusalem, the Lord was met by fathers and mothers bringing their children and asking Him to place His hands on their heads and to bless them. The disciples tried to run them off with the alibi that the Lord was too busy. Sounds like certain secretaries today, doesn't it? That didn't set too well with Jesus. "Let the little ones come to me," Jesus invited, "and do not stop them; for the kingdom of God comes only to those who are child-like, I tell you, whoever will not give himself to the kingdom of God as a little child shall never come into the kingdom." Then He cradled them in His arms and blessed them.

The absolutely best resources on family life

Christ is a personal Savior today, the same as when He lived a man among men. Mothers, I hope you will come to Jesus with your concerns about your children and your family. God will give you the best counseling in the world through His Holy Spirit. It never was easy to rear children. Today it seems far more difficult with all the distractions of so-called "peer pressure." Peer pressure existed when I was a kid, but then it was called "running with the crowd." Children and young people in this generation are confronted with the grossest of evils all around them—cursing, dirty jokes, pornography on TV, in the movies, in publications, in CDs, and on the Internet, and a thousand and one other temptations to sin through premarital sex, alcohol, smoking, or other drugs.

Fathers and mothers should think of their children as younger members of the Lord's family. Concerned parents should commit themselves to this divine calling: spiritually educating them for the here and now and for heaven later. So, the Christian home becomes a school, where the parents serve as "under teachers," while Christ Himself is the chief instructor. A few of my readers may feel, *I really don't amount to much. Haven't achieved too much either. I'll never be rich and famous or have very much.* If you are the parent of at least one Christian child, you are more than successful! One CEO of a giant conglomerate said, "I'd give everything I have simply to have my family together. While I was building a financial empire, my most important business, my home, was crumbling."

Being a Christian parent is a serious responsibility. No matter how you interpret it the Bible teaches, "Train a child in the way he should go, and when he is old he will not turn from it" (Proverbs 22:6). Dr. Spock's permissive book on child-rearing has sold more than 20 million copies around the world. But the most effective book on the subject is The Book, The Bible. It is a treasure trove of practical and workable principles about love, marriage, the family, and children.

The written Word of God teaches the sanctity of marriage and that a family is a man and woman joined together under God's aegis. Jesus declared, "For this cause shall a man leave father and mother, and shall cleave to his wife: and they twain shall be one flesh" (Matthew 19:5, KJV; see also Matthew 19:6; Mark 10:8; 1 Corinthians 6:16; Ephesians 5:31).

There is no such entity as a "same-sex marriage." Homosexuality is severely condemned both in the Old and New testaments (see Genesis 19:11; Leviticus 18:22; 20:13; Judges 19:22-30; Jeremiah 23:14; Ezekiel 16:49-50; Romans 1:26-27; 1 Corinthians 6:9-11; 1 Timothy 1:10; 2 Peter 2:6-10; Jude 7). The Hebrews punished the forbidden practice by stoning. Of course, Jesus would not stone a person, but He will ultimately judge all sin, including sexual transgressions, whether heterosexual (fornication and adultery) and homosexual (men with men or women with women).

The Bible further teaches that children should obey and respect their parents."Honor thy father and thy mother: that thy days may be long upon the land which the Lord thy God giveth thee" (Exodus 20:12. KJV). Paul gave a hearty "amen" to that commandment when he wrote: "Children, obey your parents in the Lord, for this is right. Honor your father and mother'—which is the first commandment with a promise—'that it may go well with you and that you may enjoy long life on the earth'" (Ephesians 6:1-3).

The Bible stresses the significance of the family. In one recent political campaign, liberal extremists poked fun at the idea of "family values." Yet, family values are high in God's plans for the human race. America's dreadful spiritual declension is attributable directly to the breakdown of the traditional family with a father, a mother, and children. Through decades of un-Christian brainwashing millions of Americans have departed from God's intentions. Millions of heterosexual couples are merely "living together" without commitment and marriage vows. Dr. Laura Schlessinger, who hosts a top-rated call-in show, refers to that arrangement as "shacking up," what we labeled it years ago. There are millions of single-parent homes through abandonment, separation, and divorce. It is no wonder that teenagers and young adults often drift aimlessly and have no moral compass.

"A family comprises the immediate members of a household; or the descendants of one person together with their households (Genesis 10:18; 1 Chronicles 2:53,55); figuratively in Ephesians 3:15 of the whole company of believers." [1]

Parents, especially fathers, have the divinely given responsibility of rearing (we used to call it "raising") their children according to Paul's admonition: "And, ye fathers, provoke not your children to wrath: but bring them up in the nurture and admonition of the Lord" (Ephesians 6:4, KJV). There is a danger of badgering and nagging at children to the extent that they snap and go off the deep end. We are to rear our kids with love and understanding. Oftentimes discipline is necessary but should be done in kindness and tenderness. We as parents must realize that they are not always wrong and admit that sometimes we are wrong.

The ideal is for parents to win their children for Christ. All too often Christian parents leave that up to the pastor and church staff, whereas mothers and fathers should take the initiative in pointing them to the Savior. Believing parents should create such a godly atmosphere in the home that next to "Mama" and "Dada," "Jesus" should be the word one-year olds utter. If the right example is set, at an early age children will ask, "How can I become a Christian?" Early on we must teach them to love Jesus and His church.

Christian workers may also become Christ's agents in drawing children to Jesus. Then they may see them grow up to receive the Savior. Then, trans-

---

[1] Master Study Bible *(Nashville, TN: Holman Bible Publishers, 1981), 1924.*

formed in character, they will follow Him all the days of their lives. "Of such is the kingdom of God."

Christ's humility

Satan (Lucifer, the devil) opened the door to sin by his desire for honor and supremacy (see Isaiah 14:12ff.). Christ, in order to destroy sin, humbled Himself and became obedient unto death (see Philippians 2:5-11). All of heaven beheld God's justice revealed—both the condemnation of Satan and the redemption of man.

How Does God Teach Humility?

• *God teaches humility through the reproaches of others.* Psalm 141:5 (KJV) says: "Let the righteous smite me; it shall be a kindness: and let him reprove me; it shall be an excellent oil, which shall not break my head; for yet my prayer also shall be in their calamities."

• *God teaches humility through personal failure, or the appearance of failure.* The Apostle Paul, through tough times, learned not to make comparisons about the seeming failure of his work as compared to the Christians at Corinth. In 1 Corinthians 4:10 (KJV) he testified, "We are fools for Christ's sake, but ye are wise in Christ; we are weak, but ye are strong; ye are honorable, but we are despised." If Paul had gauged his success on the Corinthians' opinion of him, he might have fallen into a deep depression and discouragement, but he was still able to write them in humility and the power of the Holy Spirit: ". . . be ye followers of me" (1 Corinthians 4:16, KJV).

• *God teaches humility through the advancement of others.* First Corinthians 12:26 (KJV) informs us that because we are all part of Christ's body, the heartaches of others should become our mutual heartaches, and the joys of fellow believers ought to be our own: "And whether one member suffer, all the members suffer with it; or one member be honored, all the members rejoice with it." Sometimes, I think, it is easier for us to bear another's sorrows than for us to celebrate their joys. When a friend is richly blessed, we are sometimes tempted to complain, "Lord, why did you send it to that person instead of me? You know how much I needed that!" Watch out! Because that is the spirit of "the old man"—carnality—rearing his jealous, ugly head.

• *God teaches humility by giving someone else credit for a job you did.* First Corinthians 10:24 (KJV) urges: "Let no man seek his own, but every man another's *wealth*" (italics mine). Face it. It is often difficult to feel or express joy when someone else is praised or honored, especially when we feel we have done the work and deserve the honor! Wait a minute. Praise God for that situation, for it is a process God uses to build Christ-like character and to help us accumulate riches in heaven.

• *God teaches humility through the correction or teaching received from a person you consider your spiritual, educational, or social inferior.* First Corinthians 1:27-29 (KJV) points out: "But God hath chosen the foolish things of the world to confound the wise; and God hath chosen the weak things of the world to confound the things which are mighty; and base things of the world, and things which are despised, hath God chosen, yea, and things which are not, to bring to nought things that are; that no flesh should glory in his presence." God often utilizes a seemingly "unworthy" person to teach us a decisive lesson—to the effect we will remember that all we have to work with was given us by God.

• *God teaches humility by bringing us to the end of our own resources.* In Psalm 73:2-3 David cried: "For I envied the arrogant when I saw the prosperity of the wicked. But as for me, my feet were almost gone; my steps had well nigh slipped. For I was envious at the foolish, when I saw the prosperity of the wicked." Puzzled and perplexed by problems he could not solve, he had to realize that God was still in charge and would do what was just, right, and merciful. Beginning with verse 22 he said: "So foolish was I, and ignorant: I was as a beast before thee. Nevertheless I am continually with thee: thou hast holden me by my right hand. Thou shalt guide me with thy counsel, and afterward receive me to glory. Whom have I in heaven but thee? And there is none upon earth that I desire beside thee . . . But it is good for me to draw near to God: I have put my trust in the Lord God, that I may declare all thy works."

God may humble you, but He will never humiliate you. God's course in humility may painfully "stretch" us, but His lessons for us are inexpressible!

Thoughts on being humble

• Be humble or you will stumble. —Dwight L. Moody

• God created the world out of nothing, and as long as we are nothing, God can make something out of us. —Martin Luther

• I do not know one millionth part of one percent about anything.—Thomas Edison

• Humble yourself in the sight of the Lord and He will exalt you. Water always fills the lowest places. The lower and emptier man lies before God, the speedier and fuller will be the inflow of divine glory. —Andrew Murray

• Great men are the ones most unconscious of greatness. Only little men must increase their size by inflation. —Anonymous

• A man can counterfeit hope, and all other graces; but it is very difficult to counterfeit humility. —Dwight L. Moody

• Lord, make me humble. And, when You do, don't let me know it. For if you let me know it, I will be proud of it. —Anonymous

Christ and the Scriptures

Jesus Christ, the living Word (see John 1:1-3), was a faithful student of the Old Testament Scriptures, constantly quoting from them as points of reference concerning His ministry and the Kingdom of God. He opened His public ministry (Luke 4:1ff.) by reading from a Messianic passage (Isaiah 61:1ff.) Matthew 4 records His temptation (testing, trial) by Satan in the wilderness. Did Jesus quote from the rabbis or from the traditions of the Mishnah and Gemarah? No. From the inspired Word of God, the Book about Himself.

After fasting forty days and nights our Lord faced His first ominous test. He answered every innuendo of the devil by referring to the Scriptures, specifically three citations from Deuteronomy. To the suggestion of turning stones into bread, He replied: "It is written: 'Man does not live on bread alone, but on every word that comes from the mouth of God'" (Matthew 4:4). To the temptation of proving His Deity by jumping down from the Temple's pinnacle, He answered: "It is also written: 'Do not put the Lord your God to the test'" (v. 7). Finally, to the temptation of gaining the world's kingdoms by worshiping Satan, He responded: "Away from me, Satan! For it is written: 'Worship the Lord your God, and serve him only'" (v. 10).

Certain liberal scholars have argued that Jesus never claimed to be God, the Messiah, the Lord, or the Son of God. Throughout the Gospels He makes all of those claims. If He were not God and the Son of God, His crime would have been blasphemy. The only charge the religious leaders could finally levy against Him was: "He claimed to be the Son of God" (also the Son of David, meaning the Messiah or "Anointed One"). All one need do is prayerfully read Matthew 21:42; Mark 12:10-11; Luke 20:17; Luke 22:22; Luke 18:31; Luke 24:25-26,44; John 5:39,46-47. "O foolish men and slow of heart to believe in all that the prophets have spoken! Was it not necessary for the Christ to suffer these things and to enter into His glory? These are My words which I spoke to you while I was still with you, that all things which are written about Me in the Law of Moses and the Prophets and the Psalms must be fulfilled" (Luke 24:25-26,44, NASB).

Either Jesus Christ was all He claimed to be, or He was a fraud and imposter . . . thus, He validated His Deity and Personage in the Godhead (Father, Son, and Holy Spirit) not only by His signs, wonders, and miracles, His marvelous teachings, and His totally sinless life . . . but also by His resurrection from the dead! The other religions of the world brag about burial sites and tombs with: "Here lies Muhammad." "Here lies Buddha." "Here lies Zoroaster." But Christians point to an open tomb and shout with the angel: "He is not here, *for He has risen, just as He said.* Come, see the place where *He was lying*" (Matthew 28:6, NASB, italics mine).

The apostle Paul summed up the Gospel in his immortal resurrection chapter, 1 Corinthians 15. Beginning with verse 1 he pointed out that we are saved by this good news. He asserted that fundamental elements of the Gospel of salvation are these:

1. "that Christ died for our sins *according to the Scriptures* . . ." (v. 3);
2. "that he was buried . . ." (v. 4a);
3. "that he was raised on the third day *according to the Scriptures* . . . (v. 4b);
4. that He proved His resurrection by appearing to more than 500 of His followers—
   "that he appeared to Peter, and then to the Twelve . . ." (v. 5);

> "that he appeared to more than five hundred of the brothers at the same time, most of whom are still living, though some have fallen asleep . . ." [have physically died] (v. 6);
> "Then he appeared to James, then to all the apostles . . ." (v. 7);
> "And last of all he appeared to me also, as to one abnormally born . . ." (v. 8).

He encouraged His disciples, and even His enemies, to continue reading and studying the Scriptures. "Jesus saith unto them, Did ye never read in the scriptures, The stone which the builders rejected, the same is become the head of the corner: this is the Lord's doing, and it is marvellous in our eyes?" (Matthew 21:42, KJV; see also Matthew 22:29; 26:54,56; Mark 12:24; 14:49; Luke 24:27,32,45; John 5:39). Thank God for laypersons and ministers who preach and teach the Scriptures, the Word of God. Pray for those who attempt either to downgrade or ignore The Book.

Sir Walter Scott, the famous author, lay on his deathbed. He called for his attendant and requested, "Please bring me the book," to which his servant inquired, "Which book, Sir?" Scott's memorable answer was: "There is only one book, The Book, the Word of God!"

> We search the world for truth. We cull
> The good, the true, the beautiful,
> From graven stone and written scroll,
> And all lower-fields of the soul;
> And, weary seekers of the best,
> We come back laden from our quest,
> To find that all the sages said
> Is in the Book our mothers read.
> —John Greenleaf Whittier

Christ and prayer

Why was it necessary for Christ to pray?

Jesus Christ was and is God Himself, yet in His incarnation He prayed to God the Father. It was not only for communication but as an example for us. He was in constant communion with the Father. He never spent a moment or performed an action without direct reference to His Heavenly Father. His thoughts were God's thoughts; His purpose was the Godhead's purpose for Him. Oftentimes Christians, and even non-Christians, will wonder, *If Jesus is God, why did He pray . . . and why did He have to pray?* The fact is that He deliberately agreed with the Father and the Spirit to limit Himself by living as a man with the makeup and emotions of a man—yet without imperfection or sin (1 Peter 2:21-22; 2 Corinthians 5:21).

How Jesus prayed

In spite of the thousands who demanded His attention, Jesus would withdraw to pray, sometimes in the company of His apostles—at other times, completely by Himself, except for the presence of the Holy Spirit and the Father (see Mark 1:35; Luke 5:16; Matthew 14:13; Mark 6:46). In our frenetic, workaday world it is sometimes almost impossible to draw aside for meditation and prayer, but our Lord did. I honestly do not believe there has ever been a busier man. Try to set aside a private time even if it is only minutes a day.

Jesus, our ideal Pray-er, recognized the necessity of being thankful. Once there was a book entitled *Prayer: Asking and Receiving.* It was an excellent book, but stopped short of prayer's scope. Prayer is far more than merely asking and receiving. Prayer is also thanksgiving, praise, petition, and spiritual communion. He always thanked the Father and blessed the food, as when He fed 5,000 (plus women and children) with five loaves and two fish (Matthew 14:17ff.). On another occasion it was 4,000 with seven loaves and a few small fish (Matthew 15:32-39; Mark 8:1-10). The Giver of "every good and every perfect gift (James 1:17, KJV) was Himself joyfully thankful at all times.

He even gave thanks for situations in which people mistreated Him, as in unbelieving towns such as Chorazin, Bethsaida, and Capernaum (Jesus did predict that it would be "more tolerable for Sodom and Gomorrah" in the judgment than for those rebellious towns!). After being sneered at He prayed, "I praise you, Father, Lord of heaven and earth, because you have hidden these things from the wise and learned, and revealed them to little children. Yes, Father, for this was your good pleasure" (Matthew 11:25-26). Another prayer of praise and thanksgiving was after

He had sent out the seventy disciples two by two (Luke 10). By God's power the disciples had even cast out demons on that mission trip. Jesus rejoiced and prayed, "I thank thee" (Luke 10:21b, KJV).

His most serious thanksgiving prayer was when He instituted The Lord's Supper. Realizing the anguish and agony that lurked around the corner He "took the cup, and gave thanks" (Matthew 26:27). You have heard this before, but Jesus would instill in us His "attitude of gratitude." Paul expressed it aptly: "In every thing give thanks: for this is the will of God in Christ Jesus concerning you" (1 Thessalonians 5:18, KJV).

Keys to praying as our Lord did

If we would walk in His prayerful steps we would relate every experience to God, remembering all the while Romans 8:28. We would have faith in the trustworthiness of God, as Christ did before raising Lazarus from the dead: "Father, I thank you that you have heard me.

I knew that you always hear me, but I said this for the benefit of the people standing here, that they may believe that you sent me" (John 11:41-42). After the two disciples walked with the resurrected Christ on the Road to Emmaus, how did they finally recognize Him? By how He broke the bread and blessed it, thanking His Father (Luke 24:30-31).

The dynamics of intercessory prayer

That term is not often heard today, but it simply means "praying for others." You have heard about the egotist's prayer, haven't you? "God bless me and my wife, my son John and his wife—these four and no more." An authentic prayer life will, of necessity, involve intensive prayer for others. Believers have often queried, "Why should I pray since God has known before the foundation of the world what is going to transpire?" Because He desires our communication—in fact, He requires it of the born-again person—He wants our prayers to include others.

Jesus constantly prayed for others, for instance Peter who seriously backslid. "But I have prayed for you, Simon, that your faith may not fail. And when you have turned back, strengthen your brothers" (Luke 22:32). John 17 is often called His "high priestly" prayer for He interceded for His apostles He would leave behind. Read it again, for the prayer also involves you as His contemporary disciple. One of His most poignant prayers was from the cross when one of His "seven last words" was: "Father, forgive them, for they know not what they do" (Luke 23:34).

The Book of Acts is crammed full of answers to intercessory prayer. One of the most striking is in Acts 12:3-17 when a group of disciples are interceding for Peter who is in prison. It reminds me of us, for they are praying for his safe release. Peter was let out and knocking on the door when a girl named Rhoda answered it and reported, "It's Peter." Those very intercessors laughed her to scorn and said, "Girl, you're crazy!" Do we ever demonstrate that lack of faith in our intercessory praying?

Jesus' principles of prayer are unfailing and practical. In the Sermon on the Mount He presented the law of asking and receiving: "Ask, and it shall be given you; seek, and ye shall find; knock, and it shall be opened unto you: For every one that asketh receiveth; and he that seeketh findeth; and to him that knocketh it shall be opened" (Matthew 7:7-8, KJV). Then he relates it to the benevolence of the Heavenly Father: "If ye then, being evil, know how to give good gifts unto your children, how much more shall your Father which is in heaven give good things to them that ask him?" (Matthew 7:11, KJV). Compare Matthew 7:1-11 with Luke 11:5-13.

In that sermon He spoke about praying without making a display, suggesting that we go into our "inner room" (Matthew 6:6, NASB; KJV: closet; NIV: room). Then in verses 9-14 He gave The Lord's Prayer as a pattern for Christians of all eras. Although we may repeat it, I believe He basically intended the prayer as a guideline for our effective prayer life. Note some arresting statements about this prayer:

- Could be called the "Model Prayer";
- Could be called the "Disciples' Prayer" because John 17 would be more like the Lord's Prayer;
- All the pronouns are plural in the prayer;
- Every clause is taken from the Old Testament;
- This prayer contains elements important for all praying;
- The Lord's Prayer can be arranged like the order of the Ten Commandments: the first part deals with God and the second part deals with mankind.[2]

---

[2] Master Study Bible *(Nashville, TN: Holman Bible Publishers, 1981), 1824.*

The miracles of Christ

Christ performed innumerable miracles, though only thirty-six are discussed in the four Gospels, Matthew, Mark, Luke, and John. Jesus used His miraculous power because He loved the people and also to attest to the fact that He was and is the Son of God. He raised the dead, healed the sick and disabled, gave sight to the blind and hearing to the deaf. One of the most touching miracles was the raising of the widow of Nain's only son.

> Jesus went to a town called Nain, and his disciples and a large crowd went along with him, As he approached the town gate, a dead person was being carried out—the only son of his mother, and she was a widow. And a large crowd from the town was with her. When the Lord saw her, his heart went out to her and he said, 'Don't cry.' Then he went up and touched the coffin, and those carrying it stood still. He said, 'Young man, I say to you, get up!' The dead man sat up and began to talk, and Jesus gave him back to his mother. They were all filled with awe and praised God. 'A great prophet has appeared among us,' they said. 'God has come to help his people.' The news about Jesus spread throughout Judea and the surrounding country" (Luke 7:11-17).

The miracles of Jesus were of two classes—those carried out on people and those effected in the sphere of external nature, such as turning water into wine, stilling the tempest of the sea, and multiplying the loaves and fish to feed thousands. When John the Baptist sent His disciples to Jesus, asking if He were really the Christ, He answered, "Go and tell John again those things which you hear and see. The blind receive their sight and the lame walk, the lepers are cleansed, and the deaf hear, the dead are raised and the poor have the gospel preached to them, and blessed is he whosoever shall not be offended in me" (Matthew 11:4-6, KJV).

Even as today there were those who merely wanted a miracle without committing themselves to being Christ's disciples. "And when the people were gathered thick together, he began to say, This is an evil generation: they seek a sign; and there shall no sign be given it, but the sign of Jonas the prophet" (Luke 11:29, KJV). We should pray for and expect miracles today—we must also thank God whether or not He grants us a miracle. After all, next to the existence of God Himself, the greatest miracle is when a person is born again and adopted into the family of God. As the songwriter put it, "It Took a Miracle."

Christ's crucifixion and resurrection

In the Garden of Gethsemane, on the night before Christ's crucifixion, the mightiest conflict in human history was being fought. All the forces of evil were gathered to do battle with our Lord. Hatred was there, as were pride, lust, greed, lying, jealousy, guilt, shame, and all the other gross influences of sin in humankind. The power of satanic darkness was so overwhelming that Jesus was submerged in the most horrendous agony of soul. He who had never known sin then stared sin squarely in its ugly face. He who had never experienced pride, greed, or lust then gazed on those vile evils in their full revulsion.

Jesus was painfully aware of all that was required of Him—i. e., "God made him who had no sin to be sin for us, so that in him we might become the righteousness of God" (2 Corinthians 5:21). The depths of His soul and spirit were opened to all of the sins committed since the Garden of Eden, B.C. and A.D. He recoiled in revulsion of soul, for it nauseated His whole being. Imagine the spotless Son of God—who is one with the Father and who shares in the glory of eternity with all its majesty, beauty, and power—having heaped on Himself the filth, stench, and shame of our lust, avarice, deception, hatred, and depravity!

So great was the intensity of His agony that drops of blood began oozing from the pores of His skin. Finally, after beseeching His Father three times for another means of providing salvation, the Lord of Glory opened wide His sinless being and accepted into Himself all the cosmic powers of darkness and the sin of humankind from the past and coming ages. "We all, like sheep, have gone astray, each of us has turned to his own way; and the Lord has laid on him the iniquity of us all" (Isaiah 53:6).

Jesus suffered, and the severity of His suffering for us is beyond human comprehension. The physical suffering of crucifixion itself was frightful enough, but Jesus suffered in His spirit far more than in His body, because He became separated from God the Father. Our alienation from God became Jesus' own in order to make possible our restoration to God. Jesus suffered until His human body could endure the stress no longer. Then He died a physical death— probably of circulatory collapse and asphyxia, together with cardiac failure and perhaps a ruptured heart— and our sin died with Him.

When His lifeless body was wrapped in a linen sheet and gently laid to rest in Joseph's tomb, hatred, pride, guilt, greed, deception, shame, jealousy, and alienation from God were buried with Him in His death. He accomplished what He had come to do: to grab hold of sin and evil and to carry them within Himself to death. The spotless Lamb of God, who became sin for us, now lay in the bonds of death. Because He died with our sin within Him, our spirits can sense that the power of the sin that seeks to destroy us was captured by Him and carried to the grave: "With His stripes we are healed." "He was raised to life three days later." Let us give thanks to the God and Father of our Lord Jesus Christ! Because of His amazing grace and mercy He gave us new life by raising Christ from death. This fills us with a living hope, and we look forward to possessing the rich blessings God has in store for His people. He keeps them for us in heaven, where they cannot decay, spoil, or fade away.

Joseph's garden tomb was empty on the third day. This is a well-established fact. The guards realized it, and so did the women, Peter, and John. Certainly the High Priest and his cronies were aware of it, for more than likely they visited the tomb to see it for themselves. Finding it empty, their only recourse was to bribe the guards to lie about it. Jesus had risen from the dead. He was no longer there. The tomb was empty! That bodyless tomb stands above all human history to proclaim that death is not the end to life. The empty tomb speaks clearly to the human spirit that the power of death, our dread enemy, was overcome when Christ was raised from death.

The meaning of the empty tomb for us today is as real as it was for the women at the tomb and for the disciples. **First,** it means that Christ triumphed over the power of death. Death had gained a momentary victory, but, with all of its destructive power, it was not powerful enough to hold in its bonds the Lord of Glory. Jesus rose from death and came forth physically from the tomb, leaving the empty graveclothes behind. Because Christ overcame the power of death, it no longer has the final word with us. When we live in union with Him, His resurrection power operates in us so we too shall be raised. His power over death is available to us.

Second, Christ bore our sin in His own body on the cross and died with our sin in Himself. When He died, the dominion of sin and evil died with Him. When He rose victoriously over death, He came forth without the sin and evil that He had carried to His death. This assures us that His power is infinitely greater than that of sin and evil, as well as immeasurably greater than the power of death.

Christ rose and is alive. He rose bodily with an eternal body not subject to the limitations of deathly bodies, not subject to disease, decay, or death. Christ is therefore the prototype of resurrected humanity. He was the first among many, among all who believe in Him. As Jesus died physically, so also every one of us will die physically of disease, trauma, or "old age" (except those believers who are alive at the time of Christ's return). As Jesus became alive with a new immortal body—no longer subject to the limitations and sufferings of mortal flesh—so we also will receive immortal bodies. Because He rose, we have a living hope of triumph over death and of resurrection into eternal life.

Jesus is our model. We can face death, confident in our ultimate conquering of it. The empty tomb is the sure sign that death is not the final event but is the passage into a life of ultimate and eternal meaning, purpose, and value. God did not make disposable people, to be thrown away when their earthly usefulness is finished. God knows our names and numbers the very hairs on our heads. By faith we may live in union with Christ who died for us and whose resurrection power is operating in us if we have accepted Him. Our eternal destiny will reflect that relationship. We shall live in eternity in the presence of the Triune God in heaven.

The Great Commission

After Jesus' death the disciples were overwhelmed by discouragement. Their Master had been rejected, condemned, and crucified. Christ had tried to prepare them for that trauma, but they had not listened. He had stated plainly that He would be crucified and that He was to rise on the third day. Crushed by grief and despair, the disciples met in an upper chamber behind closed doors. There the resurrected Savior appeared to them. For forty days Christ remained on the earth, preparing His disciples for the work before them and explaining truths they could not previously comprehend. "Then he opened their minds so they could understand the Scriptures.

He told them, "This is what is written: The Christ will suffer and rise from the dead on the third day, and repentance and forgiveness of sins will be preached in his name to all nations, beginning at Jerusalem. You are witnesses of these things" (Luke 24:45-48).

The events of Christ's life, His death and resurrection, the prophecies pointing to these events, the marvelous plan of salvation effected through Jesus' power for the forgiveness of sins— His disciples were witnesses to those events, and He commissioned them to spread that liberating message throughout the world.

Before ascending to heaven Christ, the Commander-in-Chief, issued His marching orders to the disciples.

> *All authority in heaven and on earth has been given to me. Therefore go and make disciples of all nations, baptizing them in the name of the Father and of the Son and of the Holy Spirit, and teaching them to obey everything I have commanded you. And surely I am with you always, to the very end of the age (Matthew 28:18-20).*

For thought and discussion

1. What was Jesus' purpose for entering the world?
2. List Jesus' methods of conveying God's truth.
3. Jot down several forceful lessons Jesus taught through His parables?
4. What did the religious leaders think of Jesus' disciples? Why?
5. Write down at least five lessons we learn from the Sermon on the Mount.
6. Make your own outline of Jesus' "Model Prayer" (often called the Lord's Prayer)?
7. Why is humility important in the life of Jesus' followers?
8. In what ways are you influencing your children for Jesus?
9. What specific values are you passing on to them?
10. How can you begin creating a spiritual family tree?

2
Christ Versus Self: You Have to Choose

Because we are all human, we have all sinned (Romans 3:23). On our own, none of us can escape being found guilty (Romans 6:23). But Jesus Christ, the Son of God, came to earth and accepted the punishment for our sins (2 Corinthians 5:21). His suffering, death, and resurrection have made us free to begin our lives again if we live according to His Word (1 John 1:7).

The first two chapters of Genesis recount man's creation, revealing man's intended purpose to honor God and man's value that he is a special creation of God. God created man and woman, Adam and Eve, in perfect fellowship and harmony with Him, but the first couple sinned against God in the Garden of Eden. All the pain, all the evil, and all the suffering in the world is traceable to that original act of rebellion, which is commonly called the "fall of man" (Genesis 1:27). Human beings have a spiritual, as well as a physical, dimension. The moment a baby is born, the process is set in motion for him to die physically. His spirit, however, lives forever.

Humans are unable to make themselves acceptable to God. One's inherent nature is flawed, and while he is capable of doing good, he is incapable of completely avoiding bad. God demands perfection. Since man is born imperfect, even a single flaw disqualifies him from entering into a total relationship with God (Romans 5:12). Man will live forever, and Christ has bridged the gap which sin made between man and God. That gulf is closed only as one accepts Christ as one's Lord and Savior, thus re-establishing a personal relationship with God.

Every human being must make the choice to serve Christ or self. And, as one theologian expressed it, "We have no choice but to choose." Thankfully, ". . . God is love" (1 John 4:8).

In His character and person God is the essence of love, and from that love is the extension of His grace. God loved us to the extent that He sent His "only begotten Son," Jesus, into this world to demonstrate His love and concern for each and every person. Nearly every Sunday School child can at least quote John 3:16: "For God so loved the world, that he gave his only begotten Son, that whosoever believeth in him should not perish, but have everlasting life." God offers total forgiveness for the person who trusts in Christ and willingly accepts the reconciliation God offers. Peter and other apostles preached: "Him [Jesus] hath God exalted with his right hand to be a Prince and a Savior, for to give repentance to Israel, and forgiveness of sins" (Acts 5:31, KJV).

Moderns often wildly grasp after security and purpose from mundane sources such as personal success, status, beauty, wealth, and the approval of others. The man or woman who lives only for the adoration and attention of others is never satisfied. As Christians, our fulfillment in this age depends not only on our skills to avoid life's problems, but our ability to apply God's specific solutions to those problems. An accurate understanding of God's truths is the first step toward discovering our significance and worth.

Desperately seeking "self-worth"

Real *self-worth*, often called self-esteem or personal significance, is characterized by a quiet sense of self-respect and feeling of satisfaction with who we are. True self-worth, unlike pride, is not based on an evaluation of our performance. Whether labeled "self-esteem" or "self-worth," a feeling of worthwhileness is crucial to one's emotional, spiritual, physical, and social stability. It is a driving element within the human spirit. Millions of people spend a lifetime searching for love, acceptance, and success without understanding the urgent drive that propels them.

We must understand that this hunger for self-worth is God-given and can only be satisfied by and in Him. Our value is not dependent on our ability to earn the acceptance of people, but rather its true source is the love and acceptance of God. Paul understood where self-worth and acceptance are found: "To the praise of the glory of his [God's] grace, wherein he hath made us accepted in the beloved" (Ephesians 1:6, KJV). Since He created us, He alone understands how to fulfill all our needs. If we base our worth solidly on the truths of God's Word, then our behavior will often reflect His love, grace, and power. However, if we predicate our value on our abilities and the praise of others, then our behavior will reflect the insecurity and rage that often accompany that instability. Satan wants you to believe that the foundation of your worth is your performance and the ability to please others. Remember that God "crafted" you, and He makes only "quality merchandise." As the late Ethel Waters quipped, "God don't sponsor no flops." An unknown wag has said, "God don't make no junk."

Rejecting Satan's lies and accepting God's truths lead us to a renewed hope, joy, and purpose of life. Maybe you've heard about the best-selling book by Dr. Thomas Harris, *I'm OK—You're OK.* The stark reality is that you will never be, or feel, OK until you are A-OK with your Creator and Redeemer.

The conflict of the believer's two natures

To Christians, one of the most reassuring promises of the Bible is in 2 Corinthians 5:17, where we are informed that a newness and transformation has occurred within our lives through the new birth, "regeneration" (also called "being born again"). See John 3:5,7; Titus 3:5.

Two natures beat within my breast,
One is foul, the other blest.
The one I love; the one I hate
The one I feed will dominate.

Christ vs. Self: You Have to Choose

The conflict of the two natures makes the Christian life extremely unpleasant at times. The old nature constantly harasses the new by seeking a self-centered approach to life. The old nature is sometimes referred to by Paul as "the old man." "Knowing this, that our old man is crucified with him, that the body of sin might be destroyed, that henceforth we should not serve sin" (Romans 6:6, KJV; see also Ephesians 4:22; Colossians 3:9). That old rascal has an affinity with the world. Since the believer lives in the world, the old nature finds plenty of carnality to feed upon.

Scripture candidly records that even the greatest believers, at times, became victims of their old natures. Adam and Eve walked personally with God and yet disobeyed Him; Noah, Abraham, Isaac, Jacob, Moses—the Patriarches who wore heavenly mantles—are reported as having lied, deceived, cheated, and even murdered. David had a warm, cordial relationship with God, yet he ultimately committed adultery, had his paramour's husband murdered, lied, cheated, and woefully backslid.

Paul wrote in Galatians 5:17: "For the sinful nature desires what is contrary to the Spirit, and the Spirit what is contrary to the sinful nature. They are in conflict with each other, so that you do not do what you want." Read Romans 8:3 and 1 Peter 2:11. The warfare within self is the severest battle we fight. Yielding of oneself—surrendering all to the will of God—requires a struggle, but it is priceless when one submits to God in holiness. In presenting ourselves to Christ, we must deliberately cast away all that would separate us from Him. The thinking believer, then, will recognize his status and place total dependence on Christ for deliverance, allowing the Holy Spirit to examine, rebuke, guide, and bless. "Therefore, brothers, we have an obligation—but it is not to the sinful nature, to live according to it. For if you live according to the sinful nature, you will die; but if by the Spirit you put to death the misdeeds of the body, you will live (Romans 8:12-13).

The onset of the victorious Christian life

Consistency of mastery over the old nature begins with salvation. It is developed through the intake of God's Word and maintained by walking in the Spirit (2 Corinthians 5:17; 2 Timothy 2:15; Galatians 5:16). A balanced, consistent lifestyle for Christ speaks volumes to those outside of Christ. We are to put our motivation where our mouth is. We are to walk the walk and talk the talk, keeping in mind that the two natures reveal themselves, each wishing to have supremacy.

So, we have to decide which one to submit to, which to feed, and which to honor as dominant. Our old nature is not neutral but has dynamics as in "the lust of the flesh, and the lust of the eyes, and the pride of life," which are "not of the Father, but . . . of the world" (1 John 2:16, KJV). We are at home in the world in the flesh. Our roots are physical, mental, emotional, environmental, and cultural.

When a person becomes a Christian, that old nature remains. It is true that we are immediately spiritually united with Jesus Christ at the moment of salvation, but constitutional changes occur through spiritual growth—through the inner workings of God as the Holy Spirit activates the Word of God into action.

You have to choose

You are either a slave of one master or of another. Jesus plainly drew the line: "No one can serve two masters. Either he will hate the one and love the other, or he will be devoted to the one and despise the other. You cannot serve both God and Money" (Matthew 6:24). The *King James Version* renders "Money" as "Mammon." Some translations refer to "materialism."

No neutral zone

There is no middle ground between heaven and hell. You are on the road to one or the other. The power of choice, the exercise of free-moral agency, is an awesome responsibility. The stakes are high. The consequences are eternal, and you can choose either to have your life controlled by the carnal self or by the Holy Spirit. You can opt for your own "selfish way" or you can choose "The Holy Highway."

> And a main road will go through that once-deserted land; it will be named "The Holy Highway." No evil-hearted men may walk upon it. God will walk there with you, even the most stupid cannot miss the way (Isaiah 35:8, TLB).

There must be a "crucifixion" of the principle of lawlessness within.

> I have been crucified with Christ and I no longer live, but Christ lives in me. The life I live in the body, I live by faith in the Son of God, who loved me and gave himself for me (Galatians 2:20).

There must be a dying out to self and to sin. The difficulty of this progress varies according to the individual, but the sooner we let go of all warped self-centeredness, the sooner we will receive complete deliverance. We must decide to choose the entire will of God.

> But just as he who called you is holy, so be holy in all you do, for it is written: "Be holy, because I am holy" (1 Peter 1:15-16).

A person may survive numerous problems in life staying in control, but we should always involve Christ in our decisions. Then, when we are especially helpless and weak, as in a period of illness, we will freely turn our problems over to Him.

The failure to respond to the Holy Spirit and accept Christ as Savior will separate a person from God and His heaven here and in the hereafter. The person without Christ, though physically alive, is "dead in trespasses and sins" (Ephesians 2:1b, KJV) now and later in eternity. Every sin, every neglecting of God's grace, inwardly destroys one who rejects Christ. Repeatedly answering "no" to the Holy Spirit is a gradual committing of spiritual suicide. That hardens a person's heart, twists the will, and deadens one's understanding. It makes a person less inclined and less capable of yielding to the tender pleading of the Holy Spirit. Solomon described the situation of the adamant unbeliever: "He, that being often reproved hardeneth his neck, shall suddenly be destroyed, and that without remedy" (Proverbs 29:1, KJV; see also Ephesians 4:9; 1 Timothy 4:2).

Christ stands ready to liberate us from sin, yet He does not force one's will. If a person persists in sinning against God, willfully rejecting that freedom in Christ and refusing to accept His grace, what more can God do? The determined unbeliever destroys himself by repeatedly pushing away God's loving offer to "Come to me, all you who are weary and burdened, and I will give you rest" (Matthew 11:28).

Victory over sin in a Christian's life

The Holy Spirit indwells the Christian and will convict her/him of their sins, motivating them to ask for forgiveness. The believer has the formula for combating his sins: "If we confess our sins, he is faithful and just and will forgive us our sins and purify us from all unrighteousness" (1 John 1:9). Christians will sin but do it unhappily. You may think the most miserable person in the world is a lost person. Rather, I feel that distinction goes to the believer who is out of fellowship with his Lord and Savior. Read David's "Penitential Psalm" (51) and see if you don't agree. He didn't pray, "Lord, restore unto me Thy salvation." He pled, "Restore unto me *the joy* of Thy salvation" (see Psalm 51:2a).

It is not a sin to have an evil thought traipse across "the back roads" of our minds. It is a sin when we fail to say no and don't ask our Lord (who was tempted yet never sinned) to help us overcome the lure of temptation. It is essential that we stay alert in order to defeat the devil in his attempt to make us stumble. It is a matter of moment-by-moment reliance on the Holy Spirit, by deliberate choice, to overcome the evil desires of the carnal nature. "But I say, walk by the Spirit and you will not carry out the desire of the flesh" (Galatians 5:16).

To walk in the Spirit is to have a continuing Christian faith and an attitude of reliance on the Holy Spirit, not on your own human resources. The Spirit-controlled believer will be tempted, but it is not sin until one stops trusting the Spirit to fight it. It is almost superfluous to repeat it, but God is on the side of the believer in this warfare.

> (For the weapons of our warfare are not carnal, but mighty through God to the pulling down of strong holds;) Casting down imaginations, and every high thing that exalteth itself against the knowledge of God, and bringing into captivity every thought to the obedience of Christ" (2 Corinthians 10:4-5, KJV).

Can you imagine a soldier going to battle without a weapon? Or a pilot trying to fly without an airplane? Or a carpenter without a hammer, plane, or nails? Yet, too many Christians are in the middle of warfare and don't even seem to realize it. That's what Satan longs for—the blasé, unconcerned believer who is merely going through the motions, oblivious to the prince of darkness' sneaky strategies.

This "feel-good" religion wants to ignore the cold, harsh realities—that the devil and his evil minions are at work, that every believer is embroiled in a war with hell itself, and that everything is not sweetness and light. Hard-hitting Bible truth is not popular with a large segment of society, and that's why our nation is going downhill. The victorious Christian is alert and vigilant. "Be Prepared" is the motto of the Boy Scouts. That's not a far cry from "Always be prepared to give an answer to everyone who asks you to give the reason for the hope that you have" (see 1 Peter 3:15). How are we going to prepare for warfare? Concentrate on Paul's strategy for conquest in Christ (Ephesians 4:11-18).

Christian commitment

Without commitment, faith becomes only a creed which does not carry conviction or impact. Without commitment, work is devoid of its high calling of service and becomes only a means to achieve personal gain. Without commitment, people put together dangling relationships, touching one another for convenience's sake, using one another—then are disconnected again. Without commitment life itself is suspended on quicksand sinking fast.

Commitment is a contract that is followed up by actions. It is the cement that glues relationships together. It is a stick-to-itiveness that lets no environmental factors or personal failures set back the original pledge, a marriage vow or any other kind of promise. It is the stubborn root that plows deep into the soil. It is a prioritized involvement that is willing to take the risk and the time to understand the other person. It is a growing interest in cultivating long-lasting values and is not satisfied with immediate, instant results or gratification.

Commitment, most importantly of all, means giving the best—in fact, all one has. When we commit ourselves to God, it means offering ourselves as "living sacrifices," as Paul indicated in Romans 12:1. It is not only a once-for-all sacrifice but a daily, continuous giving up of one's self-interest. It is a voluntary act that radiates from a deep surrender to God, an offering that gives God all our soul, our heart, our mind, and our strength.

In the same chapter of Romans, after urging Christians to commit themselves to God, Paul then urges them to commit themselves to one another. Seven times he employs the phrase, "let him," challenging Christians to make use of their spiritual gifts to serve one another. In verse 10 he urges them to "Be devoted to one another in brotherly love." The values of the world stress individual rights without responsibility, liberty without accountability. It is imperative that we renew our attitude of commitment to God and to our neighbors.

Growing in the Spirit is accomplished by kneeling and not running; by surrender and not by determination. Beyond these mists lies the sunshine of God's presence. For several years the so-called "Lordship" debate has continued. No doubt you've heard the statement, "Well, I accepted Jesus as my Savior but not as my Lord." The fact is: I believe that if He is your Savior, He has automatically become your Lord, whether or not you acknowledge that Lordship. He is Lord period! When people caught the real import of Jesus' teachings—that one would have to deny himself and bear the cross daily—most of them bailed out. "From this time many of his disciples turned back and no longer followed him. You do not want to leave too, do you?' Jesus asked the Twelve" (John 6:6-7; see also Luke 9:23; Matthew 16:24; Mark 8:34). Growing in the Spirit is accomplished by forgetting self and then relying on God's Spirit as our Strength, our Guide, our Confidant, and Companion—in a word, our lives.

The Christian conscience

The Holy Spirit uses the conscience as a primary avenue of communication. The conscience is that inner capacity within each of us to discern right from wrong, wise and unwise. It is that faculty which urges a person to do what he recognizes as right and thus restrains him from doing what he senses is wrong—which passes judgment on his acts and executes judgment within his soul.

Problem—Tragically, some have "seared" (dead, cauterized, insensitive) consciences (1 Timothy 4:2). That kind of conscience has been ignored to the extent that it can no longer be felt.

Paul described those who had obliterated their consciences: "Having the *understanding darkened*, being *alienated from the life of God* through the ignorance that is in them, because of the *blindness of their heart*: Who *being past feeling* have given themselves over unto lasciviousness, to work all uncleanness with greediness" (Ephesians 4:19-20, KJV, italics mine).

Such a deplorable condition cannot occur with the life of a Christian. Once a person becomes a child of God, the significance of the conscience is heightened. It becomes a divine instrument. It becomes the means through which the Holy Spirit reveals the will of God to the mind. The Holy Spirit works through the conscience to convict us of sin. A clear conscience is evidence of a life in harmony with the Holy Spirit. Paul referred to the conscience twenty-seven times and demonstrated the interaction between the Spirit and one's conscience: "I say the truth in Christ, I lie not, my conscience also bearing me witness in the Holy Ghost" (Romans 9:1, KJV).

Six basic fears of mankind

The Bible teaches, with precision and honesty, that the fleshly nature is incapable of producing true inner peace and meaning. There are at least six basic fears (or phobias) that our old nature must suffer. They fit the unbeliever, as well as the carnal believer, though he is better able to cope:

Fear of death, which always emanates from the old nature.

Fear of illness. When the mysterious pains come, the old nature becomes a prayer warrior, begging God for help.

Fear of old age. Either in actuality or in prospect, the old nature is sensitively touched here.

Fear of poverty. The love of money causes diverse problems in every level of experience. It may even cause senility, illness, or death.

Fear of loss of love. This emotional response may arise at any point in life, creating a jealous, striving mental attitude that will go to every manipulative means to comfort and appease itself.

Fear of criticism. The old nature is touchy, defensive, and self-protective. It is willing to compromise in order to avoid criticism.

It is extremely difficult even for a believer to handle the true tests of life—the losses, the illnesses, the heartaches, the breakdown of relationships, if he/she is not practicing preparedness in their daily living (see Ephesians 6:10-18).

In retrospect

If you want to have peace with God and find security for those troubled times, you must answer one important question: *Who is the ruler of your life? Either self or Christ will reign.*

For thought and discussion

1. How do you interpret self-worth or self-esteem?
2. Read Romans 6:6, Ephesians 4:22, and Colossians 3:9. What do they mean to you?
3. What separates mankind from God? What can close that gap?
4. Give your own definition of "The Holy Highway."
5. How does a Christian conscience work?
6. True or false: It is a sin to be tempted. Explain your answer.
7. List at least three of mankind's major fears. What will help us cope with those?
8. How do you define success? What influences your definition?
9. How do your attitudes and actions affect your family? Your church? Your pastor?
10. Why does God allow Christians to experience hard times?

3

Heaven or Hell—Your Eternal Home (Which Will You Choose?)

If we confess our sins, He is faithful and just and will forgive us for our sins and purify us from all unrighteousness (1 John 1:9).

As often pointed out here, God is a God of love (John 3:16; Romans 5:8; 1 John 4:8). He is not willing that any should perish, but that all should have everlasting life (see 2 Peter 3:9). However, He is also a God of justice. This is not a pleasant subject, and many pulpits and classrooms are silent about it . . . but it is terribly essential. All sin and disobedience toward God will be punished. If one doesn't repent and receive Christ, they will face eternal punishment. Yet, Christ has handled the sin problem by offering Himself as the atonement (propitiation, expiation) for sins, transgressions, and iniquities against God and our fellow man. Fantastic!

There can be no atonement, or provision for forgiveness of sins, except through the shedding of blood by one who was holy and without sin. "Without shedding of blood there is no remission" (Hebrews 9:22, KJV) The only way that God in His justice could forgive our sins was for another person, without sin, to die in our place. In His love and mercy God sent His Son, Jesus Christ, who was born of a virgin and without sin, to die on the Cross of Calvary.

God's requirements

There are certain conditions, though, that God requires us to meet, He has taken the initiative for our salvation. He has done His part; now we must do ours. In the beginning of His ministry, Jesus preached, "Repent for the kingdom of heaven is at hand" (Matthew 4:17, KJV) It is essential for sinners (and all of us are sinners) to repent (to turn from, to leave, to do a complete about face) of their sins and to trust Him as their Savior. Throughout His ministry His overriding purpose was "to seek and to save that which was lost" (Luke 19:10, KJV).

Hear His sweet words of invitation, "Come unto me all ye that labor and are heavy laden, and I will give you rest. Take my yoke upon you, and learn of me, for I am meek and lowly in heart, and ye shall find rest unto your souls, for my yoke is easy and my burden is light" (Matthew 11:28-30). There is peace and rest in Him, if you will only answer His call.

After His crucifixion on Calvary, and His resurrection from Joseph of Arimathea's tomb, Jesus issued His Great Commission. Peter preached on the Day of Pentecost, after Jesus had ascended back into heaven, "Repent, and be baptized every one of you in the name of Jesus Christ for the remission of sins, and you shall receive the gift of the Holy Ghost" (Acts 2:38, KJV). The apostle Paul testified, "Believe on the Lord Jesus Christ and you shall be saved." (Acts 16:31). The prophet Isaiah invited, "Let the wicked forsake his way, and the unrighteous man his thoughts; and let him return unto the Lord, and He will have mercy upon him; and to our God, for He will abundantly pardon" (Isaiah 55:7, KJV).

We see, then, that in order to be saved, we must repent of our sins and believe on the Lord Jesus Christ as our personal Savior. Repentance implies that the Holy Spirit has convicted us of our sins, of righteousness, and of the judgment to come (see John 16:8-11). True repentance involves a "godly sorrow" that we have sinned against God and that we are willing to confess and forsake all of our sins. It means, too, that we will make any restitution God may require. In Luke 19 Zacchaeus immediately offered to settle his accounts, even to the tune of 400 percent. After having done your part by wholeheartedly repenting of your sins, then you can have an intimate communion with God. Jesus promised that anyone who came to Him, He would accept and not turn away. We accept

Him, but He also accepts us (see John 6:37).

No doubt you would like to become a child of God, knowing that your sins are all forgiven, and that you are ready for any eventuality, whether physical death or the return of Christ. You can, if you will only believe and follow through on God's plan. "Though your sins be as scarlet, they shall be as white as snow; though they be red like crimson, they shall be as wool" (Isaiah 1:18, KJV).

Jesus is now at the right hand of God the Father in Heaven. Without hesitation He will forgive you if you come to Him with your whole heart. You don't have to be in a church building to be saved, although a church altar is a splendid place to find God. Go to your room, out in the woods, anywhere alone with God. Pour out your heart and soul to Him in sincerity. Confess your sins to Him and mean it from the depths of your heart. He has never turned down a repentant sinner.

The rich man and Lazarus

Twice during His three-and-a-half years of public ministry Jesus pulled aside, by His words, the curtain that hangs between this world and the one to come. The first time was on the Mount of Transfiguration when He appeared there with Moses and Elijah. Although I have already touched on the rich man and Lazarus, I re-emphasize this true story.

Bear in mind that the record of the rich man and Lazarus is not a parable because:

- A parable has been defined as a declaration of comparison revealing the invisible truth by the visible. This sacred record is just the opposite. It is a description by the Lord Jesus Christ of a heavenly incident with an earthly meaning.
- When the Lord Jesus Christ spoke a parable it was usually introduced by the words, "He spake this parable unto them."
- In none of the parables of our Lord were the names of persons given; but in this true account the names of three men are mentioned: Lazarus, Abraham, and Moses. Sometimes tradition has referred to the rich man as "Dives," which is a transliteration of the Greek for rich man.

Turn back to Chapter 1 of this book to read the biblical account or open your Bible to Luke 16:19-31. Remember, this is the historical account of an actual incident. Both men had died, and their bodies had been placed in their respective graves. This shocking true account describes where Lazarus is. He was in "Abraham's bosom," which meant heaven to the Jews. He was "comforted." The rich man had vision, for he could see and recognize Abraham and Lazarus. To be seen by the rich man, then, Abraham and Lazarus must have had celestial bodies. The rich man could feel, thirst, talk, and remember. He had lost neither personality nor consciousness.

Two worlds

Every mortal is a citizen of two worlds—this world and the world to come. He has a life to live here, and this life is a preparation for the next life in heaven or hell. Both worlds are real, and their existence does not admit of any reasonable doubt.

Heaven

Jesus, although loving and merciful, did not mince words."He that believeth on the Son hath everlasting life," He declared, "and he that believeth not the Son shall not see life [a foretaste of heaven here and then the actual heaven]; but the wrath of God abideth on him" (John 3:36, KJV).

Life for the believer begins at the cross where Jesus Christ died for the sins of the world and provided eternal salvation. His death and resurrection provide us eternal life. All we have to do to be saved is believe on Christ and invite Him into our hearts. John wrote, "Yet to all who received him, to those who believed in his name, he gave the right to become children of God" (John 1:12).

Heaven, the final home for Christians: A real place!

Heaven! Is it a real place? For Christians, heaven is their final, eternal home.

The word heaven, in its various grammatical usages, is found some 697 times in the Bible and is printed both in the singular and in the plural forms. The inspired Word of God is the only reliable source we have for information on the subject of heaven. Not only does it clearly teach that heaven is a place, but that it is the eternal home a Christian may secure for himself and never fear losing it. All else that the Christian may desire and seek here can only be partially obtained; then their possession is insecure and, at best, is for only a short season.

The only "sure thing" on earth is our relationship to God through Christ and the certainty that, through faith in Him, we are certain of gaining a residence in heaven. At the same time it is the highest and best that one can obtain, along with life everlasting, which can never be snatched from us. This eternal life we receive while here on earth will go with us through our earthly journey and stay with us as we enter heaven.

How many heavens?

There are at least three heavens known from the Scriptures, for Paul declares that he was "caught up even to the third heaven . . . into Paradise" (2 Corinthians 12:2-4), and there may be even more than three. The three heavens of which the Bible speaks are: the region of clouds, the place of the planets and stars, and the place of God's throne.

But however many heavens there may be, it is clear from the Word that the Lord Jesus Christ is now—in His bodily, corporeal presence—enthroned at the highest point in the universe, presiding over the world He has created. He is far above all principalities, powers, might, dominions, and above every name that is named (see Ephesians 1:21; Philippians 2:5-11). After His ascension, He was seated "on the right hand of the throne of the majesty in the heavens" (Hebrews 8:1, KJV). He "passed through the heavens"—note the word is plural (Hebrews 4:14)—and now the Lord Jesus Christ is literally above all things.

Our unsurpassed hope

All this is full of glorious meaning to us who have received Jesus Christ, for the Word of God assures us that in God's reckoning we have been crucified with Him, buried with Him, quickened (made alive) with Him, raised up together with Him, and we are seated together with Him in heaven or "heavenly places" (Ephesians 2:1-6). That is absolutely amazing for us, who once were headed for hell, to grasp! We were before our conversion "by nature children of wrath" (Ephesians 2:3, KJV).

How do we know there is a heaven?

Jesus said so!

The strongest argument for heaven being a real place, and the future home of the Christian, centers in and rests upon the foundation of the Lord Jesus' assertions. From heaven He came down to earth. To heaven He returned from the earth after His mission was accomplished. That the Lord Jesus Christ knew all about heaven, He informs us in John 3:13: "And no one hath ascended into heaven, but he that descended out of heaven, even the Son of man, who is in heaven" (KJV). Heaven is where the Father's house is. In it are "many mansions," and in addition to these mansions, our Lord Jesus Christ has gone to "prepare a place" for every Christian, that where He is, there the Christian "may be also" (John 14:1-2).

Jesus used the term "prepare a place." It means to make necessary preparations. In other words, "Get ready!" It is a figure drawn from the Eastern custom of sending ahead or going before kings, to make the road passable. Jesus is our pioneer, gone to prepare "our abiding place" in heaven for us, to make a place ready for us when we are called home.

That all Christians will be in heaven when they finish their earthly life is evidenced by the fact that the Lord Jesus Christ, in His intercessory prayer (John 17:24), so commanded the Father. It was His declared will that all Christians at death come and be with Him. Here are His revealing words: "Father, I will that they also, whom thou hast given me, be with me where I am . . ." (KJV). Mark well the two words: "I will." This is the only time He used them. That declaration is concerned with the ultimate glorification and home of every believer.

They saw heaven

Visitors from heaven: The New Testament begins by reporting that earth had visitors from heaven to announce the birth of the Lord

Jesus. In Luke 2:13, we read Luke's words concerning those heavenly visitors: ". . . "There was with the angel a multitude of the heavenly host." These learned singers were trained in a place called heaven.

Stephen saw the glory: The first martyr of the church, Stephen, shouted that he believed in heaven as a place. Here is his testimony, given shortly before he died by stoning, when he saw heaven opened and the glory of God, with Jesus standing on the right hand of God:

> But he, being full of the Holy Spirit, looked up steadfastly into heaven [singular], and saw the glory of God, and Jesus standing on the right hand of God, and said, Behold, I see the heavens [plural] opened, and the Son of man standing on the right hand of God (Acts 7:55-56).

Note that Stephen used the singular and then the plural construction of the word heaven— this was not a mere illusion of the mind but an actual revelation granted to him that his faith not fail in that trying moment.

Paul's experiences: Next to the Lord Jesus Christ, Paul had more to say concerning heaven as a place than anyone else in the New Testament. Twice, before unbelieving gatherings made up of those who were against him, Paul boldly mentioned the fact that he saw heaven opened and heard the Lord Jesus Christ speaking to him. The records of the words are found in Acts 22:1-6 and 26:9-18.

When writing 2 Corinthians, Paul informed the church members that fourteen years before he had an experience which had such a deep impact on him that it were as though it had happened that very day.

> I must needs glory, though it is not expedient; but I will come to visions and revelations of the Lord. In Christ, fourteen years ago (whether in the body, I know not; or whether out of the body, I know not; God knoweth), such a one caught up even to the third heaven. And I know such a man (whether in the body, or apart from the body, I know not; God knoweth), how that he was caught up into Paradise, and heard unspeakable words, which it is not lawful for man to utter (12:1-4).

If this occurred when Paul was stoned and left for dead at Lystra, it is clear he was not caught up in his fleshly body, for His disciples, standing guard, never lost sight of him (Acts 14:19-20). Paul, then, undoubtedly was translated or "caught up" into paradise—which now, after the Lord's resurrection—is in heaven, the home of the redeemed. Then God returned Him to earth for the body of flesh to assume control for the functioning of His soul and spirit here on earth.

The Apostle John presents another insight into this supernatural happening. In Revelation 4:1-4), while in exile on the Isle of Patmos, John writes of his experience in being out of the body and being in the heavenly or spiritual body:

> After this I looked, and there before me was a door standing open in heaven. And the voice I had first heard speaking to me like a trumpet said, "Come up here, and I will show you what must take place after this." At once I was in the Spirit, and there before me was a throne in heaven with someone sitting on it. And the one who sat there had the appearance of jasper and carnelian. A rainbow, resembling an emerald, encircled the throne. Surrounding the throne were twenty-four other thrones, and seated on them were twenty-four elders. They were dressed in white and had crowns of gold on their heads.

John informs us of "a door standing open in heaven," and a voice he could hear inviting, "Come up hither." In awe he writes that immediately he was changed and found himself in heaven. John beheld the redeemed in that celestial city, the eternal home for the saints (all born-again believers are saints, "set-apart ones," according to God's Word).

Translated saints

The Scriptures contain at least two instances of God's men who did not taste of death but were "translated" (literally carried across) directly from life on earth into heaven. From Genesis and through the Book of Revelation, we read of their extraordinary call to "Come up hither."

Enoch: The first mentioned is the translation of Enoch, as recorded in Genesis 5:24. It reads, "Enoch walked with God: and he was not; for God took him." His close relationship with God had prepared him for heavenly fellowship and—without any change other than breaking the bonds that kept him physically on the earth, he rose above it all to reach the goal of human dreams. How could this have happened? The writer of Hebrews, most likely Paul, explains it in one simple sentence: "Enoch . . . was not found, because God translated him" (Hebrews 11:5). Enoch was removed in body and soul to another dwelling place, heaven, there to live with God and those who, like him, had died in faith.

Moses: The second record of a man exchanging worlds revolves around Moses, Israel's liberator and lawgiver. In my opinion, it is the account of a transferral from the earth to heaven—of course, different from Enoch's departure.

> Then Moses climbed Mount Nebo from the plains of Moab to the top of Pisgah . . . Then the Lord said to him, "This is the land I promised on oath to Abraham, Isaac and Jacob when I said, 'I will give it to your descendants.' I have let you see it with your eyes, but you will not cross over into it." And Moses the servant of the Lord died there in Moab, as the Lord had said. He buried him in Moab . . . but to this day no one knows where his grave is (Deuteronomy 34:1,4-6).

But where did the soul of Moses go? The answer is found in the three Synoptic Gospels (Matthew 17:1-8; Mark 1:8; Luke 9:28-36). On the Mount of Transfiguration, God wanted two representative Old Testament leaders to appear with Jesus as another sign of verification. Moses, standing for the Law, and Elijah, for the Prophets, miraculously showed up. Moses had entered the Promised Land via heaven.

Elijah: The third snatching away in the Old Testament was of Elijah. That experience is revealed in 2 Kings 2.

> When the Lord was about to take Elijah up to heaven in a whirlwind, Elijah and Elisha were on their way from Gilgal. As they were walking along and talking together,

> suddenly a chariot of fire and horses of fire appeared and separated the two of them, and Elijah went up to heaven in a whirlwind. Elisha saw this and cried out, "My father! My father! The chariots and horsemen of Israel!" And Elisha saw him no more. Then he took hold of his own clothes and tore them apart (vv. 1,11-12).

For a prepared people

How does this apply to you, and you are convinced that heaven is a real place? Here it is.

Heaven is a prepared place for a prepared people: "Blessed are those who wash their robes, that they may have the right to the tree of life and may go through the gates into the city" (Revelation 22:14). So, if we are to reach the "sweet bye and bye," we must prepare for it in the "nasty here and now." Heaven is the destination of a life that is turned toward God, seeking His will now. Now! I can only feel sorry for the billionaire who more than once has publicly chortled, in essence, "I wouldn't want to go to heaven. For me that would be boring. All they do up there is pray and sing and all that stuff." At least he's honest. Now, he may not believe in hell, but that's the place he's preparing for. Preparation for heaven—and hell—begins *right now*. Here is Christ's will concerning you: "Now this is eternal life: that they [Jesus' disciples] may know you, the only true God, and Jesus Christ, whom you have sent" (John 17:3).

You can know if you're going to heaven by yielding your heart and life to Christ right now. Many people are worried about the doctrine of calling and election, fearful that maybe God will not save them. Not to worry. What should you do if you don't have the assurance of salvation? Simply follow the apostle Peter's counsel: "Wherefore the rather, brethren, give diligence to *make your calling and election sure:* for if ye do these things, ye shall never fall" (2 Peter 1:10, KJV, my italics). Call on the Lord this moment and ask Him to give you inner assurance.

After being carried to heaven, what?

Clothed with a celestial body

If you are saved it is comforting to know when God wants you to graduate from the school of life you will be "carried away by the angels," even as all the believers of history were (Luke 16:22). If you are called away before the rapture, God will immediately clothe you with a spiritual body in paradise. You will recognize that you are in eternity and will be near the Lord, meeting your loved ones and worshiping with the redeemed who have preceded you there.

At death the Christian's soul and spirit are immediately clothed with a body adapted to the function of the spirit world—one in which the soul and spirit are alive and functioning. You will not be bodiless but have a "celestial" body. Paul beautifully explains this in 1 Corinthians 15:38-40:

> But God giveth it a body as it hath pleased him, and to every seed his own body. All flesh is not the same flesh: but there is one kind of flesh of men, another flesh of beasts, another of fishes, and another of birds. There are also celestial bodies, and bodies terrestrial: but the glory of the celestial is one, and the glory of the terrestrial is another. There are also celestial bodies, and bodies terrestrial: but the glory of the celestial [this is the spiritual body—a body entirely under the control of the soul and adapted for spiritual function] is one, and the glory of the terrestrial [a body that is fleshly] is another (KJV).

Torn between two worlds

Paul again illustrates this in 2 Corinthians 5:6-8:

> Therefore we are always confident and know that as long as we are at home in the body we are away from the Lord. We live by faith, not by sight. We are confident, I say, and would prefer to be away from the body and at home with the Lord.

He stresses that his situation is a win-win one, that he cannot lose out:

> For to me, to live is Christ and to die is gain. If I am to go on living in the body, this will mean fruitful labor for me. Yet what shall I choose? I do not know! I am torn between the two: I desire to depart and be with Christ, which is better by far; but it is more necessary for you that I remain in the body (Philippians 1:21-24).

Note Paul's words carefully. What did he mean when he wrote that dying was "gain" and "better by far"? Why did he long to leave his fleshly body and to "be with Christ"? One reason was his expectation that he would not be "spiritually naked" but be consciously alive in a celestial body, in which his soul and spirit would reside and function as formerly in a fleshly body. Paul loved his life on earth but confessed that he was "torn between the two," meaning life and death here. He expressed an intense longing to depart for heaven.

The final resurrection—at the rapture

Death does not release us into the final resurrection body condition. This intermediate state of incompleteness will come about because we will not have experienced the final resurrection body. We must wait until we receive it at the rapture before we again are a complete person—body, soul and spirit back together. This was Paul's prayer for the Thessalonian Christians: "May God himself, the God of peace, sanctify you through and through. May your whole spirit, soul and body be kept blameless at the coming of our Lord Jesus Christ" (1 Thessalonians 5:23).

The Christian will discover that he has moved out of this earthly body of flesh and donned a celestial body that God has prepared for him, a body suited and fitted for him to live in. Of this Paul wrote:

> For we know that if the earthly house of our tabernacle be dissolved, we have a building from God, a house not made with hands, eternal, in the heavens. For verily in this we groan, longing to be clothed upon with our habitation

> which is from heaven: if so be that being clothed we shall not be found naked (2 Corinthians 5:1-3).

• The Christian will discover that he is now completely surrounded and breathes an atmosphere of holiness, righteousness, and love prepared for him by the Lord Jesus.

• The Christian will be reunited with his loved ones who have preceded him. The guardian angel will have informed his loved ones he is coming (Hebrews 12:1).

• The Christian will meet and have fellowship with the great saints and Christian leaders who have gone before, i. e., Adam, Eve, Abel, Noah, Abraham, Ruth, Moses, Joshua, Samuel, David, and other Old Testament patriarches and prophets ; and New Testament personalities like Mary the mother of Jesus, Mary Magdalene, Paul, Peter, James, John, Stephen, Barnabas, Silas, Priscilla and Aquila, Timothy, Titus, and others.

°The Christian will realize that he was created for two worlds—the physical he has left behind and the spiritual mansion prepared for him by the Lord: "I go to prepare a place for you" (John 14:2b, KJV).

• The Christian will experience and be conscious of seeing and standing in the presence of the Lord Jesus Christ: "They will see his face, and his name will be on their foreheads" (Revelation 22:4).

The Bible teaches that the departed soul will spend eternity in a very real heaven or a very real hell. The most fearful situation we can conceive of is to live without God and die without Jesus Christ as our Savior.

Not a renovated earth

Heaven is a household word. Most rational, thinking people are looking forward to a home where there will be no more changes and where bliss, joy, and gladness forever proliferate. But where is this place to be? What is it like? Do we have any adequate idea? The Lord Jesus Christ assured the apostles:

> Let not your heart be troubled: ye believe in God, believe also in me. In my Father's house are many mansions: if it were not so, I would have told you. I go to prepare a place for you. And if I go and prepare a place for you, I will

> come again, and receive you unto myself; that where I am, there ye may be also. And whither I go ye know, and the way ye know (John 14:1-4, KJV).

Thus the Lord emphasized the thought of our eternal abode being with Him by twice calling attention to it.

What will heaven be like?

Mind you that nothing can fully describe God, in all of His awesome majesty, and the eternal home of Him and all who have received Him through the ages. It is amazing beyond all human comprehension. Paul touched on this when he virtually shouted, "But as it is written, Eye hath not seen, nor ear heard, neither have entered into the heart of man, the things which God hath prepared for them that love him"(1 Corinthians 2:9).

God's holy angels, at the death of the believer, will carry her/him to heaven. It is a place of indescribable beauty and ecstasy. The angels transport the person's spiritual being into the very presence of God. Ezekiel in a vision beheld the awesome glory and majesty of God that produces a spectacular glow like a fire and a brilliant light surrounds Him.

> Above the expanse over their heads was what looked like a throne of sapphire, and high above on the throne was a figure like that of a man. I saw that from what appeared to be his waist up he looked like glowing metal, as if full of fire, and that from there down he looked like fire; and brilliant light surrounded him. Like the appearance of a rainbow in the clouds on a rainy day, so was the radiance around him. This was the appearance of the likeness of the glory of the Lord. When I saw it, I fell facedown, and I heard the voice of one speaking (Ezekiel 1:26-28, NIV).

Your eyes will behold God in all His beauty (Isaiah 33:17). As believers leave the throne room of God they will gaze on streets of pure gold, like transparent glass (Revelation 21:21). The twelve gates are constructed of pearls—each gate from a single pearl (Revelation 21:21). The city has no need of sun or moon to light it, for the glory of God and the lamb illuminate it. The gates never close, and there is no night (Revelation 21:23-25, TLB).

The people you will meet in heaven, like you, are believers in Jesus Christ and have their names written in the lamb's book of life (Revelation 21:27, TLB). "You will see a river of pure water of life, clear as crystal, flowing from the throne of God and the Lamb, coursing down the center of main street. On each side of the river grows the tree of life, bearing twelve crops of fruit, with a fresh crop each month" (Revelation 22:1-3, TLB). Angels no doubt will teach and guide believers in heaven.

Questions about heaven

Will we work in heaven? Yes

Our Father will have duties for each of us, "and His servants will serve Him" (Rev 22:3). Whatever we do will give us superabundant joy and satisfaction and not in sweat and drudgery as in this life.

Will we eat? Yes

Jesus after He received His glorified body ate broiled fish (Luke 24:42-43). The fruit trees mentioned in Revelation 22:1-3 will provide food for believers.

Will we wear clothes? Yes

Each of them were given a white robe (Revelation 6:11).

Will believers in heaven be married? No

They will neither marry nor be given in marriage (Revelation 20:34). We all will have fulfilling relationships but neither marriage nor sex.

Will we remember what happened on earth? No

The former things will not be remembered, nor will they come to mind (Isaiah 65:17).

Eternal rewards (Revelation 22:12; 2 Corinthians 5:10)

We are saved by grace, through faith (Ephesians 2:8-9), and that insures us a place in heaven, but we will be rewarded according to what we have done on earth. "But why dost thou judge thy brother? or why dost thou set at nought thy brother? for we shall all stand before the judgment seat of Christ" (Romans 14:10, KJV). "For we must all appear before the judgment seat of Christ; that every one may receive the things done in his body, according to that he hath done, whether it be good or bad" (2 Corinthians 5:10 KJV; see also 2 Corinthians 5:10, TLB; Jeremiah 17:10; Hebrews 6:10; Revelation 14:13; 1 Corinthians 4:5).

Many people who have lived humble lives here on earth will receive special blessings at the judgment seat of Christ (Matthew 19:30). Christians who are soul-winners will have the highest commendation from the Judge, shining as stars (Daniel 12:3).

To close out this section on heaven, I believe it appropriate to mention what will not be in Heaven. There will not be:

- sorrow, tears, regrets, broken hearts, or loneliness;
- aging, death, pain, emotional, mental, physical, or spiritual hurts, diseases, hospitals, pharmacies, nursing homes, rehab centers, or tiredness;
- selfishness, strife, jealousy, anger, or temper;
- rent, mortgages, taxes, lawsuits, or hunger;
- a devil (Satan), no sin and evil influence.

We will bask in perfect health and enjoy the ideal joy of the Lord. Throughout this book I ask this urgent question, "Have you given your heart and life to Christ?" If you have your reservation is confirmed for your trip to your eternal home in heaven. "Behold, now is the accepted time; behold, now is the day of salvation" (2 Corinthians 6:2b, KJV). God never promised us tomorrow. *His time is now*. You may think, *Oh, I can come to Christ just anytime I want to.* According to Jesus that is not the case: "No man [meaning woman as well] can come to me, except the Father which hath sent me draw him: and I will raise him up at the last day" (John 6:44, KJV). There are specific times when God is tugging on you through the convicting power of the Holy Spirit. If you sense the slightest inclination to accept Christ, *do it right this moment!*

Hell: The eternal abode of the lost

The death of the unbeliever

"Whoever believes in the Son has eternal life, but whoever rejects the Son will not see life, for God's wrath remains on him" (John 3:36). Once there was a Gospel tract. On the front it read, "What Must I Do to Be Lost?" Inside it simply said: "Nothing." Then it explained God's plan of salvation. You can reject Christ and be lost by merely failing to accept Him.

The unbeliever goes through life with one birth, yet the believer has a second birth when he accepts Christ as Savior and is born again. The unbeliever's life consists of ups and downs and may be successful or fail from an earthly standpoint . . . but the unsaved person has no future with God—only the certainty of divine judgment. Further, the unbeliever has one life but two deaths. The first is physical death and the second, spiritual death (final, permanent separation from God). Revelation 2:11; 20:6,14; and 21:8 refer to "the second death," which is not a cessation of existence but an eternity separated from God and all that is decent, lovely, and good.

When an unsaved person dies physically (they are already dead spiritually), their soul goes to an awful place called *hades* in the Greek New Testament, referred to as "hell" in most English translations. This is a temporary place where the lost person suffers until a final disposition is made at God's last judgment, the great white throne judgment (see Revelation 21:11-15). The human spirit is "quickened" (made alive) at the moment of conversion when a person receives Christ (Ephesians 2:1).

At the last judgment, hades delivers up its dead, which is the second resurrection (Revelation 20:5- 6,11-15). The first resurrection will have already occurred at the rapture of the Church when Christ comes back to receive His own (see 1 Thessalonians 4:16-18). Both soul and body will suffer as the unbeliever is cast into the lake of fire (Geénna in Greek, Gehenna in English) which has already been prepared for Satan and his angels (Matthew 25:41). It was not originally intended for human beings, but they go there if they choose the devil instead of Christ.

Hades

The first compartment, which Jesus Christ called "Abraham's bosom" (Luke 16:22), was also referred to as paradise (Luke 23:43). It was the area where the souls of all Old Testament saints were carried after death. The second compartment was where unbelievers go to torments. When Jesus was resurrected, He transferred all who were in paradise with Him when He ascended to heaven (Ephesians 4:2,9; 2 Corinthians 2:2). Unbelievers remain in the torment section of hades until the final judgment (Revelation 20:5).

Two sets of books at life's end

First—The book of life is a list of all who are believers in the true God, as revealed in Christ. Those who have not accepted Him will not have their names in the book.

Second—Groups of books consist of books of works or deeds. Deeds done on earth (2 Corinthians 5:21; Romans 4:13) are in one book at the great white throne judgment. "They were judged every man according to their works [deeds]" (Romans 4:14). As believers it is our awe-inspiring task to give the Gospel message to the world so people will not end up in the lake of fire.

The doctrine of hell

I am well aware that today the doctrine of a literal hell is highly unpopular. Since the Scriptures, including Jesus' words, are literally true, it behooves us to accept all other statements of doctrine as meaning specifically what they state. Jesus spoke more about hell and judgment than He did about heaven and justification.

It is clear from these passages—and we could examine numerous others—that the Bible teaches there is such a place as hell for future punishment. All who are willing to receive the Biblical testimony are driven to accept the fact that the Scriptures teach a place of future retribution, even as they speak of a place called heaven.

The choice is yours alone

This question is frequently asked, "How could a loving God create some of His creatures for eternal punishment?" God did not create any of His creatures for that. He created all persons (celestial and human) to love, obey, and enjoy Him forever. He created beings with the capacity of choosing for themselves either good or evil. The majority seem to choose evil. But God has not abandoned them but have sacrificed His only begotten Son to save them from their hell-driven choice. If people see fit not only to choose evil but also to deliberately and persistently refuse the free offer of salvation, then their eternal punishment is their own fault. To blame God for one's lost state is not only unjust but ungrateful and unreasonable.

People condemn themselves

Men and women condemn themselves to everlasting punishment by rejecting Jesus Christ, thus refusing the mercy and grace of God. If people will not allow God to save them from sin and its consequences, they must necessarily continue in it. And if they continue in it, they must suffer anguish as long as they do so. The time will come, sooner or later, when repentance becomes impossible; so salvation will not be forthcoming. Whether or not they are aware of it, people choose their eternal destiny. As one forceful African-American preacher put it, "The Savior and Satan are having an election. You *have* to cast your vote."

Cause—not time—effects punishment

Is it unjust to punish a few years of sin with an eternity of torment? The duration of sin's punishment can never be determined by the time it requires to commit the sin. A man can kill a person in a split second, but a just penalty would be lifelong imprisonment. Furthermore, sin involves separation from God, and separation from God is torment. The torment must continue as long as separation from God exists. When repentance and the acceptance of the Savior become impossible, one becomes eternally confirmed in one's separation from God, and eternal torment must necessarily follow.

It is not a few years of sin that cause eternal punishment. A person might continue for years in sin and still escape eternal torment *if they will only repent and accept Jesus Christ!* It is the rejection of Jesus Christ (cause) that ushers in an eternity of torment (effects).

Those who opt not to receive Christ when He is presented to them, and demonstrate no concern for God's truth and goodness, will after physical death remain without hope, eternally and consciously separated from God. Those who reject Him, after death **will never be given another chance!** "And as it is appointed unto men once to die, but after this the judgment" (Hebrews 9:27, KJV).

How dreadful and horrifying are Jesus' statements: "Then shall he say also unto them on the left hand, Depart from me, ye cursed, into everlasting fire, prepared for the devil and his angels" (Matthew 25:41, KJV). "There shall be weeping and gnashing of teeth" (Matthew 8:12, KJV).

Three words Christ used to describe Hell:

Fire—"For our God is a consuming fire" (Hebrews 12:29). Jesus employed this symbol several times. Certain scholars believe it means a thirst for God that is never quenched.

Darkness—The Bible teaches that God is light (John 1:4-9; 1 John 1:5). Hell will be exactly the opposite for unbelievers, for they will be thrown outside into darkness (Matthew 8:12). Hell is described as a fire, but that ceaseless fire will not give light! Those who have rejected Christ will be separated from this light and subsist in darkness.

Death—God is life (John 10:10; John 14:6). So, hell is separation from the life of God. "Then death and hades were thrown into the lake of fire" (Revelation 20:14). The separation from God is the second death (physical was the first).

Life is the opposite of death

We are to spend eternity somewhere. Death means spending it separated from God in eternal torment, while life indicates an eternity with God amid all the pleasures and joys He has in store for us. Everlasting life is eternity with God the Father, God the Son, and God the Holy Ghost. "Verily, verily, I say unto you, He that heareth my word, and believeth on him that sent me, hath everlasting life, and shall not come into condemnation; but is passed from death unto life" (John 5:24).

Writing this section on hell was an unpleasant experience, but the Holy Spirit compelled me. When I have heard sermons on hell, and people have given the preacher the customary, "I enjoyed it," I could not agree. Preaching on hell and judgment is not enjoyable . . . but is absolutely imperative if one is a witness who "correctly handles the word of truth" (2 Timothy 2:15).

My prayer is that God will use this book as an instrument to reveal truths resulting in many people becoming, through Christ, "*supernaturalized citizens*" of heaven.

Today is the day of salvation. Tomorrow may be too late. Situations beyond our control can instantly snatch a tomorrow from us—wrecks, heart attacks, accidents, strokes, you name them. Ask Christ to become your Lord and Savior now. "The Lord is not slow in keeping his promise, as some understand slowness. He is patient with you, not wanting anyone to perish, but everyone to come to repentance" (1 Peter 3:9).

> That if you confess with your mouth, "Jesus is Lord," and believe in your heart that God raised him from the dead, you will be saved. For it is with your heart that you believe and are justified, and it is with your mouth that you confess and are saved. . . . for "Everyone who calls on the name of the Lord will be saved" (Romans 10:9-10,13).

For thought and discussion

1. In order to be saved, one must ——— of his sins and ——— on the Lord Jesus Christ as personal ———.
2. Where does life for the believer begin?
3. How many heavens are there, and what do they constitute?
4. Name three Bible persons who saw heaven.
5. What was the Transfiguration? Who were the two persons that appeared with Jesus?
6. What is the difference between hades and the lake of fire?
7. Name three words that describe hell.
8. How do you prepare for eternal life?

Thoughts of Heaven

I ofttimes think of Heaven
　　With all its joy and peace,
When from this world of sadness
　　My soul shall find release.
I wonder how twill seem, when
　　I've reached the golden shore;
With loved ones waiting for me;
　　Where we shall part no more.
I think of many mansions
　　Prepared by Christ's dear hand;
And of His shining glory
　　In that far distant land.
How blessed it will be when
　　I'm caught up in the air;
From earth or grave He'll call me,
　　Heaven's joy with Him to share.
Twill only take a moment;
　　The twinkling of an eye;
I'll be changed and travel
　　Beyond the starry sky.
These thoughts of Heaven lure me
　　As nothing else can do.
Some day my Lord will tell me
　　My work on earth is through;
That day the trump shall signal;
　　And I shall hear the sound;
Time and earth I'll leave far behind
　　When I am heaven bound.
The time shall not be long now
　　As prophecies unfold;
Til I see my Savior
　　And walk those streets of gold.

—Author Unknown

Part II

THE CHRISTIAN LIFE

And when he [Barnabas] had found him [Saul, later called Paul] he brought him unto Antioch. And it came to pass, that a whole year they assembled themselves with the church, and taught much people. And the disciples were called Christians first in Antioch (Acts 11:26, KJV).

I have been crucified with Christ and I no longer live, but Christ lives in me. The life I live in the body, I live by faith in the Son of God, who loved me and gave himself for me (Galatians 2:20).

Then Agrippa said unto Paul, Almost thou persuadest me to be a Christian (Acts 26:28, KJV).

Yet if any man suffer as a Christian, let him not be ashamed; but let him glorify God on this behalf (1 Peter 4:16, KJV).

I press toward the mark for the prize of the high calling of God in Christ Jesus (Philippians 3:14, KJV).

4
Salvation—Then What?

Therefore we are buried with him by baptism into death: that like as Christ was raised up from the dead by the glory of the Father, even so we also should walk in newness of life. (Romans 6:4, KJV)

Salvation is a gift of God's grace. There is nothing we can do to earn it, but we must reach out in faith and receive it. I pray that, if not already, you will decide on eternal life and hope through Christ.

Christ's relationship with suffering humanity

John Wesley, the founder of Methodism, understood Jesus' emphasis that the best means of coming close to God is not by "religious" acts but our treatment of people. Christ-like treatment toward others, especially the poor and disenfranchised, grants you power with God. Jesus indicated that when we serve our fellow man, we are indirectly serving Him. "The King will reply, 'I tell you the truth, whatever you did for one of the least of these brothers of mine, you did for me'" (Matthew 25:40). "'For I was hungry and you gave me something to eat, I was thirsty and you gave me something to drink, I was a stranger and you invited me in, I needed clothes and you clothed me, I was sick and you looked after me, I was in prison and you came to visit me'" (Matthew 25:35-36).

Jesus not only saves . . . but He keeps

Jesus is not going to save us and then cut us loose to fend for ourselves. He has promised, "And surely I am with you always, to the very end of the age" (Matthew 28:20). At present He indwells us through the Holy Spirit (see Galatians 2:20). Jesus is not only our helper—He is our life. *He does not want us to work for Him. Rather, He wants us to let Him do His work through us, employing us as His instrument, even as one of the fingers on His hand.*

When we are regenerated by the Holy Spirit and become new creatures in Christ (2 Corinthians 5:17), the strength of our fallen nature is conquered but not destroyed, because sanctification—growing in God's grace (1 Peter 3:18)—is a life-long process. Christians are daily engaged in spiritual warfare with the old nature as they seek to grow in the Spirit. The old nature dies daily as the new person in Christ is empowered by the resident Holy Spirit. We as Christians will continue to face sin and temptation. This is why daily prayer and meditation, Bible reading, witnessing, stewardship, and worshiping, hopefully with fellow believers, are utterly essential.

Jesus never promised us a rose garden . . . without thorns

Living out our faith involves a certain amount of blood, sweat, and tears. Jesus called us as His lifelong learners and followers. Our discipleship never ends.

When we accept Him, He removes one set of problems—the burdens of sin, guilt, isolation, hopelessness, and separation from God. As that occurs He calls for us to become yoked with Him spiritually. "My yoke is easy and my burden is light" (Matthew 11:30, KJV). In comparison with the heavy burdens of an existence without God, the load we bear for Him is light as a feather. Yet, living a consistent Christian life—contrary to "pop" theology—is not all sweetness and light. We are to follow Him regardless of the costs, and He never promises that we will always have smooth sailing. Paul made it plain: "Endure hardship with us like a good soldier of Christ Jesus" (2 Timothy 2:3).

There is nothing on earth to compare with life in Christ, but our walk will be strewn with problems, suffering, tests and trials, and temptations. Amid all of our ups and downs Jesus will provide peace, joy, and the other fruit of the Spirit (see Galatians 5:22-23). As long as we have the assurance that our Commander in Chief is in control, no trial is too crushing, no storm too tempestuous, no crisis too overwhelming. With Paul we can exclaim, "I can do all things through Christ which strengtheneth me" (Philippians 4:13, KJV).

Heart in the Bible

In the Bible the word heart refers to a human being's inward place of thinking, loving, and deciding—the inner place where affection, emotion, passion, conscience, and faith meet and grow together. Heart, in biblical terminology, refers to the center of moral, spiritual, and intellectual life—the seat of emotions, beliefs, and decisions. " Heart" and "soul" are used interchangeably in the Bible, the heart being considered the center of *soul*-life as well as *physical*-life (Deuteronomy 6:5; 8:14; 11:13-18; Matthew 5:8). The heart is the seat of love (2 Samuel 15:6; Mark 12:30,33), of hatred (Leviticus 19:17: 2 Samuel 6:16), of joy (Ruth 3:7; Acts 2:26,46), of sorrow (Psalm 102:4; John 14:1), of wisdom (Exodus 31:6; Acts 28:27), and of pride (Proverbs 16:5; 21:4; Revelation 18:7). See also 2 Corinthians 4:6; Revelation 2:23."[1] Physically, one's heart is the propelling force of blood to keep the human body healthy. The Christ-centered spiritual heart is the enabling source for wholeness in the moral, spiritual, and intellectual dimensions of life.

Your worth to Christ

There is no greater joy than the peace and assurance of knowing that, whatever the future holds, you are secure in the loving arms of the Savior, our hope for right now and for the future. If you are a Christian, maybe He is calling you to a new commitment in which you will serve Him more fully. Whatever your spiritual needs are right now, Christ wants to provide them. He is Lord of the universe and wants to become Lord of your life as well.

Ann Graham Lotz is one of Billy and Ruth Graham's daughters. In her book, *The Vision of His Glory*, she wrote that, while waiting in a busy airline terminal, she reflected on the thought of how one individual can

---

[1]"Heart" in *Master Study Bible* (Nashville, TN: Holman Bible Publishers, 1981), 1876.

feel insignificant in the rush of business. Then Jesus Christ came to her mind as the most important person in the world, not merely in our nation or our planet, but in the entire universe. He is not merely important for four or eight years—but unceasingly throughout eternity.

Furthermore, the most important person in our universe considers how important we are. "Me? Important?" Yes, you and I. In fact, are you aware that you, one human soul, are worth more than this entire world with all of its resources? Our caring Lord proved that by posing this soul-searching question:

> For what shall it profit a man [or woman], if he [she] shall gain the whole world, and lose his [her] own soul? (Mark 8:36, KJV)

God has "pulled out all of the stops" to demonstrate how He loves us. Augustine exclaimed, "God loves you as though you were the only one to love!" Paul exulted, "But God demonstrates his own love for us in this: While we were still sinners, Christ died for us" (Romans 5:8). As the old song goes, "Tenderly He Watches Over Me." Imagine it. The Almighty God of the universe, the Creator and Sustainer of everything, who spoke the worlds and us into existence, longs to have a personal relationship with us.

The ultimate human experience is knowing God in an intimate spiritual relationship. Jesus Christ is all-powerful, fully in charge. No one is mightier than Him. One day every knee shall bow before Him and acknowledge that He is King of Kings and Lord of Lords (see Isaiah 9:6). When we are facing the impossible, we can count on the God of the impossible. Our life may be out of control, but it is ultimately under His control. Christ alone can set us free from the bondage and slavery of sin. He is the only one who can give meaning, definition, and purpose to our lives.

Filling the God-shaped vacuum

Human beings are born into this world with a vacuum at the center of their being. One may have physical life but is without a spiritual dimension through which he can know God personally. All kinds of false cults and isms are searching for God. The fact is, though, He is actually searching for us. Knowing God is only possible by accepting Christ as one's Savior. The apostles proclaimed that God so loved those whom He redeemed on the cross that He has adopted them all as His heirs, to view and share in the glory into which God's Son has come. God sent that Son to save us from condemnation by the law, that we might receive the full (adoptive) rights of sons (Galatians 4:4-15). Adoption is a family idea, conceived in terms of love and viewing God as Father. In adoption, God receives us into His family and fellowship. He establishes us as His children and heirs. Closeness, affection, and generosity are the heart of the relationship.

You and I have infinite worth apart from looks, intelligence, and performance because Christ gave His life for us and attaches inestimable value to us.

Certain basic tenets of Christianity

1. The inspiration and infallibility of scripture
2. The virgin birth
3. The Deity of Christ
4. Christ's substitutionary atonement
5. His resurrection
6. His ascension to Heaven
7. The coming of the Holy Spirit
8. Jesus' return to earth

Our precious Savior invites us to join ourselves to Him, to unite our weakness to His strength, our ignorance to His wisdom, our unworthiness to His merits.

Reviewing God's plan of salvation

1. God's love is revealed.	John 3:16; Romans 5:8
2. Humans are sinful.	John 3:18; Romans 3:23
3. Sin has a penalty.	Romans 6:23
4. Christ paid the penalty.	John 1:29; 1 Thessalonians 5:10
5. You should receive Him.	John 1:12
6. He will give you everlasting life.	John 17:3

Living a Christian life

1. Pray daily and often as you can.	John 14:13; 1 Thessalonians 5:17
2. Learn to depend on the Holy Spirit.	John 14:26; Acts 1:8
3. Attend church regularly.	Hebrews 10:24-25
4. Serve others in Jesus' name.	John 13:14; Matthew 20:27-28
5. Learn to overcome your doubts.	John 8:12; 2 Timothy 1:12
6. Learn to have peace of mind.	John 14:27; Philippians 4:7
7. Learn the blessings of suffering.	John 16:22
8. Learn how to meet temptation.	John 17:15; 1 Corinthians 10:13
9. Share the good news.	John 4:35; Acts 8:4

Time: A gift of the Lord

The Christian view of life recognizes that *all* of our time belongs to God in the sense that we should never spend our time with thoughts, attitudes, or actions contrary to His will. But God has given us 168 hours in each week. If we fail to dedicate a special portion of our time to His service, we are ungratefully neglecting to show our love for Him and our fellowman.

A Christian time survey

Driving to Church	30 minutes
Sunday School*	5-60 minutes
Sunday Morning Worship	60 minutes
Driving Home from Church	30 minutes
Driving to Church Sunday Night*	30 minutes
Sunday Night Worship*	60 minutes
Driving Home from Church*	30 minutes
Mid-Week (Including Driving)*	90 minutes
Daily Bible Reading	35 minutes (5 minutes x 7)
Prayer	35 minutes (5 minutes x 7)
Total	460 minutes
460 ÷ 60 minutes to an hour	7.67 Hours or 4.5% of your time

*A number of churches no longer have these activities. Notice that this time survey includes nothing for visitation, witnessing, counseling, and special ministries. **Are you being fair and honest with God about your time?** Think it over! The Bible makes it clear that no one's life is satisfying apart from God. No one can discover life's highest good without spending time:

- Worshiping God
- Working for God (God working through us)
- Walking in Fellowship with God

This basic rule is unchanging. It will never change as long as God is God and humans are humans. Jesus declared, "My Father is still at work and therefore I work as well" (John 5:17).

Principles in life

- We always reap what we sow (Galatians 6:7).
- The people you spend time with will influence the direction of your life (Proverbs 13:20).
- The person who hates to be corrected will eventually make stupid mistakes (Proverbs 12:1).
- Liars will ultimately be found out (Proverbs 12:19).
- What you hold onto will diminish, but what you give will be multiplied (2 Corinthians 9:6).
- God always provides for the needs of the generous (Philippians 4:19).

God's principles are timeless truths, applying to all of us at all times. In one respect they are similar to the laws of nature God has set into motion. Jump from a skyscraper without a rope, parachute, or other support, and you're a goner. Principles can be ignored but not broken. The Bible is chuckfull of them. An unknown writer has observed:

> *Principles are timeless, universal laws that empower* people. . . . principles have infinite applications, as varied as circumstances. They tend to be self- validating, self-evident, universal truths. When we start to recognize a correct principle, it becomes so familiar to us, it is almost like "common sense."

Virtually every decision you make will intersect with one or more principles of God's Word. They are that comprehensive and all-encompassing. From friends to finances, there are principles to guide you, and the principles are furthered through the leading of the Holy Spirit.

Life can have true meaning

If you feel your life lacks genuine, true meaning, have you stopped to wonder why? Likely you have. God can give your life purposeful meaning and direction if you will follow these steps:

Step 1: Remember God loves you and has a plan for your life.
His love includes you.
"For God so loved the world that he gave his one and only Son, that whoever believes in him shall not perish but have eternal life" (John 3:16).
He has new life for you.
"I have come that they may have life, and have it to the full" (John 10:10).

Step 2: Sin separates you from God and from others.
Sin is taking our way in rebellion against God's will.
"Surely the arm of the Lord is not too short to save, nor his ear too dull to hear. But your iniquities have separated you from your God; your sins have hidden his face from you, so that he will not hear (Isaiah 59:1-2, KJV).
All of us have sinned.
"For all have sinned and fall short of the glory of God" (Romans 3:23, KJV).
Sin brings death.
"For the wages of sin is death" (Romans 6:23, KJV). Sinners try, hopelessly, to find life's true meaning in the wrong ways and places.
Our own efforts cannot save us.
"For it is by grace you have been saved, through faith—and this is not from yourselves, it is the gift of God not by works, so that no one can boast" (Ephesians 2:8-9).

Step 3: Remember Jesus Christ died and rose again for our sins.

He died in our place.

"But God demonstrates his own love for us in this: While we were still sinners, Christ died for us" (Romans 5:8).

Jesus Christ is the way to new life.

"Therefore, if anyone is in Christ, he is a new creation; the old has gone, the new has come!" (2 Corinthians 5:17).

He gives innner peace,

"We have peace with God through our Lord Jesus Christ" (Romans 5:1).

And freedom,

"So if the Son sets you free, you will be free indeed" (John 8:36).

And eternal life.

". . . but the gift of God is eternal life in Christ Jesus our Lord" (Romans 6:23).

Step 4: Place your trust in Christ and receive Him as your Savior.

Christ is ready.

"Here I am! I stand at the door and knock. If anyone hears my voice and opens the door, I will come in . . ." (Revelation 3:20).

Receive Him now.

"To all who received him, to those who believed in his name, he gave the right to become children of God" (John 1:12).

Step 5: You must repent and ask God for forgiveness.

Admit and confess your sins to God.

"He who conceals his sins does not prosper, but whoever confesses and renounces them finds mercy" (Proverbs 28:13).

Repentance means:

to acknowledge your sins
to be sorry for your sins
to confess (to own up to) your sins
to be willing to forsake your sins
to have your life changed by Christ

Forgiveness is promised.
"If we confess our sins, he is faithful and just and will forgive us our sins and purify us from all unrighteousness" (1 John 1:9).

Jesus Christ didn't say, "Clean up your act, and then I'll save you." He accepts us as we are into His family. For years the only invitation hymn Billy Graham has used is *Just As I Am.* If you are truly repentant, you not only receive Him but He receives you. All we have to do is believe in the Lord's death on the cross for our sins and accept Him. Sanctification follows your initial salvation experience. However, you do not become a Christian by being a member of a church and participating in its functions. You become a Christian by personally accepting Christ. He gives you a "new birth" that turns you around and builds a new life in Him.

What to pray

Lord Jesus, I want to have new life. I know I have sinned. I need Your forgiveness and pardon. I believe You died and rose again for my sins. I now accept You as my personal Savior. I will forsake my sins. I know Your grace and power will enable me to live for You. Thank You, Jesus, for saving me and giving me eternal life and forgiveness.

If you prayed that, or an improvised prayer in your own words—and you meant it from your heart . . .

Jesus Christ has entered your life and saved you!

He has forgiven all of your sins, and God has written your name in the Lamb's Book of Life in Heaven.

You are now an adopted child of God and are an heir to all of His promises, including His indwelling presence here and an eternal home with Him in heaven when He calls you away.

The Lord Jesus promised: "All that the Father gives me will come to me, and whoever comes to me I will never drive away" (John 6:37, KJV). Now please carefully and prayerfully read the next chapter.

For thought and discussion

1. How long does sanctification require?
2. Explain the significance of "heart" in the Bible.
3. List at least five basic tenets of Christianity.
4. How can a Christian fight temptation?
5. If one would live a consistent Christian life, what is involved?
6. Jot down a schedule of how you use your time in the course of a week.
7. If you are born again, how did you come to know Christ as your Savior?

5
How Can I Know I Am a Christian?

Christ. . .
And ye shall know the truth, and the truth shall make you free (John 8:32. KJV).
I am the way, the truth, and the life: no man cometh unto the Father, but by me (John 14:6, KJV).

God created humans in His own image and offered them an abundant life. The Creator did not make them robots automatically to love and obey Him but gave him a will and freedom of choice (see Revelation 22:17). Tragically, the first human beings, Adam and Eve, deliberately chose to disobey God and "turn every one to his own way" (Isiah 53:6, KJV). Millions—probably billions—still choose self instead of the Savior. This results in separation from God.

Man through the ages has tried to bridge this gap by grasping for "religion," for, as one sage expressed it, "Man is incurably religious." He has searched every conceivable pathway, including good works, but without success.

The number-one premise of this book is: **JESUS CHRIST** is the only answer to alienation and being cut off from the true and living God. Through His death, burial, and resurrection, He has spanned that chasm between God and mankind.

The Cross—God's remedy

"That God is on one side and all the people on the other side, and Christ Jesus, himself man, is between them to bring them together, by giving his life for all mankind" (1 Timothy 2:5, TLB).

ARE YOU HERE?	**OR HERE?**
HUMANITY	**GOD**
Sin	Forgiveness
Separation	Peace
Frustration and guilt	Abundant life
Lack of purpose	Eternal life

What you must do to become a Christian

Believe by faith that Jesus Christ loves you, died on the cross to atone for your sins, and rose the third day to assure you of eternal life.

Remember God loves you and has a plan for your life.

- His love includes you.
  "For God so loved the world that he gave his one and only Son, that whoever believes in him shall not perish but have eternal life" (John 3:16).
- He has new life for you.
  "I have come that they may have life, and have it to the full" (John 10:10).

Invite Christ into your life, place your trust in Him, and accept Him as your Lord and Savior.

Place your trust in Christ and receive Him as your Savior.

- Christ is ready.
  "Here I am! I stand at the door and knock. If anyone hears my voice and opens the door, I will come in" (Revelation 3:20).
- Receive Him now.
  "To all who received him, to those who believed in his name, he gave the right to become children of God" (John 1:12).

How Can I Know I Am a Christian?

Recognize sin separates you from God.

Sin is rebellion against God's will.

- Everyone has sinned.
  "For all have sinned and fall short of the glory of God" (Romans 3:23).
- Sin brings death (Separation from God).

Confess you are a sinner.

As sinners we try, hopelessly, to find life's true meaning in the wrong ways and places. "For the wages of sin is death" (Romans 6:23).

- Our own efforts cannot save us.
  "For it is by grace you have been saved, through faith—and this not from yourselves, it is the gift of God—not by works, so that no one can boast" (Ephesians 2:8-9).

Repent by asking God for forgiveness and be willing to turn from your sins.

"If we confess our sins, he is faithful and just and will forgive us our sins and purify us from all unrighteousness" (1 John 1:9).

Commit your life to the will of God and recognize He has a plan for your life.

"Ye are the light of the world . . . Let your light so shine before men, that they may see your good works, and glorify your Father which is in heaven" (Matthew 5:14, 16).

Thank Him for giving your life new meaning and making you a new person.

He gives inner peace.

"We have peace with God through our Lord Jesus Christ" (Romans 5:1).

- And freedom.
  "So if the Son sets you free, you will be free indeed" (John 8:36).
- And eternal life.
  ". . . but the gift of God is eternal life in Christ Jesus our Lord" (Romans 6:23).

Model prayer to be saved (born again spirituality)

Dear God:

I accept You, Lord Jesus, as my personal Savior and invite You to make Your home in my heart. I surrender my life to Your Spirit and from this day forward, I will seek to carry out Your will. I believe, Lord, that You died and shed Your blood on the Cross as the only acceptable sacrifice for my sins and were resurrected on the third day so I can have eternal life. I confess to You: I am a sinner. I repent of my sins and will turn away from them.

____

Signed Date

It is this simple to become a Christian

God loves you.
Christ died for you.
You repent of your sins.
You accept Christ and receive forgiveness.
You discover the joy of God's love.
You live eternally with Christ.

Facts about Christian faith—Witnessing tools

• You may believe in God and the Church, but unless you have asked Him to enter your life as your Lord and Savior, you are not saved, and Christ is not the Lord of your life.

• If you do not receive Christ as Savior and bow to Him now as Lord of your life, the day is coming when you will bow to Him as Judge in judgment.

• The marvelous security of the Christian faith is: it is specifically designed for overcoming the storms of this life and giving us the certainty of eternal life, which starts when we are born again, now and in heaven.

• Jesus Christ will make His residence in you right now if you will turn from your sins and receive Him as Savior.

• Christ is waiting to share our sorrows, to renew our courage, to come in and fellowship intimately. He will never forsake us or let us down.

• Do you need comfort in your personal trials? Christ is waiting.

• Do you need forgiveness for your sins? Christ is knocking to come in.

What happens when we accept Christ

1. We *receive* Christ by faith into our hearts and are accepted by Him as righteous.

2. We are *pardoned* for our sins, and God will remember them no more.

3. We are *baptized* by the Holy Spirit, and He comes to live in our hearts and becomes our Comforter, Teacher, Guide, Sanctifier, and Revelator of truth.

4. We are *adopted* into the family of God. The sins of God's born-again children do not destroy their justification or nullify their adoption, but they mar the children's fellowship with their Heavenly Father. God commands, "Be ye holy; for I am holy" (1 Peter 1:16, KJV).

We are children of God through faith in Christ Jesus. The gift of sonship (and daughtership) is ours not through being born, but through accepting Christ as our Savior (being born again spiritually). "Therefore come out from them and be separate, says the Lord. Touch no unclean thing, and I will receive you. I will be a Father to you, and you will be my sons and daughters, says the Lord Almighty" (2 Corinthians 6:17-18). We are heirs and joint heirs with Jesus. "Now if we are children, then we are heirs—heirs of God and co-heirs with Christ, if indeed we share in his sufferings in order that we may also share in his glory" (Romans 8:17).

As God loves His only begotten Son, so He loves us, His spiritual sons and daughters, and adopts us into His family and fellowship. This new familial relationship arises not by natural birth but is a supernatural gift from God which we receive through accepting Christ (Galatians 4:5).

5. We are eternally *secured* in Him. Knowing God involves faith, assent, consent, and commitment. Faith expresses itself in prayer and obedience (Romans 8:29-30; Ephesians 1:13-14, 4:30; John 10: 28-30)

When you become a Christian . . .

- Pray daily. 1 Thessalonians 5:17; Luke 18:1
- Read the Bible daily. Acts 17:11; Psalm 1:2
- Confess Christ openly and be baptized. Matthew 10:32; 28:19-20; Acts 2:41
- Attend church where the Bible is preached and Christ is honored. Hebrew 10:25
- Keep Christ's commandments. John 14:15

God's Assurance of the Believer's Salvation

The Bible makes it plain

For whosoever shall call upon the name of the Lord shall be saved (Romans 10:13, KJV).

He that hath the Son hath life [right now], and he that hath not the Son of God hath not life. These things have I written unto you that believe on the name of the Son of God, that you may know that ye have eternal life, and ye may believe on the name of the Son of God (1 John 5:12-13, KJV).

All have sinned and come short of the glory of God (Romans 3:23, KJV).

For the wages of sin is death [eternal separation from God here and hereafter] but the gift of God is eternal life through Jesus Christ our Lord (Romans 6:23, KJV).

Jesus saith unto him, I am the way, the truth, and the life: No man cometh unto the father, but by ME (John 14:6, KJV, caps mine).

But as many as received Him, to them gave He power to become the Sons of God, even to them that believe on his name (John 1:12, KJV).

I have been crucified with Christ and I no longer live, but Christ lives in me. The life I live in the body, I live by faith in the Son of God, who loved me and gave himself for me (Galatians 2:20).

Here I am! I stand at the door and knock. If anyone hears my voice and opens the door, I will come in and eat with him, and he with me (Revelation 3:20).

For thought and discussion

1. If you can, read 1 Timothy 2:5 in three translations.
2. What happens when one accepts Christ?
3. After one becomes a believer, what disciplines will help in spiritual growth?
4. If you have received Christ, how would you explain it to an unsaved person?
5. Commit to memory at least three of the preceding Bible verses.

6
Faith

For a person to experience a saving knowledge of Christ, that person must first hear the Gospel. If at the time of hearing, they exercise their will positively, God will engender faith within them. "Consequently, faith comes from hearing the message, and the message is heard through the word of Christ" (Romans 10:17).

Now faith is being sure of what we hope for and certain of what we do not see" (Hebrews 11:1). Faith is accepting an idea, concept, or fact as true and depending on that. So, faith is recognition of and reliance on truth.

Faith is the key that unlocks the door to God's power among us. When Christ visited Nazareth, it was pointed out, "And he did not do many miracles there because of their lack of faith" [their unbelief]" (Matthew 13:58). Faith will grow weak if it does not have adequate spiritual nutrition on a daily basis. Ebbing faith will cause the believer to begin operating according to "the old man," the carnal nature.

God the Holy Spirit now resides in us and "gifts us" with the power to live for God's glory. The apostle Paul instructed us to be constantly filled or controlled by the Holy Spirit (Galatians 5:16-18; Ephesians 5:18). The Spirit buoys and bolsters our assurance and confidence in the promises we discover in the Bible.

Intellectual assent—not enough

Simply knowing about Christ will not save a person. Even acknowledging that Christ died for our sins and that He rose from the dead is not enough. "Thou believest that there is one God; thou doest well: the devils also believe, and tremble" (James 2:17, KJV). Satan and his minions give intellectual assent to the truth of God, but they are eternally damned. Mere head knowledge is insufficient. You must believe in Christ Himself—that is, depend on Him and trust Him. Saving faith is not believing a proposition; it is trusting a person. It is not subscribing to a creed but submitting to the Savior. "Being justified by faith, we have peace with God through our Lord Jesus Christ" (Romans 5:1, KJV).

As already explained, repentance must accompany faith. Faith, Paul wrote, "cometh by hearing, and hearing by the word of God" (Romans 10:17, KJV). Of course, people must have a certain amount of knowledge about Christ in order to have faith in Him. Faith and knowledge are inseparable. This knowledge is gleaned through reading and obeying the Scriptures (see Romans 10:14).

Faith

First, we must have a personal knowledge of Christ

Second, faith embraces belief—credence, assent, acceptance. "Believe that Jesus is the Christ the Son of God and that believing you have eternal life through His name" (John 20:31).

Third, faith demands more—not just knowledge or mere belief. There is another element in true faith, and that is commitment, a positive decision and a yielding of the will. Example: If you buy an airline ticket but remain at the terminal, you will never arrive at your destination. You must act and step on board. In other words, you must take the step of faith and actually commit yourself to the aircraft.

You must commit yourself to Christ as you commit yourself to an airplane by placing your complete trust in Him.

Fourth, there is another element in true faith: simple, even childlike **trust.**

Review: 1. Faith embraces knowledge (you can't believe what you don't know).

2. Faith embraces belief in what you have heard and know.
3. Faith embraces committal of yourself to Christ.
4. After that, it is a matter of trust and complete reliance or dependence on Him.

Faith without obedience to God and the Gospel is a vain faith. Obedience to God is an essential ingredient of true biblical faith. Less than that is "vain" (empty, hollow, vacuous) faith, since "faith without words is dead" (James 2:20, KJV).

Essential ingredients of faith

Salvation does not come to us through our own righteousness or by religious acts and rituals (see Ephesians 2:8-9).

Vain faith defined

1. *Rejection of Christ's Deity*—Unless a person believes that Jesus is the Son of God, he will not have saving faith.

2. *Rejection of Christ's Resurrection*—Believing in a Jesus who did not rise from the dead is to believe in vain.

3. *Mere intellectual assent to believe there is one God is not enough.*

4. *Believing without repentance of sin is to believe in vain.*

Acts of faith

God will do what we cannot do but will not do for us that which we are able to do for ourselves. Frequently God expects us to do something as an evidence of our faith. We act by displaying our faith; then God acts, displaying His power. At the wedding in Cana, the water was not turned into wine until the servants filled the water pots with water (John 2). The disciples did not have a miraculous catch of fish until they first gave evidence of their faith by letting down their nets (Luke 5:4-12).

Prayer itself is an act of faith, for why pray if you do not believe God will answer it? A person with his clothes on fire may believe that jumping into a swimming pool will save him, but he/she will not be spared until he dives into the pool. *Faith is acceptance plus reliance. Faith also involves trust.*

Applying principles of faith

Casting our burdens on Our Burden Bearer

When we confront a problem in our Christian life, we should immediately cast it upon the Lord (1 Peter 5:7; Philippians 4:23)—then direct our minds and faith toward one of the promises found in His Word. This will fortify our rest and assurance in the truth that God can and will meet that situation. After that, leave it there.

A few months ago I borrowed my son's new pick-up truck. Immediately after I drove onto I-40, I noticed a light on the dash indicating a problem. I pulled off the highway about four to five feet and stopped. In a few seconds I realized the emergency brake was not completely off. Suddenly I heard the worst sound of my life. A man driving at speeds of 50 to 60 miles an hour dropped a stack of papers and leaned over to pick them up. In so doing, he lost control of his car, careened off the highway, and hit the truck I was driving.

Since I was sitting still it was quite an impact. I developed a bad headache which continued for a couple of weeks. I prayed daily for deliverance from the headache. On Friday of the second week, I remember praying, "Lord, if You don't heal me soon, I'll have to go to a doctor." On Saturday I was reading and came to the Scripture, "Cast thy burden upon the Lord, and he shall sustain thee: he shall never suffer the righteous to be moved" (Psalm 56:22, KJV). I then prayed, "Lord, I'm putting my headache on your altar and leaving it there. I believe You will heal me. I don't know when, but I am leaving it with You and am not going to worry anymore." On Sunday morning I woke up without a headache.

Faith in Christ's blood sacrifice

Abel approached God to worship and commune with Him through a blood sacrifice. God set up a temporary sacrifice to regain fellowship with man through the shedding of animals' blood. Abel worshiped God in true faith. His brother Cain may have reasoned. *I see no sense in that*, and offered vegetable-fruit offerings. Cain followed reason and Abel walked by faith. Cain's sacrifice was unacceptable to God, perhaps because it was not a blood sacrifice, but also because of Cain's hateful, murderous attitude.

Today we must still approach God through faith in a blood sacrifice—the shed blood of Jesus Christ. The true faith that brings salvation is based on the divine Word of God that emphasizes, "without shedding of blood is no remission [of sins]" (Hebrews 9:22).

The walk and work of faith

It requires genuine faith to walk with God and live to please Him as we are surrounded by the grossest of evils. "By faith Noah, being warned of God of things not seen as yet, moved with fear, prepared an ark to the saving of his house; by the which he condemned the world, and became heir of the righteousness which is by faith" (Hebrews 11:7, KJV; also see 1 Peter 3:20; 2 Peter 2:5). God called on Noah to build an ark to save his family from a flood. God predicted that the flood would come and instructed Noah to preach repentance to the people so they could also be delivered. Noah and his sons worked for 120 years, and the ark was completed. The people had poked fun at him, but he was obedient to God nonetheless. Noah had never seen a flood, but he still believed God. Had he not committed himself to build that unusual ship, all of mankind would have perished. He acted on his belief and faith.

Authentic faith is always linked to obedience. "By faith Abraham, when he was called to go out into a place which he should after receive for an inheritance, obeyed; and he went out, not knowing whither he went" (Hebrews 11:8, KJV). Abraham believed God's call to leave his heathen home, Ur of the Chaldees (today probably Iraq), and travel to a place he had received as an inheritance. If he had never acted on his belief, he would not have become the heir of divine promise. Obedience is the essence and evidence of valid faith.

Lessons that unfold the mysteries of faith

Understanding is knowledge, and knowledge is power. Mark records a miracle in chapter 5 of his Gospel. Read it for yourself. This account helps us to understand more about *what faith is and how it operates.* In this story, there are five lessons which start solving the mysteries of a faith that asks and receives:

First, God's willingness to give us what we ask for;

Second, What to ask for;

Third, How to ask;

Fourth, The fourth is the place "desire" plays in asking; and

Fifth, The **necessity** for a "point of contact."

What Shall We Ask For? Ask God for precisely what you need.

How Shall We Ask? "Hitherto have ye asked nothing in my name: ask, and ye shall receive, that your joy may be full (John 16:24, KJV). Ask humbly but joyfully, not selfishly (see James 4:2-3).

Supporting Scriptures on faith

For by grace are ye saved through faith; and that not of yourselves: it is the gift of God: Not of works, lest any man should boast (Ephesians 2:8-9, KJV).

Ye are all the children of God by faith in Christ Jesus (Galatians 3:26, KJV).

Studying and applying God's Word gives us His commendation: *Study to show thyself approved unto God . . . (2 Timothy 2:15, KJV).*

All things are possible to him that believeth (Mark 9:23b, KJV).

Christian maturity comes from a constant study of the Word. *As newborn babes, desire the sincere milk of the word, that ye may grow thereby (1 Peter 2:2, KJV).*

The Word of God always is "*only believe*" (Mark 5:36), and "*with God nothing shall be impossible*" *(Luke 1:37, KJV).*

My dear children, I write this to you so that you will not sin. But we have one who speaks to the Father in our defense—Jesus Christ, the Righteous One (1 John 2:1). In God's court the defender must be, and is, sinless (1 John 2:1).

For thought and discussion

1. What is your definition of faith? What is the opposite of faith?
2. In review, what four things does faith do?
3. How does vain faith manifest itself?
4. Name two Old Testament men of faith? Were they perfect?
5. If you are born again, reflect on a recent episode of faith in your life.
6. With whom have you shared your faith?
7. How does God define obedience?

7
Love and Fear

Beloved, let us love one another: for love is of God; and every one that loveth is born of God, and knoweth God. He that loveth not knoweth not God; for God is love. In this was manifested the love of God toward us, because that God sent his only begotten Son into the world, that we might live through him. Herein is love, not that we loved God, but that he loved us, and sent his Son to be the propitiation for our sins. Beloved, if God so loved us, we ought also to love one another. No man hath seen God at any time. If we love one another, God dwelleth in us, and his love is perfected in us . . . . ***There is no fear in love; but perfect love casteth out fear:*** *because fear hath torment. He that feareth is not made perfect in love. We love him, because he first loved us. I John 4:7-12,18-19, KJV, author's bold face*

Love and Fear

Jesus gave us the supreme gift of love—His life. "Greater love has no one than this, that he lay down his life for his friends" (John 15:13). Through Christ's loving sacrifice on the Cross, God offers us full forgiveness of sins, and through the life power unleashed at His resurrection, He affords us the ability to live an abundant life pleasing to Him.

Acts of kindness have a ripple effect. They go out and affect other people who affect other people—and eventually they come back to you. Before you can assimilate joy, you must suffer sorrow. We create our surroundings by the thoughts we think. We are sent here to live life fully, to find joy in our creations, to experience both failure and success, to use our free will to expand and magnify our lives.

Love is not optional

We are to love one another. We are to be kind and to be tolerant, giving generous service. To love others as myself, I have to really love myself. If I want forgiveness, I must forgive. Jesus wants us to recognize that every person is of value and worth because he is a person. The world looks at value and measures it by two criteria—appearance and performance. Where does this leave many of the uneducated, poor, disabled, and aged? Jesus' love does not depend on what we do for Him. Our value is inborn; we are valuable simply because God made us valuable.

A man once confided that as he grew up, he loved his mother and father. When he became grown, he loved a young lady and married her. Along came a beautiful baby, and he loved her. Later at a church service he accepted Christ and loved Him. Loving his family did not cause him to love anybody else, but when he loved Jesus, he loved everybody.

The Holy Spirit makes it possible for us to follow the instructions of Jesus when He commanded, "Love your enemies, bless them that curse you, do good to them that hate you, and pray for them which despitefully use you, and persecute you" (Matthew 5:44, KJV). God's love is an exercise of His goodness toward sinners whereby, having identified Himself with their welfare, He has sent His Son to be their Savior, and now helps them know and enjoy Him in a covenant relationship.

Goodness

Goodness in God is that perfection which prompts Him to live bountifully and kindly with all His creatures. God's love is an exercise of goodness toward sinners. His love is free and spontaneous; God loves people because He has chosen to love them. God's love to sinners involves His identifying Himself with their well-being.

The measure of love

The measure of love is how much it gives, and the measure of God's love is the gift of His only Son to become human, to die for our sins, and to become the one mediator who can bring us to God. "He who did not spare his own Son, but who gave Him up for us all—how will He not also, along with Him, graciously give us all things?" (Romans 8:32). "This is love: not that we loved God, but that he loved us and sent his Son as an atoning sacrifice for our sins" (1 John 4:9-10). "God demonstrates his love for us in this: while we were still sinners, Christ died for us" (Romans 5:8), and we find the proof that . . . "the Son of God" . . . loved me in the fact that "He gave Himself for me" (Galatians 2:20).

Commitment

Love is more than a feeling. It is a commitment. We must thank God for all we receive. Gratitude is an eternal virtue. In humility we must ask, and in gratitude we must receive. The more we thank God for the blessings we receive, the more we open the avenue for further blessings. His desire to bless us is full to overflowing. If God were only love, all persons would be saved and blessed eternally, irrespective of their spiritual condition and their wills.

Love and holiness

A dominant characteristic of the Almighty's nature is His holiness. Holiness is not merely the absence of, or freedom from, evil or sin, which is the negative side of the proposition. His holiness will not countenance evil in the least (Habukkuk 1:13). If, therefore, holiness were the only characteristic of the Almighty His wrath would be stirred, and he would deal drastically with the sinner. But His love is a check upon His holiness. We, therefore, praise God for the fact that He is what He is. He can neither sanction nor tolerate sin.

That the Almighty would thus enter the human realm by becoming a helpless little baby and growing to manhood to lay down His life for man's redemption is absolutely unthinkable. It is recognized that the omnipotent God must be at the helm of the universe every moment directing it and keeping it under control. He who is called the Son, thus limited Himself temporarily by coming into the human realm to suffer for our salvation. While He was incarnate, the other personalities of the Godhead could and did run the universe.

The Apostle Matthew records that Jesus was once asked to name the most important commandment in Old Testament Law. Jesus answered by citing the command:

> Thou shalt love the Lord thy God with all thy heart, and with all thy soul, and with all thy mind. This is the first and great commandment. And the second is like unto it, Thou shalt love thy neighbor as thyself. On these two commandments hang all the law and the prophets (Matthew 22:37-40, KJV).

In the Sermon on the Mount He explained:

> Ye have heard that it hath been said, Thou shalt love thy neighbor, and hate thine enemy. But I say unto you, Love your enemies, bless them that curse you, do good to them that hate you, and pray for them which despitefully use you, and persecute you (Matthew 5:43-44, KJV).

Loving God

A man once stated that he often wondered why Christians are commanded to love, since feelings and emotions are not the sort of qualities that can be produced on demand. I replied that emotions are part of love—but only a part. Love also involves the mind and the will. The person who loves does what is best for another person, but how can we ascertain what is best for God? We evince our love for God by living in light of His revealed will, by putting His commands into practice. Matthew recorded "The Model Prayer" (often called The Lord's Prayer) Jesus shared with His disciples. The beginning petitions of that prayer focus on God and help us to understand how we can love Him.

Prayer: An expression of our love for God

To pray this prayer is one means of voicing our love for God. We make known our dependence on Him. We acknowledge that He gives us the capacity to honor and obey Him. In that relationship, we must consider the second command: "Love your neighbor as yourself." It was the Corinthian Christians' failure to love their neighbors that so dismayed the apostle Paul. Mutual love and self-sacrifice were not a part of their community life. Their self-interest and self-indulgence were so contrary to the spirit of Jesus' death that Paul denied the validity of their communion worship service. He sternly wrote them, "When ye come together therefore into one place, this is not to eat the Lord's supper" (1 Corinthians 11:20, KJV).

The Lord's Supper: A further expression of love

The Corinthian Christians had failed to recognize a persuasive truth: that the remembrance of Jesus' death in the Lord's Supper was also intended to remind them how Christians are to relate to one another. Their lack of love and their disregard for one another had produced division and discord in the community. Paul urged the Ephesian Christians, "And live a life of love, just as Christ loved us and gave himself up for us as a fragrant offering and sacrifice to God" (Ephesians 5:2).

This message is also repeatedly reflected in the Gospel of John, when Jesus commanded His followers to love one another, even as He had loved them.

A definer of genuine love

The command to love defines what it means to be a disciple of Jesus. Yet it is sometimes easier to love non-Christian neighbors than Christians in our community or church. Family relationships are not without tensions. Sometimes those who are close to us are the most difficult to love. But the Bible speaks about this as well. We show our love for God by living in light of the revelation of His will, by putting His commands into practice. Forgiveness is not optional: It is essential.

Who cares?

As Christians we are responsible for one another. "Carry each other's burdens, and in this way you will fulfill the law of Christ. Therefore, as we have opportunity, let us do good to all people, especially to those who belong to the family of believers" (Galatians 6:2,10). At no time is this truer than when suffering and death touch those around us.

Demonstrating love

Mercy and **forgiveness** are essential characteristics of God's love for us. As these passages from the Word of God show, mercy and forgiveness are also essential aspects of our love for God and for one another. Members of the family of God are to be peacemakers. Jesus stressed, "Blessed are the peacemakers: for they shall be called the children of God" (Matthew 5:9, KJV). We are to make peace, not only within our Christian communities but in the wider community of the society in which we live.

As we practice mercy and forgiveness in being reconciled one to another . . . as we demonstrate love for one another . . . as we show our love for God by honoring Him and obeying His will . . . as we proclaim the Gospel and urge people to be reconciled to God . . . as we seek to extend the family of God among the nations of the world . . . we likewise demonstrate our love for God and our love for our neighbors. God is unchanging in his love. "The Lord appeared to us in the past, saying: I have loved you with an everlasting love; I have drawn you with loving-kindness" (Jeremiah 31:3).

God loves us and has amply demonstrated His love through Christ. "He that loveth not knoweth not God; for God is love" (1 John 4:8, KJV). God loves us as individuals and doesn't oversee us as a mere mass of people. He has all-seeing eyes and knows all about us from before we were born until the day that we die. In fact, He knew us inside and out before the foundation of the world.

How do you know that God loves you?

Calvary is the conclusive proof. How can a soul doubt God's *agapé* (heavenly love) when he is confronted with the message of Good Friday and Easter? Sometimes we confuse the message of the Cross with all human suffering. We are aware that crucifixion was an ignominious death saved for traitors, murderers, and scoundrels of every ilk. We often talk of the suffering from the nails pounded into Jesus' feet, but many people died on crosses and suffered. Tradition indicates that some of Christ's early followers, including Peter, were crucified upside down. All over the world today Christians are suffering persecution, imprisonment, torture, and execution for the "crime" of professing Jesus as Lord and Savior.

What makes the cross of Christ different?

The difference is that on the Cross, Christ bore the penalty of your sin and mine. Many have suffered, but none have suffered in the horrible manner in which the Christ of God agonized. On His Cross, He suffered for the sins of every inhabitant that would ever dwell on earth, from Adam and Eve onward until the "consummation of the age." So monstrous was our sin that God the Father turned His back on His Son. Jesus cried out, "My God, my God, why hast thou forsaken me?" (Matthew 27:46, KJV; see also Psalm 22:1). Even while Jesus' physical life was slipping from Him, all He had to do was whisper, "I need help; come and get me," and 10,000 angels could have annihilated that mob from the face of the earth. But our blessed Lord stayed on the Cross, suffering that anguish, because of His love for us.

God's deliberate forgetfulness

When we appropriate the benefits of His blood, God will never again remember our sins. Although He is omniscient, all-knowing, He has the remarkable capacity to forget . . . our sins!

The psalmist sang, "As far as the east is from the west, so far has he removed our transgressions from us" (Psalm 103:12). Micah exulted, "Who is a God like unto thee, that pardoneth iniquity, and passeth by the transgression of the remnant of his heritage? he retaineth not his anger for ever, because he delighteth in mercy. He will turn again, he will have compassion upon us; he will subdue our iniquities; and thou wilt cast all their sins into the depths of the sea"(Micah 7:18-19, KJV). God spoke through Isaiah: "I, even I, am he who blots out your transgressions, for my own sake, and *remembers your sins no more*" (Isaiah 43:25, italics mine).

The essence of Calvary and the first Easter morning are wrapped up in the twenty-five words of John 3:16—"For God so loved the world, that he gave his only begotten Son, that whosoever believeth in Him should not perish, but have everlasting life" (KJV).

Love by obeying His teaching

The apostle Paul states in 1 Corinthians 12:30 that he would show Christians "the most excellent way." The way that he is referring to is "love." The apostle John recorded the words of Jesus in his Gospel (14:23): "If anyone loves Me, he will obey My teaching."

1. Study God's Word. "If you remain in Me and My words remain in you . . . you will bear much fruit, showing yourselves to be My disciples" (John 15:7-8).

2. Watch and pray. "Watch and pray so that you will not fall into temptation. The spirit is willing but the flesh is weak" (Matthew 26:41).

3. Fellowship. "May they be brought to complete unity to let the world know that you sent Me and have loved them even as you have loved Me" (John 17:23).

4. Witness. "Go and make disciples of all nations . . . I am with you always, to the end of the age" (Matthew 28:19).

Concentrate on this verse

"A new command I give you; love one another. As I have loved you, so you must love one another. By this all men will know that you are my disciples, if you love one another" (John 13:34-35).

Two examples of Christian love

1. The Parable of the Prodigal (or Lost) Son
2. The Parable of the Good Samaritan

Learning from the Parable of the Lost Son (Luke 15:11-32)

Jesus continued: "There was a man who had two sons. The younger one said to his father, 'Father, give me my share of the estate.' So he divided his property between them. "Not long after that, the younger son got together all he had, set off for a distant country and there squandered his wealth in wild living. After he had spent everything, there was a severe famine in that whole country, and he began to be in need. So he went and hired himself out to a citizen of that country, who sent him to his fields to feed pigs. He longed to fill his stomach with the pods that the pigs were eating, but no one gave him anything.

"When he came to his senses, he said, 'How many of my father's hired men have food to spare, and here I am starving to death. I will set out and go back to my father and say to him: Father, I have sinned against heaven and against you. I am no longer worthy to be called your son; make me like one of your hired men.' So he got up and went to his father.

"But while he was still a long way off, his father saw him and was filled with compassion for him; he ran to his son, threw his arms around him and kissed him.

"The son said to him, 'Father, I have sinned against heaven and against you. I am no longer worthy to be called your son.'

"But the father said to his servants, 'Quick! Bring the best robe and put it on him. Put a ring on his finger and sandals on his feet. Bring the fattened calf and kill it. Let's have a feast and celebrate. For this son of mine was dead and is alive again; he was lost and is found.' So they began to celebrate.

"Meanwhile, the older son was in the field. When he came near the house, he heard music and dancing. So he called one of the servants and asked him what was going on. 'Your brother has come,' he replied, 'and your father has killed the fatted calf because he has him back safe and sound.'

"The older brother became angry and refused to go in. So his father went out and pleaded with him. But he answered his father, 'Look! All these years I've been slaving for you and never disobeyed your orders. Yet you never gave me even a young goat so I could celebrate with friends. But when this son of yours who has squandered your property with prostitutes comes home, you kill the fattened calf for him!'

"'My son,' the father said, 'you are always with me, and everything I have is yours. But we had to celebrate and be glad, because this brother of yours was dead and is alive again; he was lost and is found.'"

The Parable of the Good Samaritan (Luke 10:30-37)

"A certain man went down from Jerusalem to Jericho, and fell among thieves" (v. 30). Highwaymen, roving bandits, were common along the trade routes outside Jerusalem. The man, possibly a wealthy merchant from Jerusalem, was in a desperate condition. The thieves had beaten him badly and left him with little chance for survival. With an exquisite choice of words, Jesus continued: "By chance there came down a certain priest that way; and when he saw him, he passed by on the other side. And likewise a Levite . . ." (vv. 31,32). "But a certain Samaritan . . . had compassion on him" (v. 33). The Samaritan, aware of the hatred between the Jews and his countrymen—and that the beaten traveler was undoubtedly a Jew—was not deterred by that but rendered aid and comfort. The words are precious: he "went to him."

The story is, of course, far more than a dissertation on prejudice. What a picture it is of grace and of the true function of the spiritual believer! Love is governed by the nature and grace of God: "The love of God is shed abroad in our hearts by the Holy Spirit . . . " (Romans 5:5b, KJV). The Good Samaritan "bound up his wounds . . . set him on his own beast, and brought him to an inn, and took care of him." The next day he gave money to the innkeeper and said, "Take care of him: and whatsoever thou spendest more, when I come again, I will repay thee." His willingness to pay the price exemplifies grace that extends itself with no thought of repayment. This man clearly fulfilled Christ's law of love.

The challenge

With the astounding skill of His divine mind, the Lord Jesus Christ had chosen the action of this compassionate man to illustrate the heavenly viewpoint and applied faith. The lesson was not without meaning to the team of seventy disciples who had just returned after actively proclaiming Christ's message to the villages of Palestine. Christ would die for those who despised and rejected Him. His followers would also minister to those who were neither responsive nor deserving. Turning to the lawyer, Christ posed the question which had only one answer: "Which now of these three . . . was neighbor unto him?" To the answer, "He that showed mercy on him" (Luke 10:36), Jesus compounded the challenge with a return to the original: "Go, and do thou likewise."

Fear not

Jesus' disciples were rugged men, physically toughened by living outdoors and traveling long distances on foot. And yet when they were caught in a sudden storm so common in the area of Galilee, they shouted in desperate fear, "Lord, save us! We're going to drown!" (Matthew 8:25). They were terrified that they were going to die. We may define fear as an emotion that speaks of dread, fright, alarm, panic, trepidation, and consternation. All human beings capable of thinking exhibit these emotions at one time or another. Fear is universal in all times and places. It is a normal, human response to the unknown. And the experience of death is an unknown.

Two types of fear

But wait. What do we do with the "fear of the Lord"? If the Bible often advises "fear not," and yet it also speaks of "fear," which does it mean? The answer is *both*. Fear is a twofold word. It refers to an emotion marked by dread and anxious concern, but it is also the word that means awe and profound reverence. This is the "fear" that inspires trust and confidence. When we fear God, we don't cringe before Him like a prisoner robbed of his freedom by a ruthless dictator. Our fear is an awe-filled, respectful love which causes us to treat Him with respect. This is what the prophet Isaiah meant when he wrote, "The fear of the Lord is the key to this treasure" (Isaiah 33:6). It is a reverence that comes when we catch a glimpse of our Heavenly Father's majesty and holiness.

Five ways to express love

- First of all, love can be communicated by touch. There is tremendous power of reaching out in the human touch.
- Love can be shown in words, both spoken and written.
- Love is often projected in gifts of objects and time.
- Our love is also displayed with facial expressions and body language.
- Finally, we can articulate our love in actions. "Actions speak louder than words."

God is love! (1 John 4:8)

Since the Bible teaches that God is love, and personifies it, as believers in the Lord Jesus let us consider the commitment our Heavenly Father wants us to make as we are being transformed into the image of His Son.

Lord	to submit to
Obedience	to respond to
Volition	to decide to
Effort	to work toward

Lord—Love is more than a word. Love is a person. JESUS is Lord! (see Romans 10:9).

"But how does man come to know that God is love? That love is because God is. That the love of God is not only available for any man to experience, it is available for any man to demonstrate. How do we come to know the true nature of love? By reading a book or embracing a particular philosophy or doctrine? Do we learn love from the Bible or from other people who expound it? Do we learn about the nature of love by practice? Is it an emotional or a spiritual exercise? It is all of these to lesser and greater degrees, but it is more . . . We can only learn of love as we learn of God. Jesus said, ". . . Learn of Me." There is no other way to learn of love."

Obedience—Jesus said that if we love Him then we will obey Him (John 14:23). Obedience is more than keeping rules; it is our reaction to our Savior's love for us.

The knowledge that God has loved me beyond all limits will compel me to go into all the world to love others in the same way. Neither natural love nor God's divine love will remain and grow in me unless it is nurtured. Love is spontaneous, but it has to be maintained through discipline.

Volition—Jesus has commanded us to love as He has loved us (John 15:12-13)! Do you allow love to make your decisions?

Effort—Love in action and demonstrated effort.

Supporting Scriptures

"Do not repay evil with evil or insult with insult, but with blessing, because to this you were called so the elect may inherit a blessing" (1 Peter 3:9).

"By this shall all men know that ye are my disciples, if ye have love one to another" (John 13:35).

"The fruit of the spirit is love" (Galatians 5:22).

"Beloved, let us love one another: For love is of God and every one that loveth is born of God " (1 John 4:7).

"Whoever has my commands and obeys them, he is the one who loves me. He who loves me will be loved by my Father, and I will love him and show myself to him" (John 14:21).

"This is how we know what love is: Jesus laid down his life for us. And we ought to lay down our lives for our brothers" (1 John 3:16).

"Humble yourselves, therefore, under the mighty hand of God, that he may exalt you at the proper time, casting all your anxiety upon him, because he cares for you" (1 Peter 5:6-7).

For thought and discussion

1. According to our loving Savior, what does genuine, heaven-sent love involve?
2. Jesus spoke of two great commandments? What are they?
3. How do we demonstrate our sincere love for God? For others?
4. Simply because we love, does that rule out occasional conflicts and carnality?
5. What is the most viable proof of God's love?
6. Quote John 3:16 from memory. Although it is short and simple, outline the aspects of that immortal verse. Also read Romans 5:8 and 1 John 4:8-10
7. What specific activities should we carry out to demonstrate our love for Christ?
8. How is earthly fear the opposite of heavenly love? What does it mean to "fear" God?
9. Why is love the essence of obedience?

Part III

PUTTING ON THE ARMOR OF GOD

Finally, my brethren, be strong in the Lord, and in the power of his might.

Put on the whole armor of God, that ye may be able to stand against the wiles of the devil. For we wrestle not against flesh and blood, but against principalities, against powers, against the rulers of the darkness of this world, against spiritual wickedness in high places. Wherefore take unto you the whole armor of God, that ye may be able to withstand in the evil day, and having done all, to stand.

Stand therefore, having your loins girt about with truth, and having on the breastplate of righteousness; And your feet shod with the preparation of the gospel of peace; Above all, taking the shield of faith, wherewith ye shall be able to quench all the fiery darts of the wicked.

And take the helmet of salvation, and the sword of the Spirit, which is the word of God: Praying always with all prayer and supplication in the Spirit, and watching there unto with all perseverance and supplication for all saints.

—Ephesians 6:10-18, KJV

We Ought Always to Pray and Not to Faint

The shadow comes and casts its length
Across their lives today,
Tomorrow is a land unknown,
And dim may be the way.
But these, as choicest saints of God,
Do not, will not, despair.
For now, just as they ever did,
They go to Him in prayer.
This then is not an alien land;
But a place they know so well.
For day by day at God's own throne,
They do serenely dwell.
His Word they love; it has first place;
They hide it in their hearts.
Now they're not strangers to His grace —
To them, God peace imparts.
How blest to be close to our God,
To know His grace and love;
To honor Him in all of life,
And all his mercies prove.
Then when the day is difficult,
And we would see His face—
It is no problem for we're never
Strangers to His grace.

—*The Family*

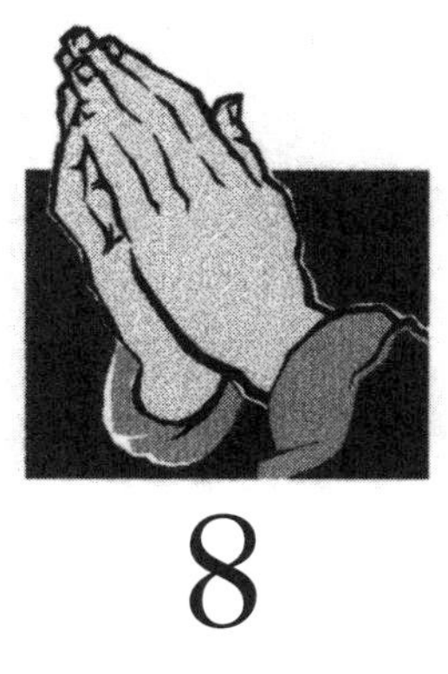

8
Prayer

If you believe, you will receive whatever you ask for in prayer (Matthew 21:22). Pray without ceasing (1 Thessalonians 5:17, KJV).

For the eyes of the Lord are over the righteous, and his ears are open unto their prayers: but the face of the Lord is against them that do evil (I Peter 5:12, KJV).

He was praying . . . one of his disciples said . . . Lord, teach us to pray . . . And he said . . . When ye pray, say, Our Father which art in heaven, Hallowed be thy name. Thy kingdom come. Thy will be done, as in heaven, so in earth. Give us day by day our daily bread. And forgive us our sins; for we also forgive everyone that is indebted to us. And lead us not into temptation, but deliver us from evil (Luke 11:2, KJV).

This prayer points to the fact that we're in this together. Our lives are linked to others as well as to God.

Teach us	Learn the "habit" of prayer.
Give us	Trust your daily needs to God.
Forgive us	Forgive in order to be forgiven.
Lead us	God will help deter you from entering temptations.
Deliver us	God is able to deliver you.

God will attempt to lead you away from temptations of sin, but the devil is working to entice you into sinful situations. "No temptation has overtaken you except such as is common to man; but God is faithful, who will not allow you to be tempted beyond what you are able to withstand, but with the temptation, He will also make the way of escape that you may be able to bear it" (1 Corinthians 10:13, NKJV).

After all, what is prayer?

Prayer is coming to God our Father, in the name of Jesus Christ, His Son, and the power of the Holy Spirit, with a sincere desire for His blessing, believing with faith He will bestow it, but willing to be denied if it is not His will for one' s life (see Romans 12:2).

We must remember that God sees a bigger picture than we do. He can see the future, other relating circumstances, and all of the events that will affect our lives.

When we pray for a specific blessing, we must ask:

- Is it God's will? (Do the Scriptures prohibit it, allow it, or promise it?)
- Is it for God's glory? What is our motive—pleasure, prestige, or honoring Christ.
- Is it in God's timing? (Are there conditions to be met? Does He want us to wait?)

Luke the evangelist, who presents Jesus as The Perfect Man, emphasizes His teaching on prayer. Our Lord began and ended His earthly life in an attitude of prayer. He was praying at His baptism, and His last word from the cross was a prayer. He spent the night in prayer before appointing The Twelve. After feeding the 5,000, realizing a crisis, He withdrew into a mountain to pray. He was in prayer when He was transfigured. In Gethsemane, anticipating the dread of the Cross, He agonized in prayer. And on the Cross the Lord Jesus prayed. In Luke 18:1, He asserts that "men ought always to pray and not to faint." In many a trial and difficulty we would soon give up if we could not resort to prayer.

Jesus helps us pray

"Who will bring any charge against those whom God has chosen? It is God who justifies. Who is he that condemns? Christ Jesus who died—more than that, who was raised to life—is at the right hand of God and is also interceding for us" (Romans 8:33-34).

What a magnificent thought! Jesus is our advocate, our defense lawyer, pleading our case before God the Father, testifying that the person being presented for heaven must be admitted on the basis of God's grace alone. If human beings were judging us, they might consign us to the pit of Gehenna, "the lake of fire."

Many people are deceived by Satan into thinking that God is a vengeful taskmaster, gleefully consigning to hell all those who offend Him. Those skeptics are plainly not familiar with the love of God through Christ. True, God does hate sin, but He loves the sinner. Since we are all sinners, our only right for admission to heaven lies in the provision He made for our sins.

The Holy Spirit helps us pray

"The Spirit helps us in our weakness. We do not know what we ought to pray for, but the Spirit himself intercedes for us with groans that words cannot express. And he who searches our hearts knows the mind of the Spirit, because the Spirit intercedes for the saints in accordance with God's will" (Romans 8:26-27).

To abide in Christ is to be in spiritual fellowship and communion (prayer) with Him. If we have faith and live in Christ, we will receive all we ask, provided it is God' s will. Jesus waits for us to pray, whether in "the closest" or elsewhere. John Donne, the noted English preacher-poet, observed that "pray and stay are two monosyllables." Edwin Keith, also from Britain, said, "Prayer is exhaling the spirit of man and inhaling the Spirit of God." Christ lives at the place of prayer. Of necessity, we need to linger there and become better acquainted with Him, sharing our ups and downs with Him.

Our Heavenly Father knows best

Years ago *Father Knows Best* was a top-rated TV show, yet more than that, our Heavenly Father knows best. What a thought of consolation and comfort. The psalmist was on target: "No good thing will he [God] withhold from them that walk uprightly" (Psalm 84:11, KJV).

Lord, teach us to pray

The Model Prayer that Jesus taught His disciples is really the Disciples' Prayer. It is built on a beautiful relationship where, through faith in Christ and by the Holy Spirit' s power, we have become members of God's family. Jesus explained, "Your Father knows what you need, before you ask Him. Pray, then, in this way . . .

> Our Father who art in heaven, hallowed be thy name. Thy kingdom come. Thy will be done, on earth as it is in heaven. Give us this day our daily bread. And forgive us our debts, as we also have forgiven our debtors. And do not lead us into temptation, but deliver us from evil. For thine is the kingdom, and the power, and the glory, forever. Amen (Matthew 6:9-13, KJV).

No relationship can thrive without constant, heartfelt communication. This is true not only in human interaction, but also in our communion with God. If we are to nurture a "winning walk" with our Savior, we must stay in constant touch with Him. We do that with prayer, actually conversation with God, our primary means of communicating with Him. Our persistence in prayer reveals how serious we are.

The prophet Micah assured us, "Though I sit in darkness, the Lord will be my light" (7:8). A Christian has access to light. We ought to pray, in essence, "Lord, I will follow You even if I don't know the way. You are my Way. I don't need any other road map. I need to quit worrying about tomorrow and trust You to guide me one day at a time."

We should never study our Bibles without prayer. Before opening its pages, we should ask for the enlightenment of the Holy Spirit, and it will be given.

How can we . . . present our bodies as living sacrifices?

> Therefore, I urge you, brothers, in view of God's mercy, to offer your bodies as living sacrifices, holy and pleasing to God—this is your spiritual act of worship. Do not con-

form any longer to the pattern of this world, but be transformed by the renewing of your mind. Then you will be able to test and approve what God's will is—his good, pleasing and perfect will (Romans 12:1-2).

First We must be born again. This comes as a result of God's salvation through Christ.

Second By maintaining an intimate relationship with the Almighty, through studying His word, prayer, and singing hymns and songs of praise.

Through that we will conform to His will and pleasure.

Five kinds of prayer

Adoration/glorification of God;
Confession—report of sins;
Thanksgiving—thanks for supplying our needs—and for everything;
Intercession—praying for others;
Petition—asking God for our needs according to His will.

Adoration/glorification of God

"Bless the Lord, Oh my soul; and all that is within me, bless his Holy Name" (Psalm 103:1, NKJV). Adoration creates an awareness of God's nearness in daily events and recognizes that God is the source of all power and creation.

Confession

Confession frees us from damaging guilt as sins of omission and commission are admitted to a loving Father. Jesus, in The Model Prayer taught, "Forgive us our debts as we have also forgiven our debtors" (Matthew 6:12, RSV).

Thanksgiving

Give thanks for all blessings. Thanksgiving draws attention away from self and directs it to blessings we have already received—food, clothing, home, health, job, family, ad infinitum.

"Oh Lord my God, I will give thanks unto thee forever" (Psalm 30:12).

Intercession

Pray for others, a soul cry to God for another. This aggressive kind of praying kindles faith for both intercessor and receiver. Example: the small group of believers who prayed Peter out of prison (Acts 12:5). When we pray, we link ourselves with the inexhaustible power that spins the universe. Intercessory prayer demonstrates love and places self behind the love for another.

Petition

Petition is the most prevalent of prayer forms and expresses urgent desire. This kind of prayer deals with the whole of human needs, including heartfelt pleas for daily bread, deliverance from temptation, and our comfort and health needs. Of course, we should always ask for our needs according to God's will. Prayer as an act of faith changes those who pray. A life of prayer involves us in a continuous remolding process by the Master Potter. Prayer shapes us into Christ-likeness. If a person stays committed, keeps believing, and persists in prayer, he has the inner assurance that in God' s time, His power will move in the pray-er's life. A proud person who prays is reminded that without God there is no food, sun, water, or oxygen. This ought to shatter arrogance.

Further principles of prayer

Sin poisons the reservoirs of our inner life and poisons our self-worth and joy. On the other hand, prayer frees us from self-centeredness. Prayer is a vital work in the world, and it blesses those who give and those who receive. You can't locate a Christian who does not pray, even as you can't, a living person without a pulse. Prayer is as necessary to inner wholeness as the circulatory system is to physical health. Prayer creates friendship with God. A person should pray every day and throughout the day. However, every believer should set aside a "quiet time" for close sharing with God. We should pray with expectancy and respond fully to the assurance of His faithfulness. Prayer is an offering of our desires to God for matters agreeable to His will. *Patience and persistence* are essentials.

Persistence means "hanging in there"

Jesus related this parable to illustrate that they should keep on praying and never become discouraged. This parable is called "The Parable of the Unjust Judge" or "The Persistent Widow" (Luke 18:1-8). "In a certain city," He said, "there was a judge who in his rule did not try to do right, but was often unjust and wicked; for he had no fear of God and no care for what men said about him. And in that city there was a widow who came many times to this judge, crying over and over again, 'Do for me what is right against the man who has done me wrong!'

"For some time the judge paid no attention to her, for right and wrong were both the same to him. But after a while the judge said to himself: 'Although I have no fear of God and no care for man, yet as this widow is so troublesome to me, and gives me no rest, I will do what she asks, for I am tired of her coming and of her calling out for her right every day.'

"Listen," said the Lord Jesus, "to what this unjust judge says. And if a man who does not care for right or wrong will at last answer a prayer, how much more will your heavenly Father listen to his own children when they call upon him day and night, even though he seems to make them wait long for the answer to their prayers? I tell you that God will do right by them and answer their prayers, and that very soon! Yet when the Son of Man comes, will he find on earth those who are looking for him and who believe in him?" (Luke 18:1-8).

Jesus' sweeping statements about prayer

"And when thou prayest, thou shalt not be as the hypocrites are: for they love to pray standing in the synagogues and in the corners of the streets, that they may be seen of men. Verily I say unto you, They have their reward. But thou, when thou prayest, enter into thy closet, and when thou hast shut thy door, pray to thy Father which is in secret; and thy Father which seeth in secret shall reward thee openly. But when ye pray, use not vain repetitions, as the heathen do: for they think that they shall be heard for their much speaking. Be not ye therefore like unto them; for your Father knoweth what things ye have need of, before ye ask him" (Matthew 6:5-8).

Prayer is the means by which we open the door of our spirits for God to enter and work out His grand plans for our lives.

Some reasons why our prayers are not answered

1. *One must be saved (born again) to have power in prayer.* A non-believer can pray to God for salvation and be heard, but as long as he refuses to accept Jesus, heaven's door is closed to his every plea (1 Peter 5:12). Paul wrote to Timothy about our linkage with God: "There is one God and one mediator between God and men—Jesus Christ" (1 Timothy 2:5).

2. *One must walk in fellowship to have power in prayer.* "If I regard iniquity in my heart, the Lord will not hear me" (Psalm 66:18). Pray that God will deliver you from sins, both known and unknown. Seek constantly to abide in Him and let His words abide in you.

3. *An unshakable faith is another condition that must be met for our prayers to be answered.*

If we pray without faith that we will receive it, our prayer is to no avail. Just believing that God can is not believing that God will.

Three reasons for prayerful faith

God's present power
God's past performance
God's precious promises

Sometimes our prayers are not answered because we have misplaced faith. It isn't prayer that changes things: It is God.

4. *Selfishness is the foundation of much praying, and God pays no attention to such.* If we ask with a desire to bless others and to glorify Him and His Son, then we are on the ground where prayers are answered. Elijah would never have stopped the heavens from raining with his praying had he wanted God to do it *in order that all of the people would recognize what a great prophet Elijah was.* It was God's glory that the great prophet had in mind. *So, God heard and answered his unselfish prayer.*

5. *We must be right with our fellowmen to have power in prayer.* Jesus teaches that we cannot receive prayer answers when we have unforgiveness in our hearts toward each other. Hear Him: "For if ye forgive not men their trespasses, neither will your Father forgive your trespasses" (Matthew 6:15). How many of us pray with grudges in our hearts toward

a friend (or possible friend) or brother? If God's Word is true, and it is, then we cannot reach God with such a spiteful, unforgiving attitude.

6. *Many of our prayers are not answered because we are too impatient.* Again and again God emphasizes the value of waiting on Him for the full answer to our prayers. We have no right to expect the God of the universe to jump like a frog the moment we call on Him. He realizes that it is for our own good to keep us praying and waiting, so we will grow in grace and appreciate the answer all the more when it arrives.

7. *God doesn't always answer our prayers with a positive answer because a negative response is sometimes best for us.* Often the best answer God can give us is, "No!" Many of us ask for things that would hurt us if we received them. If you ask the Lord for something, and don't receive it, first search your life to make sure that you have met all other conditions that govern answers to prayer. If you have, and no answer comes, then thank God that He is answering in the negative. Of course, it is possible that He wants you to continue to pray and wait for the answer later.

8. *It may not be God's will to answer our prayers.* Another reason God does not always answer our prayers is because it is not always His will to do so. Jesus repeatedly emphasized that we must pray according to the Father's will. In The Model Prayer He admonishes us to pray, "Thy will be done." He Himself prayed, even in Gethsemane, "Not My will, but Thine be done."

9. *Prayers that are cold are not answered.* Still another reason that our prayers are not answered is because we are so cold and indifferent in our praying. In James 5:16 we read: ". . . the effectual fervent prayer of a righteous man availeth much." Notice carefully God moved James to write the "*fervent prayer*" of "*a righteous man availeth much.*" God knows that many of our prayers are not from the depths of our hearts. There is nothing wrong with a prayer that is read provided it was composed, and repeated, in spiritual sincerity. It isn't the many words we utter that count; rather, it is the spirit of our hearts. Are your prayers unanswered? Then search your heart and life before God to discover which of these hindrances to prayer are robbing you of prayer power "before the throne of grace" (see Hebrews 4:16, KJV).

Summary of prayer scriptures

The heart's cry for God: Psalm 42:1-2; 63:1-3; 84:2; 143:6-9
Prayer in the morning: Psalm 5:3; 88:13; 143:8; Isaiah 33:2
Two times a day: Psalm 88:1
Three times a day: Psalm 55:17; Daniel 6:10
All night: Luke 6:12
Without ceasing: 1 Thessalonians 5:17
Called for: Hebrews 4:16
Prayer for deliverance: Exodus 33:12,18
Secret: Genesis 24:63; Matthew 6:5ff.
Silent: Psalm 5:1
With weeping: Ezra 10:1
Prayer for wisdom: 1 Kings 3:7-14; 2 Chronicles 1:10-12

For thought and discussion

1. To you what is prayer? Why is it necessary to pray if God knows everything?

2. How does the Holy Spirit help us to pray?

3. Besides "The Lord' s Prayer," what else is it sometimes called?

4. List the five kinds of prayer. How do they appy in your life?

5. If God already knows what we need, why should we persist in prayer?

6. State three reasons for prayerful faith.

7. God answers our prayers in three ways. What are they? Write down several reasons why our prayers are sometimes unanswered.

8. Is there a specific time when we must pray?

9. How can a person possibly pray without ceasing?

10. What are you praying for God to do?

11. What is the "ideal" quiet time and how do you spend it?

12. Name one significant answer to prayer you have experienced.

13. How do you balance your time between your family, career, God, and your church?

9

The Word of God—Living and Written

For there are three that bear record in heaven, the Father, the Word, and the Holy Ghost: and these three are one (1 John 5:7. KJV).

Thy Word have I treasured in my heart, That I may not sin against Thee . . . I shall delight in Thy statutes; I shall not forget Thy word. . . . Thy word is a lamp to my feet, And a light to my path (Psalm 119:11,16,105, NASB).

The Bible is God's written revelation to mankind. Not only were the writers' thoughts inspired but also the words which expressed them in the original tongues—Hebrew, Greek, and Aramaic—were unerringly conveyed through the Holy Spirit. "The Lord said exactly what He meant and meant exactly what He said."

> All Scripture is God-breathed and is useful for teaching, rebuking, correcting and training in righteousness, so that the man of God may be thoroughly equipped for every good work (2 Timothy 3:16-17).

> For the prophecy came not in old time by the will of man: but holy men of God spake as they were moved by the Holy Ghost (1 Peter 1:21, KJV).

Truth without any mixture of error

My Southern Baptist friends approved a confession of faith, "The Baptist Faith and Message" statement, in 1963, in which the framers of the document declared:

> The Holy Bible was written by men divinely inspired, and is a perfect treasure of heavenly instruction. It has God for its author, salvation for its end, and truth without any mixture of error for its matter. It reveals the principles by which God will judge us. It shall remain, to the end of the world, the true center of Christian union, and the supreme standard by which all human conduct, creeds and opinions shall be tried.

God's indestructible truth

For hundreds of years every ungodly totalitarian regime has tried to eradicate The Book from the face of the earth or either keep it away from the masses. Communists, fascists, and certain non-Christian fanatics have confiscated and burned copies of God's written Word. During the Middle Ages the predominant church chained the Scriptures in church buildings and cathedrals. Translators of the Scriptures, John Wycliffe and William Tyndale to mention two, were imprisoned, tortured, and executed. Their crime: making the Bible available in the language the common people could understand. Every state church and government-sponsored religion has minimized its principles, including freedom of conscience and soul. Yet, it still exists and is the best-selling book in history. Considering all of the hateful, concerted opposition against the Bible, it would have disappeared centuries ago—were it not of Divine origin.

Generations follow generations—yet it lives.
Nations rise and fall—yet it lives.
Kings, dictators, presidents come and go—yet it lives.
Torn, condemned, burned—yet it lives.
Doubted, suspected, criticized—yet it lives.
Damned by atheists—yet it lives.
Exaggerated by fanatics—yet it lives.
Misconstrued and misstated—yet it lives.
Its inspiration denied—yet it lives.
Yet it lives—a lamp to our feet,
a light to our paths,
a standard for childhood,
a guide for youth,
a comfort for the aged,
food for the hungry,
water for the thirsty,
rest for the weary,
light for the heathen,
salvation for the sinner,
grace for the Christian.
To know it is to love it;
To love it is to accept it;
To accept it means life eternal.
— Willard Johnson

Incomparable benefits of the Bible

Faithful reading and study of God's Word over a period of time make it part of your interior vocabulary and your thought processes. Then, amazingly its counsel and strength will surface when least expected and most essential. We are fortified and grow spiritually as the Scriptures serve us as friend, teacher, "strength coach," life's "tour guide," and motivator.

Obvious hindrances to a closer relationship with God occur when the "old man," the carnal nature, raises his ugly face: "sexual immorality, impurity and debauchery; idolatry and witchcraft; hatred, discord, jealousy, fits of rage, selfish ambition, dissensions, factions and envy; drunkenness, orgies, and the like" (see Galatians 2:19-21). When the old man messes with us, we should summon the Word, as our Lord Jesus often did, and rebuke the devil with: "Away from me, Satan! For it is written: 'Worship the Lord your God, and serve him only'" (Matthew 4:10). The Word, activated by the Holy Spirit, will enable us to overcome temptations. We can master them, talk about them, expose them, and refuse to give in-to them.

James stated that the outgrowth of wisdom is Christlikeness, peace, humility, and love (James 3:17), all built on faith in Christ (1 Corinthians 3:18; 2 Timothy 3:15). Do you want to know God more deeply and intimately? Do you want to discover His will for your life? Then read and study the Scriptures daily. Not only do that, but set up a personal goal to memorize key Scripture verses. Incorporate them into your thought processes. The psalmist hid them in his heart and continually meditated on God's Word, whether in scrolls or the Word delivered by God's Spirit (see Psalm 119).

If you are depressed by the immensity and complexity of your problems, read God's Word! Most of us like sweet stuff. The Word gives us a sweet taste, even though life is sometimes bitter. "How sweet are thy words unto my taste! yea, sweeter than honey to my mouth!" (Psalm 119:103, KJV; see also Psalm 141:6). Let the still waters of the Word drown out all other sounds and voices.

As a *relief for loneliness*, the Word pledges: "Be strong and of good courage, fear not, nor be afraid of them: for the Lord thy God, he it is that doth go with thee; he will not fail thee, nor forsake thee" (Deuteronomy 31:6). For frightening fears, the Bible promises: "Peace I leave with you, my peace I give unto you; not as the world giveth, give I unto you. Let not your heart be troubled, neither let it be afraid" (John 14:27, KJV).

The Bible as *a source book for healing stress* causes us to see ourselves as we actually are. Hebrews 4:12 says, "The word of God is quick, and powerful, and sharper than any two-edged sword, piercing even to the dividing asunder of soul and spirit, and of the joints and marrow, and is a *discerner of the thoughts and intents of the heart*" (KJV, italics mine). But this new self-awareness should not disturb believers, because the Bible also reveals how to close the gap between who they are and who they can become. The Bible helps eliminate the tension between being and becoming by making the journey both possible and enjoyable.

It teaches deep lessons about God

A view of the seven letters to the seven churches in Asia Minor (today's Turkey) by John (in The Revelation) presents profound lessons about God:

First—We recognize that God cares about us as individuals. Our risen Lord cares about each of us personally and knows us as a mother does her child. He is present in the spirit of every believer.

Second—He views us as sharing our lives with other believers in the church.

Third—The issues the risen Lord dealt with then are as contemporary as those concerns of today. Our sins, temptations, and weaknesses are no different from theirs.

The Bible points to God as its author, yet it was written by human hands. The God of glory, through the Spirit, enlightened the minds and hearts of His servants. Through dreams, visions, symbols, and figures, He has opened up His truth, embodying His thoughts and principles into human language.

The Ten Commandments, however, were spoken by God Himself and written by His own hand. The Bible, with its God-given truths couched in the language of human beings, presents a union of the Divine and the human. Such a union existed in the nature of Christ, who was the Son of God and the Son of Man. Thus, it is true of the Bible, as it was of Christ, that "The word was made flesh and dwelt among us" (John 1:14, KJV).

It presents God's plan for our lives

In His Word, God has committed to us truths necessary for salvation. From Genesis 1:1 through Revelation 22:21 it is a book of salvation history. The Scriptures afford authoritative, unfailing directions concerning God's will, i. e., what God wants for our lives. They are the standard of character, the revealer of doctrines, and the test of experience. Yet the fact that God has uncovered His will to us through His word, has not rendered expendable the Holy Spirit's continued presence and guidance. On the contrary Jesus promised that the Spirit would open the Word to the believers, illuminating and applying its teachings. And since it was the Spirit of God who inspired the Bible, it is impossible that His teaching should ever be contrary to the written revelation.

No substitute for the Bible

The Heavenly Father did not send the Spirit to supersede the Bible, for the Scriptures explicitly state that the Word of God is the standard by which we must test all teaching and experience. The apostle John cautioned, "Believe not every spirit, but try the spirits whether they are of God: because many false prophets are gone out into the world" (1 John 4:1). And Isaiah wrote how to spot a false prophet: "To the law and to the testimony; if they speak not according to this word, it is because there is no light in them" (8:20).

Do you ever doubt God's promises?

When we seem to doubt God's love and distrust His promises, we dishonor Him and grieve the Holy Spirit. His words are facts that not even Satan and his hosts can at heart deny. Where the heart is yielded to Christ, with love focused on Him, there is faith that works by love and cleans up our inner selves. Through this faith, the heart is renewed in the image of God. "These things write I unto you, that you sin not, and if any man sin, he has an advocate [defense attorney] with the Father, Jesus Christ the righteous" (1 John 2:1, KJV).

We should always evaluate our life experiences based on the truths of God's Word. The Holy Spirit and the Word of God will instruct you and help you in understanding how and where God is working in your life and the lives of others.

The Holy Spirit: Our present teacher

On the night before His crucifixion, Jesus foretold how the Holy Spirit would become intimately involved with the apostles and all of His subsequent disciples. In John chapters 14—16 our Lord conducted a virtual "seminar" on the person and work of the Spirit. He assured them: "But the Comforter, who is the Holy Spirit, whom the Father will send in my name, he shall teach you all things, and bring all things to your remembrance whatever I have said unto you" (John 14:26, KJV; see also vv. 16-18). This statement is extremely significant because it has vital implications about the divine nature of the New Testament.

The Holy Spirit: Conveyor of God's truth

By this, Jesus indicated that, after His upcoming Ascension, the Holy Spirit would prompt the apostles not only to remember Jesus' teachings but would "teach you [them] all things." This activity of the Holy Spirit has a tremendous implication concerning the divine nature of the New Testament. The Gospels are the records of Jesus' ministry and teaching during His three-and-a-half-year ministry. Two of the Gospels, Matthew and John, were written by two of Jesus' apostles. Neither of these Gospels was written until several decades after Jesus' Ascension. Since human beings quickly forget and have faulty memories, on what basis can we trust the accuracy and reliability of these Gospel accounts?

Jesus Himself revealed the basis of that truth. The Holy Spirit would help them recall the events and teachings of their Lord's ministry; He would fulfill the major role in the apostles' oral and written accounts of Jesus' teaching, working supernaturally with those men to produce accurate, reliable documents.

Jesus: The Living Word

With all of the biblical evidence it is incredible that any conscientious person would doubt the Deity of Christ. In the very first verse of his Gospel, the apostle John asserts, "In the beginning was the Word, and the Word was with God, and the Word **was God**" (1:1). He then refers to Jesus as "life" and "light." In the original the Greek for "Word" was "Logos." Jesus as the living "Logos" means that He was and is the embodiment of God's pronouncements to mankind. As the way, the truth, and the life, He was the truth of God walking around in human form. "The Word became flesh and made his dwelling [pitched His tent, tabernacled] among us. We have seen his glory, the glory of the One and Only, who came from the Father, full of grace and truth" (1:14). So, the people of God have access to the Word incarnate and the Word written.

Seven Truths About the Living Word

In the beginning was the Word.

- The Word was with God.
- The Word was, and still is, God.
- Through Him all things were made. He was the Godhead's agent in every act of making.
- In Him was life, given and maintained by the Word.
- He, as the life, was, and is, the light of mankind.
- The Word became flesh, incarnate. The baby in Bethlehem's manger was none other than the eternal Word of God, God Himself—God made man. The Creator of the universe became a man that He might empathize with us.

Interpretation of the Bible

We should interpret the Word of God in its most normal and natural sense. When the Bible uses a metaphor or a figure of speech, it should be instantly apparent, and one should interpret it accordingly. So, when Jesus affirms that He is "the door" (John 10:7) it's clear He isn't talking about wood and hinges. Because the Author of the Scriptures, the Holy Spirit (2 Peter 1:21), resides within each child of God (1 Corinthians 3:16), he or she is in a unique position to receive God's illumination (1 Corinthians 2:9-11). The Spirit of truth not only provides insights that permeate the head, but also provides the light of truth that shines into one's heart.

Scriptural harmony . . . means that individual passages of Scripture must always harmonize with the Scripture as a whole. One text can never be interpreted in such a manner that it conflicts with other passages. If a particular passage can seemingly be interpreted in several ways, the only choice is that interpretation which harmonizes with the rest of God's Word. Paul referred to this as "comparing spiritual things with spiritual" (1 Corinthians 2:13, KJV).

Why Four Gospels?

In the writers of the four Gospels, we have independent witnesses. Each one relates a consistent account. Each one presented Jesus from his particular point of view, using the material that would assist in reaching his objective. Of course, in the testimony of independent, truthful witnesses, there are similarities and dissimilarities, but they will agree in the main. Any perceived differences, when all the facts are known, will be seen as presenting a remarkable harmony. While all speak of the same person, Jesus, and the same events, disparities are due to the differences in personalities and habits of the writers.

Matthew—Because of the Messianic predictions in the Old Testament, the Jewish people were anticipating the appearance of their Messiah, who was to be born of a virgin (Isaiah 7:14) and of the Davidic line (Isaiah 11:1). In writing for the Jews, Matthew traced the regal line of the house of David from Abraham to Jesus. The Hebrews always reckoned the progeny from the father—never from the mother. There is no exception to this rule in the Old Testament. Holding to this rule, Matthew gave the lineage of our Lord from the standpoint of Joseph; then stated, "and Jacob begat Joseph *the husband* of Mary, of whom was born Jesus, who is called Christ" (Matthew 1:16, KJV, italics mine). Matthew decisively declared that Joseph was the husband of Mary, and it was of Mary that Jesus was born (see also Luke 3:23). Through Mary, Jesus was a descendent of David. Through Joseph, His foster father, He had a legal right to the throne of Israel, for Joseph was also a descendent of David.

Throughout his record, Matthew recognized that his intended readers would have an unquestioned acceptance of the Old Testament as the revealed Word of God. It is a literary unit, the type of Book that would be written by a Jew of the first century to prove to his brethren that its hero, Jesus of Nazareth, was and is the Messiah. The force of the evidence is accumulative. The implications of the miraculous conception and virgin birth are confirmed by the material in the subsequent discussions of the Book. The Gospel of Matthew has a marvelous message for the Jewish people today who are acquainted with Old Testament teachings concerning the Messiah's true nature—that He is the God-man—and who realize that, according to prophecy, He was to make atonement for sin. To those who are not into these implications, the Gospel record of Matthew is somewhat of an enigma.

Mark—According to discoveries of New Testament scholars, Mark was the first of the Gospels. He obviously wrote for the Romans who liked men of action. So, Mark, led by the Holy Spirit, selected those materials from Jesus' deeds and teachings that would present Him in a light that would have appeal to Roman citizens. In studying this Gospel carefully, we may see that—though Mark emphasized what Jesus did and taught—he also assumed His Divine-human nature.

Mark wrote nothing about the virgin birth because the Romans were not particularly interested in that subject. It appears that his plan was to present Jesus as a man of action who related to the masses of common people. After giving a brief statement about John the Baptist's ministry, and then Jesus' baptism and temptation—Mark plunged into the great Galilean Ministry. His short Gospel has an attraction for the hearts of those wishing to get the facts in the shortest space and time.

Luke—It appears that Luke, a Gentile, wrote especially for the Greeks, who loved beauty and grandeur. His ideal was to display Jesus as a perfect man, which He was. At the same time, he recognized that Christ was the God-man Savior of the world. When laying Luke's Gospel beside Mark's, one may note that the material is parallel, likewise chronological. But Luke purposed to give a complete account, going back to the birth narrative and the genealogy of Jesus which he traces to Adam. He does not tie the miraculous conception and virgin birth accounts to Old Testament predictions as Matthew did, because he did not particularly have the Hebrews in mind. Since his intended readership was not conversant with the Old Testament, a different tack would not have aided his purpose.

The miraculous elements in the birth narratives of John the Baptist and Jesus are strengthened and confirmed by the data of the entire book. Since Jesus was begotten of the Holy Spirit and born of the virgin, the portrait throughout the Book is in perfect conformity with chapters 1 and 2. The cumulative evidence of Luke therefore confirms that Jesus was God who entered the world by virgin birth.

In chapters 9:51—18:34 Luke presents a wealth of information not given by the other writers and supplements them greatly. His contribution concerning the events of the last week of our Lord's life is of inestimable value. No one can claim to be well-educated who is not familiar with this matchless account of Jesus' life.

John—Scholars have noticed the vast difference between this Gospel and the other three, calling them Synoptic Gospels. A close examination of this Gospel discloses that John stressed Jesus as the God-man. It was necessary for him to buttress the material already appearing in the Synoptics. He treats the matchless discourses and discussions Jesus had with the religious authorities. The material lightly touched upon in the other three Gospels is boldly asserted here.

John assumed that his readers had a general knowledge of Jesus as He had ministered throughout Palestine. The discussions recorded were naturally centered around the person of Christ and His claim to be the "only begotten Son of God" (see John 1:18; 3:16). John deals not so much with what Jesus did as *who and what He was.*

The testimony of four witnesses—instead of two or three

According to the law of Moses, every matter that came up for investigation in the court of Israel was to be substantiated by the testimony of at least two or three witnesses (Deuteronomy 17:6; 19:15). In keeping with this custom, God has given us the testimony of His servants who have written accounts of Jesus' life which have been miraculously preserved for us to this day.

History of the Bible

Literally, the Scriptures are composed of sixty-six books. They were written by approximately fifty different authors, living under varying conditions in many civilizations and environments. Notwithstanding the numerous diversities related to these authors, they all treat the single story which runs through all the Scriptures. Each book is a literary unit, while at the same time a part of the whole, making its own distinctive contribution to the revelation of God.

The writers

It is believed there were approximately fifty writers. Among them were Moses, the great lawgiver; Joshua, a skillful military strategist; Samuel, a pious, godly judge and prophet; David, a king, statesman, warrior, and poet-musician; Solomon, a king, practical philosopher, and writer; Isaiah, a statesman, poet, and dramatic orator; Amos, a rugged, rustic sheepherder; Jeremiah, "the weeping prophet" who cried over the gross sinfulness of God's people; Daniel, a capable administrator and fearless servant of God; Ezra, a devoted scribe; Matthew, a tax-gatherer; Peter an impetuous, impulsive fisherman; John, who called himself "the disciple whom Jesus loved";

Luke, a skilled physician, historian, and lover of sea lore; and Paul, the former rabbinic Pharisee who became a peerless missionary, a matchless expositor of the Gospel, and a humble bondslave of Christ. From diversified vocations God called men and spoke through them His life-giving Word.

The Divine Library

The sixty-six Books of the Bible might be considered chapters in **The Book**. Each Book has a distinctive purpose and special teaching, yet all the books are related to one main theme: God's plan of redemption. Its lifeline or bloodline runs from Adam, through Seth, to Jesus Christ, "the son of David, the son of Abraham" (Matthew 1:1). The *Divine Library* is departmentalized as follows:

The Old Testament is divided according to the nature of the contents of its thirty-nine books into four divisions, with the forth subdivided into two:

The Pentateuch (Torah or Law—five Books): Genesis, Exodus, Leviticus, Numbers, and Deuteronomy

Historical (twelve Books): Joshua, Judges, Ruth, 1 Samuel, 2 Samuel, 1 Kings, 2 Kings, 1 Chronicles, 2 Chronicles, Ezra, Nehemiah, and Esther

Poetical (five Books): Job, Psalms, Proverbs, Ecclesiastics, Song of Solomon

Prophetical (seventeen Books):

1. *Major Prophets* (five Books): Isaiah, Jeremiah, Lamentations, Ezekiel, Daniel

2. *Minor Prophets* (twelve Books): Hosea, Joel, Amos, Obadiah, Jonah, Micah, Nahum, Habakkuk, Zephaniah, Haggai, Zechariah, Malachi

The New Testament contains twenty-seven Books, which may be divided into three main divisions and several subdivisions. The names of these divisions are helpful in indicating the character of the contents of the Books and Epistles (Letters):

Historical (five Books):

1. *Biographical:* the Life of Christ (four Books)—Matthew, Mark, Luke, John;

2. *Church History* (one Book)—Acts

Doctrinal and practical (twenty-one Books):

1. *Pauline Epistles* (fourteen Books):

a. Ecclesiastical—to the churches (nine Books)—Romans, 1 Corinthians, 2 Corinthians, Galatians, Ephesians, Philippians, Colossians, 1 Thessalonians, 2 Thessalonians;

b. Pastoral—i. e., to pastors-ministers-bishops-elders (three Books)—1 Timothy, 2 Timothy, Titus;

c. Personal (one Book)—Philemon

d. To Hebrew Christians (one Book)—Hebrews (though the name of this Book's writer is unknown, most reliable scholars believe that it was written by Paul).

2. *General Epistles* (seven Books):

a. to the Hebrew Christians (three Books)—James, 1 Peter, 2 Peter;

b. John's Epistles (three Books);

General—1 John;

Personal—2 John, 3 John;

c. Jude's General Epistle,

Prophetical (one Book)—Revelation (written by John)

Bible thoughts to ponder

1. Even as Christians, we may be tempted to doubt our salvation. Read John 3:16; 5:24; 6:47. How do these verses show us that through our salvation we have already received God's gift of eternal life?

2. We sometimes question our worthiness to receive the gift of eternal life. Read Romans 5:9-11; 6:23. What do self-worth or personal merit have to do with receiving the gift of eternal life? Consider Titus 3:5-6.

3. Study 2 Corinthians 5:1. How are we sure that this gift of eternal life will last forever? Now look at Hebrews 9:11-15.

4. Carefully consider 2 Corinthians 4:17—5:9. How should the promise of eternal life influence our everyday living?

For thought and discussion

1. Name practical benefits of reading, studying, and applying God's Word.
2. Although the Bible is accurate in other areas as well, what is its primary purpose?
3. During this age Who guides us into God's truth? Write down at least two verses concerning this Teacher.
4. Why did John refer to Jesus Christ as "The Word" (Logos)?
5. Sum up several truths about Christ, the Living Word.
6. What is meant by Scriptural harmony?
7. What did each Gospel writer distinctively stress about Jesus?
8. Without looking list the names of several writers of Bible Books.
9. Why are prayer and Bible reading essential to understanding God's will?

10
The Body of Christ—The Church

And he is the head of the body, the church; he is the beginning and the firstborn from among the dead, so that in everything he might have the supremacy. For God was pleased to have all his fullness dwell in him (Colossians 1:18-19, author's italics).

The Church is God's appointed agency for the salvation of mankind. It was organized for service, and its mission is to carry the Gospel to the world. From the beginning God planned that His Church would reflect His fullness and sufficiency. The members of the Church—those He has called "out of darkness into His marvelous light" (2 Peter 2:9, KJV)—are to reflect His glory.

The Church: The vehicle of God's grace

The Church is the repository of Christ's riches of grace. Through the Church the final and full display of God's love will eventually be shown, even to "the principalities and powers in heavenly places" (Ephesians 3:10, KJV). The Church alone can provide a moral vision to a wandering people. Only the Church can step into the vacuum and demonstrate that there is a sovereign, living God who is the Source of truth. According to the New Testament every saved person is a member of the

Church but should also align himself with a local congregation. The Church (in this sense I use a capital; lower case for a specific local church) includes born-again believers from "ev'ry kindred, ev'ry tribe, On this terrestrial ball" (Edward Perronet in "All Hail the Power of Jesus' Name"). The writer of Hebrews refers to the family of the redeemed as "the general assembly and church of the firstborn, which are written in heaven" (13:23, KJV).

What we do of ourselves does not matter. What does make an eternal difference is what a sovereign God does through us, His church (*ekklesía*, " the called-out ones"). God doesn't want our success. He merely wants us. He doesn't demand our achievement; He does require our obedience. Let's stop praying, "Lord, bless what we're doing," and start praying, "Lord, help us to do what You're blessing."

Our calling

One of Christianity's most daunting challenges is for churches to live out the Christ life so the lost world will embrace Him. Unfortunately, all too many churches are appalling rather than appealing! When a church demonstrates God's presence and activity, it will allow God to shake and stir even hardened sinners and cynics. *How can your church be that kind of church?* First, you must understand who you are in relation to God and to one another:

A church is a creation of Christ. He builds His church (Matthew 16:18), using Spirit-directed pastors and leaders (Ephesians 4:11-13), and arranges the members in it according to His will (1 Corinthians 12:18). Therefore, spiritual leaders and members should have respect for the pastor and every member God has placed in their church.

A church is a living body of Christ with many members (1 Corinthians 12:27). The church is not a building or an organization. It is a group of people built up into a living body.

A church is uniquely related to Christ as Head of the body (Ephesians 1:22; 4:15-16). All matters in a church are to come under His lordship.

Members of a church are exceptionally related to every other member (Ephesians 4:11-16; 1 Corinthians 12). All members are interdependent on one another and need one another.

A church is on mission with Christ carrying out Christ's Great Commission (Matthew 28:18-20; 2 Corinthians 5:17-20). "We are God's fellow workers" (1 Corinthians 3:9).

The beginning of the body of Christ, the Church

Shortly after Christ ascended to the Father, God moved through the Jerusalem believers to officially establish the Church, even though that organism, in essence, already existed. The full-blown Church was inaugurated on the Day of Pentecost, when on that Jewish holy day the apostle Peter, filled with the Spirit, delivered the first Gospel sermon in the name of the risen Christ. Three thousand people responded and were drawn together into an organic, spiritual union (Acts 2). That day the Holy Spirit was sent to permanently indwell the hearts of all believers, whereas previously He would enter a person on occasion and then depart. Jesus Christ founded the Church, died for the Church, sent His Spirit to the Church, and will one day return for it (1 Thessalonians 4:13-18).

Building Christ's Church

So, you'd like to build a healthy and growing church? Then you must expend time and energy laying a solid foundation. Every church should adopt a mission statement based on God's Word, so the entire membership will understand why their church exists. Once you have clarified your church's purpose, you can develop goals to implement your mission for Christ. A sample purpose statement might be: "First Church seeks to be a body of loving, sharing Christians who are united in fulfilling Christ's commission by proclaiming Him as Lord and Savior and, through the power of the Holy Spirit, winning unsaved persons to Him, nurturing and educating believers, and keeping God's commandments." Of course, the length of your statement is up to you. Then, as the leadership and laypersons plan activities, approaches, and programs, they should always do so in light of the mission statement. Having a stated purpose builds morale, reduces frustration, and allows concentration on specifics. It also attracts cooperation of members and assists in measurement of progress.

The five purposes of the Church

Worship: The church exists to worship (which may include singing, praising and thanking God, prayers, messages from the minister and sometimes others, personal testimonies, drama, etc., all with the intention of glorifying and magnifying the King of Kings and Lord of Lords). The worship services help us focus on God, preparing us spiritually and emotionally for the week ahead.

Ministry: Christ teaches us to love our neighbors as ourselves, especially through ministry to them. Ministry is demonstrating God's love to others by meeting their needs. Ministry helps us find and develop our talents and spiritual gifts and use them in serving others.

Discipleship: This is the lifelong process of aiding people to become more Christ-like in their thoughts, feelings and actions. A major responsibility of the church is to help believers reach spiritual maturity, equipping the saints for the work of ministry (Ephesians 4:12), fortifying their faith by learning the truths of God's Word and applying biblical principles in their lifestyle.

Evangelism: This fulfills our mission of reaching for Christ: our families, friends, acquaintances, and all peoples, near and far. We are "ambassadors for Christ" (2 Corinthians 5:20, KJV), and our number-one assignment is to evangelize the world (Matthew 28:18-20; Acts 1:8).

Baptizing them: Water baptism is not only a signal of salvation, it is a symbol of fellowship. It is an outward sign of an inward change. It does not save but, as Jesus expressed at His baptism: " Let it be so now; it is proper for us to do this to fulfill all righteousness.' Then John consented [and baptized Him]" (Matthew 3:15). Baptism verifies our walk with Christ and follows His example. Water baptism is also the visible expression of the Spirit's baptism when we were saved. "All baptized by one Spirit into the body of Christ."

Five elements of the Christian lifestyle

The purpose of the Church is to facilitate these elements:

• Every believer is a **missionary**. "Go make disciples of all nations," Jesus commanded. Our purpose: To *evangelize* the world.

• Every believer is a **member** of Christ's Family. "Baptize them in the name of the Father, Son, and Holy Spirit." Our Purpose: To *encourage* one another.

• Every believer needs **maturity**. "Teach them to obey everything I have commanded you." Our Purpose: To *edify* (build up) one another.

°Every believer is to **magnify** the Lord. "Love the Lord your God with all your heart." Our Purpose: To *exalt* Christ in worship.

• Every believer is a **minister**. "Love your neighbor as yourself." Our Purpose: To *equip* for service. Loving your neighbor is what ministry is all about.

There are numerous analogies for a Christian disconnected from a church: a football player without a team, soldiers without a platoon, a sheep without a flock, a child without a family.

Maturity of the believer

Spiritual maturity is demonstrated more by behavior than stated beliefs. Genuine spiritual maturity includes having a heart that worships and praises God, building and enjoying loving relationships, using one's gifts and talents in building up the Body of Christ, and sharing faith with those outside the spiritual family of God. We are to become mature, attaining to the whole measure of the fullness of Christ (Ephesians 4:13). God is far more concerned with our character than with our comfort. His plan is to perfect us, to make us fulfilled and complete in Him. For this reason, He allows a variety of character-building circumstances, conflicts, and disappointments in order to develop our character in preparation for carrying out His will.

How does God SHAPE us for ministry?

S Spiritual gifts
H Loving hearts
A Abilities
P Personality
E Experiences

The church practices stewardship by assessing the SHAPE of its members.

God's plan for us

God creates each of us as unique. There is nobody else in the entire world who is exactly like you; no two sets of fingerprints are alike, and all of us have different DNA characteristics. Deep within our makeup He planted the seeds of the ministry for which he has prepared us. If we believe Psalm 139:13-16 and Jeremiah 1:4-5; 29:11, then we are sure that God has specific plans for us! Living a life of yieldedness and obedience and being attentive to the Spirit's leading allows God to work out those plans through us.

The church's pastor

The heart of the God-called, sincere minister is filled with an intense longing to reach people for Christ. Since he has caught the vision of the living Christ, he will bend every effort to share God's joy- and peace-giving truths with others. God's Spirit will empower Him. He will shepherd souls as one who will give an account. An unknown preacher of a previous generation summed up the pastor's awesome role:

> With his eyes fixed on the Cross of Calvary, beholding the uplifted Savior, relying on His grace, believing that He will be with him until the end, as his shield, his strength, his efficiency, he works for God. With invitations and pleading, mingled with the assurances of God's love, he seeks to win souls to Jesus, and in heaven he is numbered among those who are "called, and chosen, and faithful" (Revelation 17:14).

The two ordinances of the Church

Baptism

The ordinance of baptism in the name of God the Father, God the Son, and God the Holy Spirit symbolizes the believer's faith in a crucified, buried, and resurrected Savior. It also stands for the believer's death to sin, the burial of his old life, and—through Christ's resurrection—his new life. Paul explained, "We were therefore buried with him through baptism into death in order that, just as Christ was raised from the dead through the glory of the Father, we too may live a new life" (Romans 6:4). When the Christian minister baptizes the believer in water to typify the work of the

Spirit, the rudiments of the Gospel message are pictured (see 1 Corinthians 15:3-4). A few far-out cults and "churches" have cast aside baptism as archaic and non-essential. Christ requested that John the Baptist baptize Him to set an example for us to follow (Matthew 3:17).

The Lord's Supper—Communion

The Lord's Supper represents the atonement of Christ as the only means of our justification (God's receiving us as righteous), and the only support for the new life we have in Christ. There is no magic in it. The supper is memorial in nature (1 Corinthians 11:23-26). It "shows forth" and dramatizes the agonizing death of our Lord on the Cross.

When we partake of the Lord's Supper, it means that we believe Christ has made an all-sufficient substitutionary sacrifice for our sins.

The purpose of the Lord's Table

The gathering of the Lord's people to observe the Supper has a sacred meaning that is essential to the spiritual well-being of the church's members. For that reason Communion is a special object of Satan's attack. Christ taught:

• **The purpose** of this gathering is to "remember" Him and His death until He comes again.

• **The symbols**—the bread and the cup—speak not only of His complete gift of Himself but also of our own total identification in it. He lives within us (see also Matthew 26:26-29; Mark 14:22-25; Luke 22:17-20).

During the interval between His Ascension and His second coming, we are to keep His atoning death central in the practice and preaching of the Church, His Body. Most evangelicals believe this ordinance is essential because it honors the Lord's request but do not feel it bestows saving grace as a few churches do.

Churches grow when they are:

- **Warmer** through fellowship
- **Deeper** through discipleship
- **Stronger** through worship
- **Broader** through ministry and larger through
- **Evangelism**

The necessity of fellowship

The writer of Hebrews urged: " Let us not give up meeting together, as some are in the habit of doing, but let us encourage one another—and all the more as you see the Day [the Lord's return] approaching" (Hebrews. 10:25). Coming together as fellow believers helps us to face life's problems, because we mutually encourage and support one another.

Such a Christ-centered *family*, called the Church, offers the instruction of a school where learning is a joy; the healing of a supernatural hospital where inner health is assured; the resources of a wealthy bank where human needs are abundantly met; and the acceptance of a home where love is supreme. As a network of joyful friends, the Church becomes a channel through which people strengthen one another.

A society of love

It is a fact of this life together that receiving love enhances the ability to give love, thereby creating a supportive circle of enabling relationships. In such an environment, it becomes almost automatic for people to return affirmation for affirmation, encouragement for encouragement, and affection for affection. Every believer, regardless of talent or training, is called and resourced by God to build these kinds of relationships with other Christians. We enjoy the privilege of edifying one another. Paul implored: " Let us therefore follow after the things which make for peace, and things wherewith one may edify another" (Romans 14:19, KJV). "Wherefore comfort yourselves together, and edify one another, even as also ye do" (1 Thessalonians. 5:11, KJV). Positive words and helpful actions encourage others to a stronger commitment of servanthood and to lasting friendships centered around our shared love for Christ.

Renewal of family commitments

A loving family is among life's richest blessings. Apply that lovely word family to all primary relationships—including spouses, children, parents, grandparents, siblings, cousins, aunts, and uncles—and you can develop support groups in the church or community. Believers may serve as a substitute family, even if one's biological family is nonexistent or broken. Many churchgoers have testified, "Church is the only place where I hear the words, I love you.'"

Giving the gift of yourself

Of all the gifts you give your family, none is as precious as the gift of yourself. Open a line of emotional credit for every member of your real or adopted family, in which you become the "co-signer," signifying that you will make yourself available to them. Then become a second-mile Christian, going out of your way to be helpful and affirming and to listen fully.

Giving a gift of yourself means your presence. People—whether family, friends, or acquaintances—who are ill in body, battered in spirit, or disappointed by life don't need empty cliches. More than all else they need a gentle presence, a listening ear, and a caring heart. Time and attention are among the most precious gifts you can give. Remember that your gift of being there usually becomes a serendipity, because you will often receive far more than you give. Never cease cherishing people; express your love and gratitude for them.

Church—A family everyone needs

A divorcee in her early thirties moved to a strange city with her young children. Though she longed to begin a new life, her past drove her to places where she formed dead-end relationships. One evening in a near-drunken state, her heart questioned her about the purpose of her existence. At nearly the same moment, a young neighbor couple appeared at her door and cordially invited her to attend church with them the next morning, Sunday. Though she hesitated, their friendly persuasion was hard to resist. True to the couple's promise, they carried the mother and her children to a small church close to her house. As the tiny congregation offered her friendship, she felt drawn to Christ and surrendered the shards of her broken life to Him. Along with her newfound faith, her sense of belonging increased as the people of God offered her unconditional love and overlooked her weirdness. Her new church friends provided such wholehearted support that she began calling them "the family I never had."

Restoration of broken relationships

Since love and forgiveness are always intentional acts, set your will to nurture relationships at home, at work, wherever you are. Though it is not easy to control our feelings, we can often strengthen even the most sandpapered relationship with Christ-motivated thoughts, words, and actions. Avoid anger and retaliation. Like Lincoln, whose heart had "no room for the memory of a wrong," forgive quickly. Enrich each person you meet with an act of unexpected kindness. Rejoice in another person's good fortune as quickly as you would sympathize with his pain or sorrow. Make affirmation and support a habitual part of your conversations. *Remember that a one-minute discussion of someone's faults often destroys a lifelong friendship.*

When an unfortunate attitude or unkind action fractures a relationship, take the first step toward reconciliation. Your action may build a bridge on which the other person can walk back into your heart. Far more people than we can imagine would like to right a wrong—but don't have the slightest notion of how to start, or don't have the spiritual energy to try. Why not make the first move?

Following Jesus will cost you your life!

"What?" you may query. "Throughout this book you've said that we're not saved by works but by the grace of God. Huh?" Salvation is free to us, but Jesus bought and paid for it. Yet, discipleship follows our regeneration—and that does cost . . . our lives. We cannot divorce the integrity of church membership from discipleship. Jesus is calling disciples, not club members or cliqué groupies. The churches with relevant worship styles; Christ-centered, prophetic proclamation; and social sensitivity will make an impact on their communities.

God's expectations of interpersonal relations in the Church:

Romans 14:1, 12-13: "Accept him whose faith is weak. Without passing judgment on disputable matters . . . each of us will give an account of himself to God. Therefore let us stop passing judgment on one another. Instead, make up your mind not to put any stumbling block or obstacle in your brother's way."

1 Corinthians 10:24: "Nobody should seek his own good, but the good of others."

Ephesians 4:25: "Each of you must put off falsehood and speak truthfully to his neighbor, for we are all members of one body."

Ephesians 4:29: "Do not let any unwholesome talk come out of your mouths, but only what is helpful for building others up according to their needs, that it may benefit those who listen."

Ephesians 4:31-32: "Get rid of all bitterness, rage and anger, brawling and slander, along with every form of malice. Be kind and compassionate to one another, forgiving each other, just as in Christ God forgave you."

Ephesians 5:19-20: "Speak to one another with psalms, hymns and spiritual songs. Sing and make music in your heart to the Lord, always giving thanks to God the Father for everything."

Ephesians 5:21: "Submit to one another out of reverence for Christ."

Colossians 3:13-14: "Bear with each other and forgive whatever grievances you may have against one another. Forgive as the Lord forgave you. And over all these virtues put on love, which binds them all together in perfect unity."

Christ's Prayer for the Church: In Jesus' great intercessory prayer to the Father, He asked, "Neither pray I for these alone, but for them also which shall believe on me through their word; that they all may be one; as thou, Father, art in me, and in thee, that they may also be one in us: that the world may believe that thou hast sent me" (John 17:20-21, KJV). We can fully trust in the answer to this prayer, for the Church as a unity is developing out of it. Jesus Christ, the Head of the Body, continues to intercede for us as our Great High Priest! (Hebrews. 4:15-16).

Samuel J. Stone wrote the stirring lyrics to *The Church's One Foundation*:

The church's one foundation is Jesus Christ her Lord;
She is His new creation, By Spirit and the Word;
From heav'n He came and sought her To be His holy bride,
With His own blood He bought her, And for her life He died.
Elect from every nation, Yet one o'er all the earth,
Her charter of salvation, One Lord, one faith, one birth;
One holy name she blesses, Partakes one holy food,
And to one hope she presses, With ev'ry grace endured.

For thought and discussion

1. What is the meaning of the Greek word for the Church, *ekklesía*?
2. Set down several definitions of what the Church is. How does your church measure up?
3. What are several purposes for the Church?
4. Fill in the blanks. Spiritual ——— is demonstrated more by ——— than by stated beliefs.
5. Name the two ordinances of the Church and comment on them.
6. Initially, what is the best gift you can give? Explain why.
7. Read John 17, Christ's high priestly prayer. What all did He pray for?
8. How do you go about making disciples?

Part IV

The Holy Trinity

Holy, holy, holy! Lord God Almighty!
Early in the morning our song shall rise to Thee;
Holy, holy, holy, merciful and mighty!
God in three Persons blessed Trinity!
— *Reginald Heber*

And God said, Let **us** make man in our image, after our likeness:. . . (Genesis 1:26a, KJV, author's bold face)

Therefore go and make disciples of all nations, baptizing them in the name of **the Father** and of **the Son** and of **the Holy Spirit** (Matthew 28:19, author's bold face).

As soon as **Jesus** was baptized, he went up out of the water. At that moment heaven was opened, and he saw the **Spirit of God** descending like a dove and lighting on him. And **a voice from heaven** said, "This is my Son, whom I love; with him I am well pleased" (Matthew 3:16-17, author's bold face).

For there are three that bear record in heaven, **the Father, the Word,** and **the Holy Ghost**: and **these three are one** (1 John 5:7, KJV, author's bold face).

The Word of God is filled with mysteries our finite minds cannot grasp. Because God teaches them in The Book, by faith we accept them. God, the uncreated Creator, Himself is a mystery. As the old song goes, "We will understand it better bye and bye." In heaven, Paul wrote, we will know even as we are known (1 Corinthians 13:12, KJV) Yet, because we are not God, He will limit our knowledge even then.

One of those unfathomable mysteries is the doctrine of The Trinity (although the term is not used in the Bible, the reality of God's Tri-unity is there), God in three Persons. From a human standpoint there is no logical explanation. God may operate as He pleases, and He has chosen to reveal Himself as The Triune God—God the Father, God the Son (Jesus Christ), and God the Holy Spirit. All three Persons were manifested when God the Son was being baptized by John the Baptist. The Holy Spirit descended in the form of a dove, and God the Father spoke approvingly from heaven: "This is my beloved Son, in whom I am well pleased" (see Matthew 3:16-17).

God the Son was baptized; God the Holy Spirit came down in a visible form; and God the Father spoke (see also Matthew 28:19; John 15:26; 1 Corinthians 12:4-13; 2 Corinthians 13:14; Ephesians 2:18; and 1 Peter 1:2).

The vision of Revelation 4–5

Tremendous truths are revealed in those chapters.

° There is a powerful God at the center of creation, and He is worthy of our trust and praise in the tempestuous days ahead.

° The mediator between God and man is Jesus Christ (see also 1 Timothy 2:5).

° The third Person of the Trinity reveals all of this to us. The Holy Spirit (God living within us) is the unfailing agent of our cleansing and sanctification.

The Triune God . . .

While God is one in nature, essence, and being, He is three Persons. The unity of essence does not forbid plurality of purpose. God is the absolute sovereign over the entire universe, the eternal God in whom "we live, and move, and have our being" (Acts 17:28a, KJV). To Him all human creatures are responsible and will eventually render an account of their lives and deeds. He has endowed them with free-moral agency and has placed them in various locales where He has ordained they should live. In their exercise of choice, He expects them to serve and worship Him, the Creator and moral Governor of the cosmos.

The remarkable theologian, W. T. Conner, observed: "The New Testament conception is not that Father, Son, and Holy Spirit mutually and successively co-operate in carrying out a plan previously agreed upon, but rather that all work in and through each. The work of the Son is the work of the Father, and the Father works in and through the Son. The work of the Spirit is the work of Christ, and Christ works in and through the Spirit. The work of each is the work of all, and the work of all is the work of each . . . Yet there is a distinction of office' or function. The Father is the source and origin of all things; the Son is the medium of the outgoing energy and power of God; the Holy Spirit works to complete all things. But each works not so as to exclude the others, but so that the work of each is the work of all—not all separately but of the Godhead as a unity."[1]

God is an infinite, intelligent Spirit, the Maker and Supreme Ruler of the universe. In the unity of the Godhead, the three Persons, Father, Son, and Holy Spirit, are equal in every divine perfection and execute distinct but harmonious offices in the grand work of human redemption.

All three Persons were involved in creation. Likewise, they collaborate in the salvation of those who receive the Savior. The Godhead devised the plan of salvation, and Christ carried it out. Without the Holy Spirit, though, no one could be saved. Further, the Spirit, through those who minister God's Word, is convicting the lost to become reconciled to God through faith in Christ.

God is three Persons but one in essence and substance. All illustrations to demonstrate The Trinity are rather futile. However, here is one: Water can appear in three forms—liquid, steam, or ice. All three are still water but in different forms.

---

[1]Walter Thomas Conner, *Christian Doctrine* (Nashville, TN: Broadman Press, 1937), 125-126.

Mankind has willfully sinned against the Triune God

Sadly, beginning with Adam and Eve humans have abused their God-given autonomy, which has resulted in deliberate, willful acts of pitting themselves, with finite wills, against the Infinite One. Without fail every human being has chosen to become corrupt and alienated from the life of God. Isaiah proclaimed, "All we like sheep have gone astray; we have turned every one to his own way; and the Lord hath laid on him [Jesus] the iniquity of us all" (Isaiah 53:6, KJV). Without Christ, as Paul put it, one is "dead in trespasses and sins" (see Ephesians 2:1, KJV). In a Christless condition persons are in a state of hopelessness (see Ephesians 2:12, KJV).

11
God The Father

Let your light so shine before men, that they may see your good works, and glorify your Father which is in heaven (Matthew 5:16, KJV).

After this manner therefore pray ye: Our Father which art in heaven, Hallowed be thy name (Matthew 6:9, KJV).

The God who creates, rules, and sustains the universe is the caring Father who loves *you* as if you were the only one to love! God wants the best for you. Imagine it. The awesome God of glory wants to have intimate fellowship with you, to wipe the tears from your eyes, and to fill your life with incredible happiness. This sovereign God, as revealed in Jesus Christ, is supreme. He has a plan and purpose for everything and has done nothing accidentally. He "works out everything in conformity with the purpose of his will" (Ephesians 1:11b). God is a unity. "Hear, O Israel: The LORD our God, the LORD is one" (Deuteronomy 6:4).

The prophet asked the rhetorical question: "Hath not one God created us" (Malachi. 2:10, KJV). God endowed each of His angels, and man who followed, with the power of free choice. He never bullies anyone's will but uses moral persuasion, always stopping short of coercion or forcing one's will. God could have created us as robots or puppets, but He wanted us to have a loving, personal relationship out of our *free will.*

God's divine government

In eternity past the Triune God determined to create all things for His own pleasure and purpose (see Revelation 4:11; Ephesians 1:11). God the Father would design the divine plan; God the Son would become its unique executor; and God the Holy Spirit would reveal through the Scriptures its marvelous blueprint. God designed a moral government and divided it between two classes of created beings—angelic creatures and man. Within this government, God set up an ethical system based on His goodness and justice. These absolutes are His basis for framing a moral government for His creatures. "For by him [Jesus Christ] all things were created: things in heaven and on earth, visible and invisible, whether thrones or powers or rulers or authorities; all things were created by him and for him" (Colossians 1:16, KJV).

God's creation

God's wisdom and power as the world's architect were so immense that He could visualize beautiful images and then turn them into reality. "And God saw every thing that he had made, and, behold, it was very good"(Genesis 1:31, KJV). "The earth is the Lord's and the fullness thereof, the world and they that dwell therein" (Psalm 24:1, KJV). "He loveth righteousness and judgment: the earth is full of the goodness of the Lord" (Psalm 33:5, KJV). "We are created in Christ Jesus for good works which God prepared beforehand that we should walk in them" (Ephesians 2:10, NKJV).

God's image

Man was created in the image of God—*imago Dei.* Then God said, "Let us make man in our image according to our likeness (Genesis 1:26). "And God created **man** in His own image, in the image of God, He created him: **male and female** He created them" (Genesis 1:27, NKJV, bold face mine).

The **us** must refer to God alone: God the Father, God the Son, and God the Holy Spirit.

That humans are created in God's image simply means that they share, in a finite and imperfect manner, the communicable attributes of

God. Among these attributes are personality, spirituality (John 4:24), rationality, including knowledge and wisdom (Colossians 3:10), and morality, including goodness, holiness, righteousness, love, justice, and mercy (Ephesians 4:24).

These attributes give us the capacity to enjoy fellowship with God and to develop relationships with one another:

God	**Man**
God is eternal (Psalm 90:2).	Man was created at a point in time (Genesis 11:26-33).
God has life in Himself (John 5:26).	Man is dependent on God to sustain him (Acts 17:18).
God is all powerful (Job 42:2).	Man is weak (1 Corinthians 1:25).
God is all knowing (Isaiah 40:13).	Man is limited in knowledge (Isaiah 55:8-9).
God is everywhere present (Jeremiah 23:23-24).	Man is confined to a single space of time (Psalm 139:1-12).

The Law of God (The Ten Commandments)

There are four basic reasons why God gave the Law.

First—To show man what sin is, to set standards against which to compare our lives. Like pain it indicates to us that something is wrong. The law of conscience cannot be depended on because it can be seared or "cauterized" into senselessness (see 1 Timothy 4:2). Within the few hundred years between Adam to Noah, mankind had so deadened its conscience that God was sorry He ever created humans.

Second—The Law was given to reveal man's sin in comparison to the holiness and righteousness of God. God wanted human beings to recognize how woefully they had missed the mark. Paul wrote that the Law was "a schoolmaster to bring us unto Christ" (Galatians 3:24-25, KJV).

Third—To drive us to despair of self-effort when we have despaired of concocting our own self-worship.

Fourth—To bring the unbeliever to Christ for **salvation** and the believer to the Holy Spirit for His empowering.

Grace replaces law

The Law escorted the unbeliever to the end of himself until his only recourse was to plead for God's offered grace and mercy. Once one has received Christ, he no longer needs the Law except to recognize that The Decalogue (The Ten Commandments) is a code of moral rules set up by God. "Christ is the end of the law so that there may be righteousness for everyone who believes (Romans 10:4). "Now that no one is justified by the law before God is evident; for the righteous man shall live by faith'" (Galatians 3:11-12). If righteousness comes through the Law, then Christ died needlessly (Galatians 2:21). "For the law was given through Moses; grace and truth came through Jesus Christ" (John 1:17).

God's provisions for new life in Him

In order to live a righteous and obedient life one must walk in the Spirit by faith in His ability to produce righteousness and obedience within us (see Romans 8:4). In the Christian life there is only one source of power: the indwelling of God the Holy Spirit. There is only one means of releasing that source: faith. Obedience is a result of a Spirit-filled relationship with Christ.

God has removed us from under the jurisdiction of the law and placed us under His grace. He did not do away with the Law, since it is a standard for evaluating the conduct of our lives. "But now we have been released from the Law, having died to that by which we were bound, so that we serve in newness of the spirit and not in boldness of the letter"(Romans 7:6).

When a person becomes a true believer in Christ, he is born into God's family (adopted) and out of Satan's hellish household. Satan does all he can to keep people blinded to the offer of forgiveness in Christ. Multiplied millions, even billions in history, have thrown off his shackles and gone from death to life (see John 5:24). God has no hostility toward mankind. He loves us but hates our sin. By God's grace in Christ Jesus, we may have victory over the enemy (see 1 Corinthians 15:57).

He is a righteous God who required atonement for our sins. This is why He became a man—so he could bear the judgment and punishment due us and remove every barrier that our sin had erected between Himself and us. God never needed to be reconciled. Rather, we are the ones who need it. "God was in Christ reconciling the world to himself, not counting men's trespasses against them . . . for he made Him who knew no sin to be sin on our behalf, that we might become the righteousness of God" (2 Corinthians 5:19-21, NKJV). God absorbed our sins and gave us His righteousness.

The apostle John wrote the believers: "My dear children, I write this to you so that you will not sin. But if anybody does sin, we have one who speaks to the Father in our defense ["advocate," KJV, meaning defense attorney]—Jesus Christ, the Righteous One. He is the atoning sacrifice for our sins, and not only for ours but also for the sins of the whole world" (1 John 2:1-2).

Why the Ten Commandments?

Why did God formulate Ten Commandments if He realized we were going to violate them? He gave them to demonstrate that we are sinful and weak. I look into the "mirror" of the Ten Commandments and exclaim, "I'm a sinner!" Then I am driven to plead, "God, have mercy on me, a sinner" (Luke 18:13c).

God never changes. His moral precepts are absolute and irrevocable forever. God will judge us by them. The Ten Commandments are God's outline for human behavior, and we have broken them. Actually, they cannot, in the truest sense, be broken. They break us unless we repent. We have sinned against His clearly defined will, and that is what sin means: "Sin is the transgression of the law" (see 1 John 3:4, KJV). The law becomes like a schoolmaster that drives me or leads me to the Cross of Christ because I cannot save myself. I must open my heart and allow Jesus to bridge the gap.

Our liberation from dire consequences

Because we have violated God's law, we deserve judgment and hell—but God has taken the initiative to provide for our liberation from the curse of the law. God laid on Him all of our breaches of the law. We do not have to suffer condemnation and hell (see Romans 5:1; 8:1). We can have the peace of God which passes all understanding (see Philippians 4:7). We can possess fulfillment and the joy Christ produces when we turn our sin-cursed lives over to Him.

The Ten Commandments declare that our first priority is to love God (see Matthew 22:37-38). The first four Commandments deal with our relationship to God. The last six treat our relationship with our fellow human beings, whom we also are to love.

The Ten Commandments as given by God

I

Thou shalt have no other gods before me.

II

Thou shalt not make unto thee any graven image, or any likeness of any thing that is in heaven above, or that is in the earth beneath or that is in the water under the earth: thou shalt not bow down thyself to them, nor serve them: for I the Lord thy God am a jealous God, visiting the iniquity of the fathers upon the children unto the third and fourth generation of them that hate me; and showing mercy unto thousands of them that love me, and keep my commandments.

III

Thou shalt not take the name of the Lord thy God in vain; for the Lord will not hold him guiltless that taketh his name in vain.

IV

Remember the Sabbath day, to keep it holy. Six days shalt thou labor, and do all thy work; but the seventh day is the Sabbath of the Lord thy God; in it thou shalt not do any work, thou, nor thy son, nor they daughter, they manservant, nor thy maidservant, nor thy cattle, nor thy stranger that is within thy gates: for in six days the Lord made heaven and earth, the sea, and all that in them is, and rested the seventh day; therefore the Lord blessed the Sabbath day, and made it holy.

V

Honor thy father and thy mother: that thy days may be long upon the land which the Lord thy God giveth thee.

VI

Thou shall not kill.

VII

Thou shalt not commit adultery.

VIII

Thou shalt not steal.

IX

Thou shalt not bear false witness against thy neighbor.

X

Thou shalt not covet thy neighbor's house, thou shalt not covet thy neighbor's wife, nor his manservant, nor his maidservant, nor his ox, nor his ass, nor anything that is thy neighbor's.

—Exodus 20:3-17

The character and attributes of God

SOVEREIGNTY: God is the supreme Ruler of the Universe. He is called the King over all that He has created (Psalm 103:19; 47:7-8). In accordance with His absolute will God does whatever pleases Him (Psalm 135:6; Daniel 4:25). God demonstrates His will within His moral government in the three following categories:

• In **His sovereign will** God controls all the circumstances within His kingdom but does not directly interfere with the operation of anyone's volition. This is exemplified in the lives of Jonah and Peter. His rulership also includes control over Satan and all fallen angels who, despite their willful rebellion and disobedience, become instruments of God's sovereign will in His moral government. God will use every situation and circumstance and cause them to work together for the believer's good and for His own ultimate goals (Romans 8:28).

• In **God's permissive will** He will permit humans to reject the Gospel even after hearing it repeatedly. He will not violate the will He created within us, yet God will do all within His power—not withstanding the limitations He Himself originally imposed within His moral government—to draw an unsaved person to a saving knowledge of Jesus Christ (2 Peter 3:9; Revelation 22:17; John 3:36). If a person then rejects the Gospel, God's justice must condemn this unbelief and rejection of His grace. That willful unbeliever will be judged at the great white throne.

God in His permissive will also allow Christians to exercise their volitions in what Paul calls carnality (1 Corinthians 3:1). For example, believers may choose non-believing partners in marriage. This opens the door to divisive misery that they might have avoided. Paul warned Christians against such unions with: "Do not be yoked together with unbelievers" (2 Corinthians 6:14). *It is God's will that all Christians be constantly controlled and guided by the Holy Spirit* (see Ephesians 5:17-18).

• **God's directive will** for all Christians is found in the Word of God. That is why we, as His people, are instructed to study (be diligent, apply ourselves) to show ourselves "approved unto God" (2 Timothy 2:15). Jesus said, "Man shall not live by bread alone, but by every word that proceedeth out of the mouth of God (Matthew4:4, KJV). God's directive will toward the unbeliever is that he believe on His Son (John 3:36).

RIGHTEOUSNESS: God is absolute righteousness. Because of His character and essence, He does everything right. His righteousness always requires that He be perfectly right within His own character. God never asks anything that is not right, and He never commands that which will make us do wrong. "The Rock, his work is perfect, and all his ways are just. A faithful God, without deceit, just and upright is he" (Deuteronomy 32:4, NRSV).

HOLINESS: Holiness may be called the purity of God's substance. The Lord has always been and always will be the embodiment of purity in the highest sense of the term. He is the personification of absolute righteousness. Holiness has been attributed to all three Persons of the Godhead. Jesus addressed the Father as "Holy Father" (John 17:11). The Holy Spirit's title is found all through Scripture. In announcing the coming of the Lord Jesus, the angel informed Mary, "The holy thing which is begotten shall be called the Son of God" (Luke 1:35, KJV).

LOVE: "God is love" (1 John 4:8b). The attribute called *love* in the Scriptures is God's inherent, eternal love that was expressed within the Trinity long before angels or mankind were created. The Holy Spirit is revealed in the Bible as the Spirit of love (Romans 5:5; 15:30). Jesus speaks of the Father loving Him before the foundation of the world (John 17:24). Love is an attribute that requires an object to express itself. That facet of God's essence can only be found and grasped through special revelation. Where else do you find such statements? "For God so **loved** the world, that he gave his only begotten Son." It is the greatest love story ever related, all in one verse of the Bible (John 3:16).

OMNIPRESENCE: God is ever-present, everywhere, at once.

God is not in everything, however. The mistaken concept that He is in everything of creation posits that God and nature are one. This is often called pantheism—the idea that God, nature, and even animals are actually deity. Eastern mysticism—especially Hinduism and Buddhism—propound this twisted religion-philosophy that has exposed itself in the so-called "New Age" movement. They teach reincarnation or the transmigration of the soul.

If God were in everything, then all people would have to do is bow down and worship whatever is present in his immediate environment—their car, dog, television, or nature itself. Actually, such deluded persons generally end up worshiping themselves because they believe they are God! While the one and only God is not in everything, He is everywhere present (see Psalm 139:7; Proverbs 15:3). That the Lord Jesus Christ, as the second Person of the Trinity, possessed this attribute while here on earth is shown in John 1:48; 3:13; and Matthew 28:20.

OMNIPOTENCE: God is almighty and all-powerful. "The Lord our God, the Almighty, reigneth" (Revelation 19:6, KJV). Jesus declared "with God all things are possible" (Matthew 19:26). All that can limit God is God Himself. By His omnipotence He willed to create all things, including angelic creatures and man, placing these creatures within a moral government and endowing them with a choice. God's power also extends to the control of all inanimate creation (Psalm 147:4); over Satan and all angels (Job 1:22; 2:6; Revelation 20:2); and over death and hades (Revelation 1:18). Jesus displayed power over diseases, death, winds and the sea, and demons.

OMNISCIENCE: God is all-knowing and all-wise. There is a difference between His wisdom and knowledge. Knowledge, of course, comprises what is known. His wisdom is the discerning, intelligent application and flawless display of that knowledge in plan and purpose. All things have and will be chosen to the best interests of God's glory (Revelation 4:11; Romans 11:33). He knows everything (1 John 3:20). Scripture discloses that He has numbered the billions of stars and knows them all by name (Psalm 147:4). Jesus told His disciples that if a teeny sparrow falls God knows it; in fact He knows it beforehand (Matthew 10:29). God the Father knows all of our needs (Matthew 6:8). He knows every thought that enters every human mind (Psalm 139:2; 94:11). God's omniscience covers all His works from the beginning of the world (Acts 15:18). He knows the past, the present, and the future at any instant in time.

ETERNALITY: John opened his Gospel with: "In the beginning was the Word, and the Word was with God, and the Word was God" (1:1, KJV). Jesus Himself declared, "Verily, verily, I say unto you, before Abraham was, I AM"—not "before Abraham was I was," but "before Abraham was, I AM." With that statement His foes clearly understood He was referring to Himself as Deity, declaring Himself to be the eternal "I AM" (John 8:58, KJV). Remember that God had introduced Himself to Moses with: "I AM WHO I AM. This is what you are to say to the Israelites: 'I AM [Elohim] has sent me to you'" (Exodus 3:14). That name means "He that was and is and ever shall be, without beginning or ending—thus eternal.

Even in the Old Testament we have pronouncements concerning the eternality of Jesus who was to be born in Bethlehem: "But thou, Bethlehem Ephratah, though thou be little among the thousands of Judah, yet out of thee shall he come forth unto me the one that is to be ruler in Israel; whose goings forth have been from of old, from everlasting" (Micah 5:2, KJV). Isaiah foretold, "For unto us a child is born, unto us a son is given; and the government shall be upon his shoulder; and his name shall be called Wonderful, Counsellor, mighty God, everlasting Father, the Prince of Peace" (9:6, KJV). "Jesus Christ the same yesterday, and to day, and for ever" (Hebrews. 13:8).

IMMUTABILITY: His being, attitude, and acts are without change. God states in Malachi 3:6; "I, Jehovah [*Yahweh*], change not." James wrote, "Every good gift and every perfect gift is from above, coming down from the Father of lights, with whom can be no variation, neither shadow that is cast by turning" (1:17). There was a pop song, "Everything Changes." Everything but God and His providence does. No doubt people have changed, hurting and betraying you. Maybe your spouse left; a child turned against you; even a trusted church member let you down . . . but God never changes. This comforting characteristic can anchor our faith in the security and hope of our dependable, faithful Lord.

VERACITY: God is perfectly truthful and incapable of deceit, falsehoods, or treachery. His truth endures forever (Psalm 117:2). In fact, it is impossible for God to lie (Titus 1:2, Hebrews. 6:18). Christ is the embodiment of God's truth—"the way, and the truth, and the life" (John 14:6). His Word contains stupendous promises that provide our daily needs and carry us through all of our problems and trials (Psalm 91:4; 1 Peter 5:7). The Holy Scriptures constitute the written truth of God; we can trust His Word without fail (2 Timothy 3:16).

God's providence toward believers

- God's grace—pardons us.
- God's power—protects us.
- God's goodness—relieves us.
- God's wisdom—directs us.
- God's mercy—crowns us.

A warning to those who have not accepted God in Christ

Many comment, "I just don't get it. If God is love, why does He condemn and judge people, and why does He send them to hell?" Yes, God is perfect love, but He is also just and righteous. He does not consign people to hell. They *choose* to spurn His love. In so doing, they *send themselves there*. To those who adamantly rejected and opposed Him, Jesus spelled it out: "You belong to your father, the devil, and you want to carry out your father's desire" (John 8:44a).

Christians will follow Jesus to heaven; non-Christians will follow their "daddy" to hell.

In the first place, hell was not originally intended for humans. Engrave this on your mind: "Then he [God] will say to those on his left, 'Depart from me, you who are cursed, into the eternal fire prepared for the devil and his angels'" (Matthew 25:41). If a person continues to resist God's calling to become His child, there is no recourse but eternal fire.

Like the old spiritual, 'Everybody Talkin' 'bout Heaven Ain't Goin' There'

Universalism, the perverted idea that everybody is going to be saved, regardless, is bunk. Think about it. If universalism were true, Christians would be in heaven with mass murderers Mao tse-tung (listed in the *Guinness Book of World Records* as the worst, responsible for the deaths of 26 million of his own people!), Adolph Hitler, Joseph Stalin, Attila the Hun, and Pol Pot of Cambodia, along with a horrific assortment of civilization's scum—rapists, child molesters, and sadists, including the Marquis de Sade himself. Enough said. If universalism were true it would prove that God is neither just nor righteous.

God destroyed all who rejected Him by a flood in Noah's day. He obliterated Sodom and Gomorrah in Abraham's day. As King of Kings and ruler of the universe, He will soon return to earth. He will exercise His judgment and pour out His wrath on those who have willfully turned Him away. God is all-powerful but never forces Himself on a person. God is love but is also righteous. God is righteous but is also wrathful.

> And to you who are troubled rest with us, when the Lord Jesus shall be revealed from heaven with his mighty angels, In flaming fire taking vengeance on them that know not God, and that obey not the gospel of our Lord Jesus Christ: Who shall be punished with everlasting destruction from the presence of the Lord, and from the glory of his power (2 Thessalonians 1:7-9, KJV).

For thought and discussion

1. Why did God create human beings? Read Revelation 4:11 and Ephesians 1:11.
2. What does being created in God's image imply?
3. True or false. We are saved by keeping The Ten Commandments.
4. What provisions does God give to produce new life in Him?
5. Explain the advocacy of Jesus Christ, the Righteous One.
6. What do you think about the concept of God's permissive will?
7. Review the section on God's attributes. Which of those attributes may we attain through Him? Which will always be unattainable?
8. How do you go about receiving guidance from God?

12

God The Son—Jesus Christ

No man hath seen God at any time; the only begotten Son, which is in the bosom of the Father, he hath declared him (John 1:18, KJV).

But these are written, that ye might believe that Jesus is the Christ, the Son of God; and that believing ye might have life through his name (John 20:31, KJV).

e is Risen!

"Truly this was the Son of God," was the Centurion's fearful cry as the Earth was in upheaval during the crucifixion (see Matthew 27:54, KJV). Through the centuries billions have agreed with that awe-stricken affirmation. Even today millions of Christians are undergoing torture, imprisonment, and death for believing and declaring, "Jesus is Lord." All sincere seekers of the truth may determine Christ's Deity and Lordship for themselves. Jesus guaranteed, "Then you will know the truth, and the truth will set you free" (John 8:32). His hearers were staring the personification of the truth squarely in the face.

To the artist He is the One Altogether Lovely,
To the architect He is the Chief Cornerstone,
To the baker He is the Living Bread,
To the banker He is the Hidden Treasure,
To the builder He is the Sure Foundation,
To the doctor He is the Great Physician,
To the educator He is the Great Teacher,
To the farmer He is the Planter and the Lord of the Harvest,
To the florist He is the Lily of the Valley and the Rose of Sharon,
To the geologist He is the Rock of Ages,
To the judge He is the Righteous Judge,
To the lawyer He is the Counselor, the Lawgiver, and the Advocate,
To the newspaper person He is the Good News of Great Joy,
To the humanitarian He is the Inexpressible Gift,
To the philosopher He is the Wisdom of God,
To the preacher He is the Word of God,
To the lonely He is the Friend who sticks closer than a brother or sister,
To the worker He is the Giver of rest,
To the sorrowing He is the Comforter,
To the bereaved He is the Resurrection and the Life,
To the sinner He is the Lamb of God that takes away the sins of the world.
To the Christian He is the Son of the Living God, the Lord, Savior, and All in All.

— Author Unknown

The greatest story ever told

Years ago Fulton Oursler published a best-selling book, *The Greatest Story Ever Told*. It was about none other than Jesus. His is the greatest story ever told. Jesus came to reveal who God is and that God may become our spiritual Father. When we allow Christ to enter our hearts, we may call on the Heavenly Father, even as a child may make requests of a caring, loving earthly father. Jesus plainly declared His kinship with the Father, "Anyone who has seen me has seen the Father" (see John 14:19; also John 10:30). As the second Person of the Trinity, Jesus has all of the characteristics of the Father. In essence, He was stressing, "I am like my Father."

The stage was set

For centuries the Jews had longed for the Messiah (The Anointed One, "The Son of David") to arrive and deliver them from their oppressors. They had suffered at the hands of warring tribes in Canaan and were either harassed or enslaved by Egypt, Syria, Assyria, Babylonia (Iraq today), Medea and Persia (now Iran), Greece, and Rome. The populace was desperate for a charismatic figure to lead them in overthrowing the Romans and their puppet kings and procurators, especially if the Messiah were to emerge.

There are far in excess of 300 distinct Messianic prophecies in the Old Testament, the majority of them now fulfilled. When the Messiah, Jesus ("Yeshua," equivalent to "Joshua," meaning "*Yahweh* [Jehovah] is salvation" or "God saves") finally arrived, His own people did not recognize Him, and He was executed on a Roman cross. The charge: He claimed to be the King of the Jews and the Messiah, the Son of God. The Roman governor, Pontius Pilate, disagreed with the multitude that screamed for His blood, and announced: "I find no fault in this man" (Luke 23:4, KJV; see also 23:14; John 18:38; 19:4,6).

Miracles surrounding Jesus' birth

Jerusalem was and is known as "The Holy City" because it was home of the Temple. Jesus called the Temple "the house of God." In the Temple stood an altar, which was like a huge box made of stone, hollow inside and covered with a metal grating. On that altar, a fire was kept burning night and day. On the fire the priest, who led the worship of God, laid the offerings of sheep and oxen, which were burned as gifts to God. Around the altar the people prayed to God in thanksgiving.

Beyond the holy place was another room called "The Holy of Holies." Into that exclusive area no one entered except the High Priest, and he only one day in the year (*Yom Kippur*, "The Day of Atonement"), for this inner room was set apart for the dwelling place of God. Years before a heavenly shaft of light (the *shekinah* glory) had beamed onto the altar in The Holy of Holies. Because of the people's disobedience God had withdrawn the glory, which represented His awesome, holy presence.

One day an elderly priest, Zechariah (Zacharias, KJV), was offering incense on the golden altar in the Holy Place. Suddenly an angel from God, Gabriel, appeared to him, asking him not to be afraid. Gabriel announced: "You shall have a son and shall call his name John." The angel continued, "When your son grows up he will give joy to God's people and will be great in the kingdom. His words will prepare the Jews for the coming of the long-awaited Messiah-King. He must live a pure life, neither drinking wine nor strong drink, for he will be set apart to serve God only and to preach the message that their King and Savior has come."

The priest was filled with surprise and fear, inquiring, "I and my wife are old. How can this possibly be?" Because Zechariah did not believe the angel, he was stricken dumb and could not speak until John was born.

In Nazareth lived a girl, probably a teenager, named Mary. Nazareth is about seventy miles from Jerusalem. Only Matthew and Luke give accounts of her. Mary was a pure-hearted, lovely girl, who served the God of Israel with all her heart and lived a holy life. She, like her prospective husband, Joseph the carpenter, was a descendant of King David. It is clear that she understood the Old Testament. From all we can surmise, Mary and Joseph's families were honest, hard-working people.

Gabriel was on assignment to report miraculous events. He visited Mary. In a sweet voice, trying not to terrorize her, he said, "Peace be with you, Mary! You are in high favor and love, for the Lord is with you!" The sight of this shining form filled the young girl with alarm. Gabriel reassured her, "Do not be afraid, Mary, for God has chosen you among all women for this special favor. You shall have a son, and you shall give Him the name of Jesus, because He shall save His people from their sins. He shall be great and shall be called the Son of the Highest. God shall give to your Son the throne and the kingdom of his father David."

Puzzled, Mary asked, "How can this be since I haven't had relations with a man?" Gabriel's answer is of decisive significance for our affirmation of the virgin birth. **"The Holy Spirit will come upon you, and the power of the Highest will overshadow you . . . for with God nothing will be impossible" (Luke 1:37).** Gabriel further announced that Mary's Holy Child would be called "the Son of God" and that her cousin, Elizabeth (Elisabeth, KJV), would soon have a son in her old age. Mary humbly responded, "I am the Lord's servant . . . May it be to me as you have said" (1:38). Mary felt she must talk with a confidante about this astounding development, so her mind turned to Elizabeth. Since it was more than 100 miles to Elizabeth's home, she probably traveled in a caravan and rode a small animal. When Mary arrived Elizabeth exulted, "Blessed, most blessed are you among women! And blessed among men shall be the son born to you."

Meanwhile, one night Joseph dreamed that an angel by his side declared, "Joseph, son of David, do not be afraid to take Mary home as your wife, because what is conceived in her is from the Holy Spirit. She will give birth to a son, and you are to give him the name Jesus, because he will save his people from their sins" (Matthew 1:20-21). Joseph married Mary and carried her to his home, where he plied his trade as a carpenter.

John the Baptist

Not long after Mary's visit with Elizabeth, John was born and he grew up to be a strong, righteous boy. When John became a young man, he left home and lived in the desert, alone with his thoughts and his communion with God. John lived simply and dressed ruggedly. In the Judean wilderness he preached repentance and, as prophesied by Isaiah, was "The voice of one crying in the wilderness: Prepare the way of the Lord, make his paths straight" (see Matthew 3:1ff., NRSV).

The trek to and sojourn in Judea

One preacher from the past quipped, "God hits straight licks with crooked sticks." God hit a straight lick with Caesar Augustus, who issued a decree that all persons in the Roman Empire must travel to their original homes to enrol for taxation, a severe inconvenience for the commoners. Since both Joseph and Mary had descended from David—who was born in Bethlehem more than a millennium before—legally they had to make the trip, but God was behind it all.

Maybe innkeepers didn't post "no vacancy" signs then, but the inn was full, so they were offered a stable. When I was young sometimes people would joke, "Were you born in a barn?" I wasn't, but my Lord and Savior was. Imagine it. The God of glory, who spoke the universe into existence, condescended and became a Babe in a manger with animals!

The King of Kings, before whom every knee will one day bow, was born as a peasant.

In his sermons Billy Graham has often referred to his son, Franklin, who will continue his father's ministry. When Franklin was a little boy he and his dad were out walking when they accidentally stepped on an ant bed. Franklin cried because several of the ants were crushed, and somehow he wanted to apologize. Billy then told his son that the only way he could contact those ants was to become an ant and live with them. He used that simple analogy to teach about how Christ became one of us. He had to become a human being in order to reach us personally.

Shepherds were out tending to their sheep. Then a glorious angel shared the good news with those bedazzled men: "Do not be afraid. I bring you good news of great joy that will be for all the people. Today in the town of David a Savior has been born to you; he is Christ the Lord" (Luke 2:10b-11). Could God have planned this special encounter because "the son of David," the Messiah, was born—and before becoming a mighty warrior and then King, David was a shepherd boy? Those outdoorsmen were guided to the newborn Baby and paid their homage. We are not sure how old the Child was when the Magi, "Wise Men," found Him. However, a bright star directed them, and they presented their gifts to Him.

Joseph and Mary later found better quarters and sojourned in Bethlehem for a while. When Jesus was forty days old, they carried Him to Jerusalem, which was only six miles away. In the Temple a ceremony was conducted, demonstrating that He was consecrated to God and would be reared according to the precepts of the Old Testament.

While at the Temple, an elderly man of righteousness, Simeon, appeared. The Holy Spirit had revealed that before his death, he would see the Messiah. Simeon cradled the Child in his arms and blessed God and prayed that he was ready for heaven, "For mine eyes have seen thy salvation, which thou has prepared before the face of all people; a light to lighten the Gentiles, and the glory of thy people Israel" (see Luke 2:21-35).

Christ's person: Simeon recognized that the infant Jesus was "the Lord's Christ," thus relating Him immediately to all the Messianic prophecies of the Old Testament.

Christ's mission: Simeon realized, too, that the Baby was destined to be "a light to lighten the Gentiles, and the glory of thy people Israel." Even the order of these words is momentous, for in the outworking of God's purposes Jesus became the light for the Gentiles and will yet be acclaimed by Israel as their glory.

Christ's death: But Simeon recognized as well that Jesus would be a stumbling stone to many. His death on the Cross would be misunderstood by many Jews as God's curse on Him (Deuteronomy 21:23; Galatians 3:13), and without further thought they would dismiss His claims. He would be "spoken against" and rejected (Psalm 22; Psalm 53). And in His rejection Mary, His mother, would experience profound grief and sorrow.

The birth of Jesus reported by Anna (Luke 2:36-38)

Dr. Luke then briefly mentions another godly, elderly person, Anna the prophetess, who continually "served God with fastings and prayers night and day . . ." Note her character. She was a prepared woman. If the pure in heart shall see God, then her vision was crystal clear, and she beheld God incarnate. Maybe God had prepared her heart with Scriptures such as Malachi 3:1: "The Lord, whom ye seek, shall suddenly come to his temple, even the messenger of the covenant who ye delight in: Behold, He shall come, saith the Lord of hosts."

Likewise, she was a prayerful woman. "Fastings and prayers night and day." Perhaps she cried out in the words of Job: "Oh, that I knew where I might find him! that I might come even to his seat!" (Job 23:3). She was seeking the fulfillment of prophecy about Israel's Redeemer. She was a perceptive woman. Finally, the woman who reported the birth of Jesus to the godly remnant in Jerusalem was insightful. As she observed all that was going on, God confirmed in her heart that this Babe was The Promised One of Israel. As fast as her aged feet could carry her, she rushed out to spread the good news of His birth.

The Messiah's childhood and youth

Joseph and Mary carried Jesus back to their home in Bethlehem. An angel appeared to Joseph and instructed him to flee to Egypt. Insanely paranoid Herod had heard about the birth of a King and was bent on finding and killing that King. For that reason he commanded that every infant under two years old in the Bethlehem area be murdered. The holy family remained in Egypt until the death of Herod.

Then, Joseph (who, of course, was not Jesus' biological father—the Holy Spirit was!), Mary, and the young Child returned to Nazareth where He lived until His ministry (Luke 2:39). Joseph earned his living as a carpenter and lived in a house with six sons and several daughters. Jesus also plied that trade. Jesus no doubt attended school at their village synagogue after he reached the age of six, where the pupils studied the Old Testament, especially the Torah. He was referred to as "the carpenter's son" (Matthew 13:55). The people were not aware of His divine origin. We have reason to believe that He was liked by the people, although little is known about His childhood and youth in Nazareth. In those days it was the Jewish custom for a boy to drop out of school at twelve unless he planned to study for the priesthood or the rabbinate.

At twelve, the usual time for a boy's Bar Mitzvah—Hebrew confirmation—His parents traveled to Jerusalem for the Feast of the Passover (see Luke 2:41ff.). The Passover celebrated the Israelites' escape (Exodus) out of Egypt and to freedom, when the death angel passed over the Hebrews' homes, since their doors were sprinkled with blood, but slew every firstborn Egyptian son (see Exodus 12:11; Matthew 26:17; Luke 22:15; John 18:39; Acts 12:4; 1 Corinthians 5:7).

After their caravan had gone a day's journey, Mary and Joseph, to their chagrin, discovered that Jesus was not with them. They returned to Jerusalem and three days later found Him amid learned scholars in the Temple. His hearers were amazed at His precocious grasp of the Law. But his parents weren't happy about it, so His agitated parents implored, "Son, why have you treated us this way?" (see Luke 2:48, NASB). His misunderstood reply was: "'Why were you searching for me?' he asked. 'Didn't you know I had to be in my Father's house?'" (2:49). The last we read of Him until His ministry is in Luke 2:52: "And Jesus increased in wisdom and stature, and in favor with God and man."

The beginning of His ministry

Eighteen years had passed. At thirty Jesus sensed the Father's leading to follow through on the Godhead's plans for Him. John the Baptist, His cousin, was preaching repentance and baptizing his followers, preparing them for the coming Messiah. At Bethabara near Jerusalem, John was baptizing in the Jordan River. When Jesus came walking up John exclaimed, "Behold the Lamb of God, which taketh away the sin of the world" (John 1:29, KJV).

John protested because, through the Spirit, He recognized that Jesus had never sinned and was not a candidate for the rite. John argued, "I need to be baptized by you, and do you come to me?" (Matthew 3:14b). The Lamb of God didn't need to be baptized but did it as an example for us.

As Jesus rose out of the water, the Holy Spirit in the form of a dove descended upon Him, and the Father spoke from heaven: "This is my beloved Son, in whom I am well pleased" (Matthew 3:17, KJV). At that instant an enormous power permeated our Lord. The Spirit of God had always been with Him in the accomplishment of the Father's will. In that moment, however, Jesus was **filled** with the **Spirit** of God as no man—not even the greatest of the prophets—had ever been before.

John the Baptist's martyrdom

John had lambasted King Herod for taking his brother's wife Herodias. Herod was offended but not to the hellish extent of Herodias. On Herod's birthday, Herodias' daughter danced for the vain ruler; he was elated and promised to give her whatever she wanted, "even half of his kingdom." Herodias insisted that her daughter ask for John's head on a platter. Weak-kneed like many Roman puppets, including Pilate, the king was "grieved," but had the grisly murder carried out (see Matthew 14:1-12; Mark 6:14-29). Jesus had given John the consummate tribute:

> Then what did you go out to see? A prophet? Yes, I tell you, and more than a prophet. This is the one about whom it is written: "I will send my messenger ahead of you, who will prepare your way before you." I tell you the truth: Among those born of women there has not risen anyone greater than John the Baptist; yet he who is least in the kingdom of heaven is greater than he (Matthew 11:9-11).

Miracle of loaves and fishes

At Bethsaida a huge crowd gathered to hear this young Preacher. At the close of the day the people were famished. The disciples found a boy with five loaves of barley bread and two little fish. Little did that unnamed boy realize that he was providing the "seed" for the blossoming of a miracle. The people were arranged in companies with 50 to 100 in each company. Jesus blessed the boy's lunch—then gave a piece of the bread and fish to each disciple. His power transformed little into much as 5,000 men, *plus women and children*, were amply fed. There were twelve baskets of left-overs—maybe one each for The Twelve!

Early events

Christ sensed that the people were envisioning Him as their King. They were thinking, *If this Man could feed perhaps 15,000—20,000 from practically nothing, and perform signs, wonders, and miracles, what could He do as a Liberator King?* Likewise that idea appealed to His disciples, for that might mean favored positions. All of them were upset because Jesus refused to accept Kingship . . . then. However, at His first coming His kingdom existed in the hearts of those who loved Him. The kingdom was not to be won by armies. Jesus sent His disciples and the people away and "withdrew again to the mountain by Himself alone" (see John 6:1-15, NASB).

On the night after the multitude was fed, the disciples were rowing on the Sea of Galilee toward Capernaum. Suddenly, a treacherous storm arose. From the mountaintop, Jesus could see that they were in danger of their lives. His followers cried out in terror, both from the storm and from the fact that a man was walking on the water! Jesus' voice was heard over the stormy sea: "Be of good cheer! It is I; do not be afraid!" Then they realized it was not a ghost (see John 6:16-20). Impetuous Simon Peter wanted to walk on the water, too. He called out, "Command me to come to you on the water; and the Lord said come." Peter stepped onto the water but became obsessed with the peril instead of the Prince of Peace who rules the waves. "The Rock" began to sink. Peter hollered, "Lord, save me," and the Lord did, and the sea suddenly became calm. When they reached land the disciples fell down at Jesus' feet and confessed, "Truly you are the Son of God" (see Matthew 14:25-32).

A Canaanite woman threw herself at Jesus' feet and begged Him to cast an evil spirit out of her daughter. The disciples insisted that the Lord send her away because she was a Gentile. As He often did Jesus taught His disciples that a Gentile could have the same faith as a Jew. After testing her faith Jesus said, "'Woman, you have great faith! Your request is granted.' And her daughter was healed from that very hour" (see Matthew 15:22-28).

Later at Decapolis, Jesus spoke to a multitude. Jesus caused the lame to walk, the blind to see, and the deaf, healing all kinds of diseases. The crowd followed Jesus for three days, and the food ran out. This time there were 4,000, not including women and children, seven loaves, and a few small fish, and after the people were filled, seven baskets of food were picked up.

The number of those who ate was four thousand, besides women and children (Matthew 15:33-38).

A pivotal point in Jesus' ministry

At Caesarea-Philippi, our Lord continued teaching the disciples. One of His methods was to ask questions—in fact, sometimes even asking a question in order to answer one. So, put in today's language, He inquired, "Men, what do people really think of Me?" They replied: "John the Baptist returned to this life; Elijah, even Jeremiah or another prophet." The most crucial question, though, was: "Who do you say I am?" Outspoken Peter declared, "You are the Messiah, the Christ, the Son of the living God" (see Matthew 16:13-19).

Not long after that experience Jesus tried to prepare His disciples. "We are going up to Jerusalem, and the Son of Man will be betrayed to the chief priests and the teachers of the law. They will condemn him to death and will turn him over to the Gentiles to be mocked and flogged and crucified. On the third day he will be raised to life!" (Matthew 20:18-19).

Jesus' statement of the two greatest commandments:

- The Lord our God is one and thou shalt love the Lord thy God with all thy heart, and with all thy soul, and with all thy mind, and with all thy strength (Luke 10:27).

• The second commandment is this, like unto it, "Thou shalt love thy neighbor as thyself." There is no other commandment greater than these two (Matthew 22:39).

To love our neighbor is to have an interest in our fellow human beings and to do for them whatever we would like for them to do for us. That is the essence of Jesus' "Golden Rule." "So in everything, do to others what you would have them do to you, for this sums up the Law and the Prophets (Matthew 7:12).

"The Widow's Mite"

On the last day of Jesus' teaching in the Temple, Jesus observed people leaving their money in a box for the poor. The rich were ostentatious in contrast to a poor woman who gave what amounted to a quarter of a cent. Jesus commended her, "I tell you the truth, that in the sight of God this poor widow has put into the box more money than any of the others. All the rest have been putting in money they could spare and did not need. But the widow woman in her need gave all she had, her whole living"(Mark 12:42ff., KJV; also Luke 21:2ff.).

Parable of the vine and branches (John 15:1-5)

> I am the true vine, and my Father is the gardener. He cuts off every branch in me that bears no fruit, while every branch that does bear fruit he prunes so that it will be even more fruitful. You are already clean because of the word I have spoken to you. Remain in me, and I will remain in you. No branch can bear fruit by itself; it must remain in the vine. Neither can you bear fruit unless you remain in me. I am the vine; you are the branches. If a man remains in me and I in him, he will bear much fruit; apart from me you can do nothing.

The Garden of Gethsemane

During the Last Supper, Christ promised the coming Holy Spirit that would indwell them (see John 14—16 and Chapter 13 of this book). With all of His being He endeavored to brace His followers for the betrayal, torture, humiliation, and death that lay ahead. They still did not seem to understand.

It was around midnight when Jesus and the apostles (then reduced to eleven by Judas Iscariot's defection) departed from the upper room. They arrived at an orchard of olive trees, the Garden of Gethsemane. He then sighed, "My soul is overwhelmed with sorrow to the point of death. Stay here and keep watch with me" (Matthew 26:38ff.). Accompanied by Peter, James, and John, He entered the Garden to commune with the Heavenly Father. Realizing that He would literally become the embodiment of sin for us, His righteous mankind recoiled against the thought of it (2 Corinthians 5:21). "Oh, my Father, my Father,You can do anything. Take this cup away from me, I pray. Yet, I do not ask to have My will, but only what is Thy will." Christ prayed this prayer three different times. During the third prayer he cried, "My Father, if this cup cannot be taken away, if I must drink it, then Thy will be done!"

President Franklin Delano Roosevelt called December 7, 1941 (when the Japanese bombed Pearl Harbor, Hawaii), "a day that will live in infamy." That Passover night in the Garden would live not only in infamy but, conversely, in glory. Judas Iscariot and a mob of soldiers and religionists burst into the Garden, and Judas betrayed Christ with a kiss. Christ was arrested and carried away for a series of seven trials—then condemned to die on the Cross. But that is not the end of the story. In fact, He is alive, and the story is perpetuated in the hearts and lives of multiplied millions and billions who have not betrayed Him, but rather have identified with Him.

The Deity of Christ

The holy Son of God

Christ's virgin birth was a matter of prophecy. Isaiah the prophet designated that He should be called "Immanuel" or "God with us" (Isaiah 7:14). This was approximately 750 years before the angel informed Mary that she would give birth to the Son of God" (Luke 1:35).

Jesus, the Son of David and Abraham

The Old Testament is clear on the matter of the Messiah's coming as a man—"the son of David, the son of Abraham" (Matthew 1:1). To be a man He had to be born of a woman as are other men. Humanly speaking, His coming depended on one of three means: by human parents through procreation; by an entirely new creation; or by the substitution of Divine operation for a human father. Human parentage would simply have produced another man with an inherent fallen nature. Another created being from Adam's race could not have championed mankind's cause as a Savior. The only other possibility was that of substituting Divine intervention in lieu of a human father. Thus, there would be no taint or element of sin.

More importantly is the fact that we have heavenly confirmation of this matter: The explanation given by the angel and the apostle's inclusion of the angel's words and quotation, serve as a divine seal certifying to the truthfulness of the record. Perfect harmony exists between the original prophecy and the fulfillment of the prediction. They complement, or throw light on, each other.

Jesus is the Christ

What prophetic proofs have we that Jesus is in reality the authentic Christ? What are His credentials? There are four tests we may apply:

• **Was He born of the right line?** He was to spring from Eve, not Adam, and He did. "I will put enmity between thee [the serpent] and the woman, and between thy seed and her seed; it shall bruise thy head, and thou shalt bruise his heel" (Genesis 3:15). He was to come of Abraham, not of Lot, and He did! "And the Lord said unto Abram, after that Lot was separated from him . . . I will make thy seed as the dust of the earth" (Genesis 13:14,16a). "To Abraham and his seed were the promises made. He saith not, And to seeds, as of many; but as of one, And to thy seed, which is Christ" (Galatians 3:16). He was to come of Isaac, not of Ishmael, and He did! "There shall come a Star out of Jacob, and a Scepter shall rise out of Israel . . . Out of Jacob shall come he that shall have dominion" (Numbers 24:17,19). He was to come of David (of the line of Judah, not of Saul, a Benjamite), and He did! "David shall never want a man to sit upon the throne of the house of Israel" (Jeremiah 33:17). "He [Joseph] was of the house and lineage of David" (Luke 2:4b). Yes, He passes the genealogical test. Yes!

• **Was He born in the right place?** He was! Biblical prophecy pinpointed the little town that would be His birthplace. "But thou, Bethlehem Ephratah, though thou be little among the thousands of Judah, yet out of thee shall he come forth unto me that is to be ruler in Israel" (Micah 5:2a). ". . . Jesus was born in Bethlehem of Judea" (Matthew 2:1). He passes the geographical test. Yes!

• **Was He born in the right manner?** This is the most searching test of all. The prophet had foretold the wonder in terms of solemn grandeur: "Behold, a virgin shall conceive, and bear a son, and shall call his name Immanuel" (Isaiah 7:14b). Did it happen like that? Here is the answer of the New Testament: "Now the birth of Jesus Christ was on this wise: When as his mother Mary was espoused to Joseph, before they came together, she was found with child of the Holy Ghost" (Matthew 1:18). ". . . The angel Gabriel was sent from God unto a city of Galilee, named Nazareth, to a virgin espoused to a man whose name was Joseph, of the house of David; and the virgin's name was Mary" (Luke 1:26- 27). "The virgin shall conceive a child. She shall give birth to a Son and He shall be called Emmanuel [" God with us"] (Matthew 1:23). Yes!

• **What did our Lord Himself believe about His own identify?**

Let the recorded incident in the New Testament answer. It is noon in Samaria. The sun is high and hot overhead. Jesus is sitting on the coping of Jacob's Well at Sychar. Over the skyline appears a woman coming to draw water. As they talk together the Savior tenderly touches on a sore point in her moral life. To hide her embarrassment she "changes the subject" and makes a stab at discussing theology. As she does, our Lord unfolds to that sinful woman several of the profoundest truths. In mock "piousity," the woman remarks, "I know that Messiah cometh, which is called Christ: When he is come, he will tell us all things."

In words, simple but also sublime, Jesus draws back the veil of anonymity which, in His modesty, He wore during His incarnate life. **"I that speak unto thee," He says, "am he!" (see John 4:1-26). Yes!**

Other proofs of Christ's deity

There are incidental proofs of Christ's absolute Deity that are in some facets even more convincing than the direct assertions of it.

• **"Come unto me** . . . I will give you rest" (Matthew 11:28): No one can give rest to all who "labor and are heavy laden" unless he is God, and yet Jesus Christ offers to do it. Innumerable multitudes who have labored and were heavy laden and crushed—for whom there seemingly was no help—have come to Jesus Christ, and He has actually given them rest.

• **"Believe in God,** believe also in me" (John 14:1): Christ demands the same absolute faith in Him that is exercised toward God the Father. Jesus was perfectly familiar with Jeremiah 17:5 where we read, "Thus saith Jehovah: Cursed is the man that trusteth in man." Yet He demands that we put trust in Him, even as we believe in His Heavenly Father. It is the strongest possible assertion of Deity on His part that billions have found that—when they do believe in Him—their hearts are delivered from trouble, regardless of their circumstances.

• "He that loveth father or mother more than me is not worthy of me; and he that loveth son or daughter more than me is not worthy of me" (Matthew 10:37; see also Luke 14:26,33). There can be no question that this is Jesus' demand for supreme and absolute love to Himself, a love that lowers even the dearest relations of life to a secondary plane. No one but God has a right to make such demands.

• "I and the Father are one" (John 10:30). The Lord Jesus claimed complete equality with the Father.

• "He that hath seen me hath seen the Father" (John 14:9). Jesus claims here to be so consummately God that to see Him is to see the Father who dwells in Him.

• "And this is life eternal, that they should know thee the only true God, and him whom thou didst send, even Jesus Christ" (John 17:3). In other words, He claims that the knowledge of Himself is as essential a part of eternal life as knowledge of God the Father.

The glorious truth

There is no room left to doubt the unquestionable Deity of Jesus Christ. It is a glorious truth. The Savior in whom we believe is God, a Lord for whom nothing is too hard, who can save us from the "guttermost to the uttermost." We should rejoice that we have no merely human savior—but a Savior who is God Himself! Denying Christ's Godhood does not make His Deity any less a fact, but it does make the denier guilty of abysmal sin against the God of the universe.

Jesus, the Savior on the Cross

When a person was crucified, the Romans customarily put a sign above the victim's head detailing the charges against him. Over the protests of the religious authorities, Pilate commanded that the sign over Jesus' head read:

> This is Jesus of Nazareth
> The King of the Jews.

It was written in the language of three prominent cultures: in Hebrew, the tongue spoken by the Jews; in Latin, the language of the Romans; and in Greek, the language of many non-Jews throughout the Empire. Pilate had asserted, "What I have written I have written" (John 19:22, KJV). In Pilate's Latin, he meant "Stet"—" Let it stand." The procurator was indicating, "This is the official position because I have declared it." How sad that Pilate did not receive the One about whom he confessed, "I find no fault in this man." That trilingual sign mutely preached a powerful sermon: that Jesus is The King.

Along with the crowd a gathering of religious leaders stood around the cross staring at Him hanging there. For them it was not enough that He was suffering the death of a common criminal. They booed, jeered, mocked, and railed on Him. They taunted Him with, "Ah! you would destroy the Temple and build it again in three days, would you? Then come down from the cross and save yourself if you can!" And they chortled, "He saved others . . . but he can't save himself! He's the King of Israel! Let him come down now from the cross, and we will believe in him. He trusts in God. Let God rescue him now if he wants him, for he said, 'I am the Son of God'" (Matthew 27:42-43).

One of the two robbers crucified on both sides of Jesus called out to Him, joining in the abuse: "Are you not the Christ, the King of Israel? If you are, why don't you save yourself and save us with you?" But the malefactor on the other side of Jesus rebuked him: "Have you no fear of a just

God? You are suffering the same sentence as this man and you and I are suffering only what we deserve for our deeds; but this man has done nothing wrong." Then this man from his cross implored, "Jesus, do not forget me when you come into your kingdom." And Jesus answered him, "I tell you truly, this very day you shall be with me in the heavenly land." At this time, near Jesus' cross, was standing John the apostle (later to write the Gospel, 1, 2, and 3 John, and The Revelation). With him were Mary, the mother of Jesus, also her sister, and two other women named Mary—Mary, the wife of Clopas, and Mary Magdalene or Mary of Magdala.

When Jesus viewed his mother and John He said, "Woman, there is your son." Then he said to John: "Son, there is your mother." And from that time Mary, the mother of Jesus, lived with the disciple John, as though he were her own son (John 19:26-27).

Since the crucifixion three agonizing hours had passed. Exactly at noon a sudden darkness enshrouded the sky and the earth until 3 in the afternoon (Matthew 27:45). Precisely at 3 Jesus "cried with a loud voice, . . . Eli, Eli, lama sabachthani? that is to say, My God, my God, why hast thou forsaken me?" (v. 46, KJV). Then Jesus "yielded up the ghost" (v. 50, KJV). Pandemonium reigned as the veil of the temple was torn in two, there was an earthquake, and numerous bodies of the saints were resurrected and appeared to many in Jerusalem (vv. 51-53, KJV). The Roman centurion, in charge of the contingent guarding the crosses, in fearful awe gave a succinct testimony, "Truly this was the Son of God" (v. 54, KJV).

Christ forsaken for you and me

In that moment God collected all of our sins and laid them on His only begotten Son. In that ghastly moment He had called out, "My God, my God, why hast thou forsaken me?" Peter later described that event: "Who his own self bare our sins in his own body on the tree, that we, being dead to sins, should live unto righteousness: by whose stripes ye were healed" (1 Peter 2:24, KJV). God the Father and God the Holy Spirit turned their backs on him momentarily. As He died on our behalf all the powers of the devil and his angels were marshaled against Him . . . but He would conquer Satan.

The broken fellowship between God and man is restored by Christ's having abolished death on our behalf. "The last enemy to be

destroyed is death" (1 Corinthians 15:26). On Calvary, He executed the Divine plan through which He can restore our fellowship with God if we will only accept His atoning sacrifice and ask Him into our lives. Christ Shouted, "It Is Finished!"

First, the sufferings of Christ as man were finished.

Second, the amazing work of atonement (propitiation, substitutionary sacrifice; see 1 John 2:2) was finished. In dying He assumed our punishment and paid for our salvation.

Third, the kingdom of Satan was finished. The seed of the woman, in the person of Christ, there bruised the head of the serpent, Satan (see Genesis 3:15).

Christ's death on the cross atoned for our sins and re-established fellowship with God. The "second death" is when unbelievers are permanently separated from God. Jesus on the cross cried, "Father, into your hands I commit my spirit" (Luke 23:46; John 19:30).

When Jesus was released from the self-imposed limitations of His mortal body, He was free to exercise His unlimited powers. Upon entering the place of departed spirits, He seized the keys of death and hell (*hades*) from Satan. Christ affirmed, "I was dead, I am alive forevermore, and have the keys of death and hell" (Revelation 1:18, KJV). **He put a robe of righteousness around every one of the departed who had trusted God.** Then He opened the gates of the place of departed spirits for all believers and led them forth to heaven. The unsaved stayed in their separate compartment in hades and will remain there until the final judgment. See Chapter 3 on "Heaven or Hell—Your Eternal Home."

When Christ returned from that mission, His spirit re-entered and immortalized His physical body that lay in the tomb. He emerged as the glorified, victorious Lord and Savior.

The power of His Resurrection

Christ's resurrection proves conclusively that the believer is raised from the dead and there is a blessed immortality beyond this life. The souls of all believers go immediately to heaven and into the presence of God (2 Corinthians 5:6-8). If our Lord's body had remained in the tomb, there would be no resurrection for anyone. Paul, in essence, wrote that without Christ's resurrection, we'd all be "sunk." "If in this life only we have hope in Christ, we are of all men most miserable" (1 Corinthians 15:19, KJV). He willingly endured the Cross because of our transgressions and was resurrected to insure eternal life for us who embrace Him as Savior (Romans 4:25).

Soon after the appearance of Jesus to seven disciples by the Sea of Galilee, many disciples met with Him on a mountain in Galilee. It is thought that more than 500 followers were present as Jesus revealed Himself to them. When they gazed on Him, they bowed and worshiped Him. Even then, though, a few were in doubt whether they had really seen the Lord.

The basis of Christianity—the resurrection

First Corinthians 15 shows that the foundation of Christianity is the resurrection of our Lord Jesus Christ. His coming forth from the tomb is a guarantee and pledge of our resurrection and fellowship with Him and with the saved throughout all eternity. "The first man Adam became a living being; the last Adam (Jesus Christ) a life-giving spirit" (1 Corinthians 15:45). The resurrection of Jesus Christ is a well-attested fact of history:

- **Empty tomb**
- **Appearances of Christ**—after the resurrection, Christ appeared to more than 500 eye witnesses (1 Corinthians 15:6).
- **Radical transformation of Christ's disciples**

We cannot adequately comprehend all that was involved in Christ's abolition of death, but we are sure that Satan's power over death was broken when Christ died and rose again for us.

Justification and being "Born Again"

Christ died on the Cross alone for our sins. We are justified when we believe in Him, confess those sins, and repent of them (Acts 20:21). A Christian may continue to sin. Rest assured, though, that he/she won't enjoy it, for his/her sins will make him/her wretched. The indwelling Holy Spirit will severely convict the believer. God will forgive the Christian's sins, but he will not want to grieve the Spirit by continual sinning (Ephesians 4:30. KJV) and will own up to his wrongdoing. "If we confess our sins, he is faithful and just to forgive us our sins, and to cleanse us from all unrighteousness" (1 John 1:9, KJV).

Our sins neither annul our justification nor nullify our adoption, but they do grieve God and mar our fellowship with Him. If a person continues to sin deliberately, one has to question whether He has actually received Christ.

Grace is . . . amazing!

A surprising number of Americans know nothing about grace except most of them have heard John Newton's old hymn, "Amazing Grace." Back in the early 70s Judy Collins had a number-one hit with her a cappella rendition of the tune. Expressing the meaning of grace in human words is difficult. The New Testament word is from the Greek *charis* which means graciousness, bestowing benefits, favors, or gifts, including liberality, pleasure, and thanks. Grace is often described "as God's unmerited favor toward mankind." It is inseparable from His love, and it is how He operates with us.

Christ as our advocate with God (Hebrew 9:11-24)

"For there is one God and one mediator [advocate, arbitrator, go-between, peacemaker) between God and men, the man Christ Jesus" (1 Timothy 2:5). Christ tasted death for every person and through His atonement, satisfaction was made *provisionally* for our sins—but *practically* atonement is granted only to those who accept Christ as Savior.

Although Jesus rules as our Judge, the Father has also appointed Him our Advocate. He is our high priest forever (see Hebrews. 6:20—all of Hebrews. 7) whose sacrifice was His own body on the Cross. As you read this He is in heaven interceding for us on earth. A priest not only offers sacrifices for sins but also intercedes in powerful prayer. As our Intercessor He intervenes, forgives, and strengthens us, all because of His blood of the everlasting covenant (see 1 John 2:1-2).

Christ as our example and pattern (1 Peter 2:21; Hebrews 4:16-17)

Controversy has raged over whether Jesus could have sinned. His overcoming the temptations (trials, testings) of the devil would have no practical application for us if He could not have chosen to sin. What counts is that He did not. Except for one recorded "brief season" when the devil left Him, Jesus was assailed by the enemy, yet never yielded, "For we have not an high priest which cannot be touched with the feeling of our infirmities; but was in all points tempted like as we are, yet without sin. Let us therefore come boldly unto the throne of grace, that we may obtain mercy, and find grace to help in time of need" (Hebrews. 4:15-16, KJV). Peter wrote that God's Son "did no sin, neither was guile found in his mouth" (1 Peter 2:22, KJV). Because Jesus was tempted, yet never sinned; because He suffered like us from every standpoint and stood His ground, He is able to help us who are being tempted. I cannot overemphasize how important this is. If Christ had given in to only one temptation, He could not have served as the atoning sacrifice for our sins.

Our vision of what Christ means to us

The vision of His glory ignites our hearts with passionate anticipation, challenging us to live faithfully every moment in the light of His imminent return. He is:

- The Anointed One who was the atoning sacrifice for our sins (Romans 5:11);
- The Son of Man (Daniel 7:13);
- The Son of God (Daniel 3:25);
- The Great High Priest (Hebrews 4:14);
- The Light of the World (John 8:12);
- The Everlasting Father (Isaiah 9:6);
- The Bread of Life (John 6:35);
- The Lion of Judah (Revelation 5:5);
- The Word of God (John 1:1);
- The Resurrection and the Life (John 11:25);
- The Lamb of God (John 1:29);
- The Advocate and Intercessor with God for us (1 John 2:1);
- The Mighty God (Daniel 7:13; Isaiah 9:6);
- The Chief Shepherd of the sheep (1 Peter 5:4);
- The Author and Finisher of our faith (Hebrews 12:2)
- The Prince of Peace (Isaiah 9:6);
- The Way, The Truth, and The Life (John 14:6);

• The Lord of Lords (Revelation 19:16);
• The King of Kings (Revelation 19:16);
• A Friend Who Sticks Closer than a brother (Proverbs 18:24) . . . and infinitely more!

The obsession with parapsychology

Today people are obsessed with the supernatural. God Himself has installed curiosity in His creatures. One tabloid advertises with the phrase, "Enquiring minds want to know." Once predominantly a Christian society, this nation is now "multi-cultural." Millions of persons from Third World countries are, like the song goes, "Coming to America." Instead of embracing Jesus Christ, millions of them are continuing in their culture-based religions like Mohammedanism (Islam), Buddhism, Shintoism, Hinduism, and even "voodoo" and animism. Strange cults are allowed to practice without government's questioning, except in rare cases like the Branch Davidian tragedy. According to the polls, perhaps 90 to 95 percent of our citizens claim to believe in God . . . but what God or gods?

Untold thousands are caught up in consulting costly "psychic" networks that are copiously advertised on television, in the print media, and on the Internet. Inquiring minds rely on a thousand and one superstitions, including fortune tellers, Tarot cards, crystals, palm reading, tea-leaves interpretation, "channelers" (those who claim to give forth prophetic messages from the departed—i. e., one woman who supposedly "channels" for a 36,000-year-old warlord), and forms of "black" and "white" witchcraft. The list is almost endless. Admit it or not these people are searching for meaning and truth, only they are looking in the wrong places. Most of them have heard the Gospel at one time or another, but often it was an untrue universalism. If everybody is going to be saved, regardless, what difference does it make if one worships anybody but himself and his own selfish desires? Or they heard a message from a minister who watered down his belief in God's Word because he was afraid of offending his hearers.

Christ—the supernatural source

We as believers are as challenged today as were those of the previous two millennia. We must direct all of the above "seekers" to the supernatural Lord and Savior. If curious people long for contact with eternity and the spiritual world, if they want answers to human dilemmas and the future, there is only one Source—the true God as revealed in Jesus Christ. When one turns oneself over to Him, God immediately moves in and lives within. Paul encountered similar "inquirers" on Mars Hill in Athens. Luke wrote of his confrontation: "For as I walked around and looked carefully at your objects of worship, I even found an altar with this inscription: TO AN UNKNOWN GOD. Now what you worship as something unknown I am going to proclaim to you" (Acts 17:23). Paul then directed the Athenians to Christ. Perhaps billions are trying to worship an unknown god when God the Son is The God who may be known personally!

For thought and discussion

1. What is the significance of the Messiah to the Jews? What did the term, "Son of David," mean to them?
2. Name the two elderly people who blessed the baby Jesus in the Temple.
3. What is meaningful about the expression, "Jesus had no earthly father and no heavenly mother"?
4. Since He was not a sinner, why did Jesus submit to baptism at the hands of John the Baptist?
5. What is important about Jesus' teaching to His disciples at Caesarea-Philippi?
6. List several prophetic proofs of Jesus' Messiahship. How are they linked with His Deity?
7. Cite at least one evidence that Jesus knew His identity as Savior and God.
8. Why are the crucifixion and the resurrection equally important in the plan of God?
9. Write down as many designations and titles of Jesus as you can.

13
God The Holy Spirit

And I will pray the Father, and he shall give you another Comforter, that he may abide with you for ever; Even the Spirit of truth; whom the world cannot receive, because it seeth him not, neither knoweth him: but ye know him; for he dwelleth with you, and shall be in you. —John 14:16-17, KJV

The Holy Spirit is the Third Person of the Trinity.

The promise of the Spirit

Christ promised His apostles the coming of the Spirit as He was nearing the close of His earthly ministry. "I will pray the Father and He shall give you another Comforter, that He may abide in you forever, even the Spirit of the truth; whom the world cannot receive, because it seeth Him not, neither knoweth Him: but you know Him; for He dwelleth with you and shall be in you" (John 14:16-17, KJV).

After His triumphant resurrection He promised, "And surely I am with you always, to the very end of the age" (Matthew 28:20 [other translations have it "to the consummation of the age" and "to the end of the world']). And how would He do that? Through the Comforter, the Spirit of truth. To every believer since Pentecost, the Holy Spirit has come as a Counselor, Sanctifier, Guide, and Witness. That means He is always with us, wherever we go and whatever we do.

The "Host of Holiness"

Since the Holy Spirit is holy, He cultivates holiness and righteousness within us. When we allow the Spirit to control our lives—which means entire surrender of our wills to God's will—we will live by every word that proceeds from the mouth of God (see Matthew 4:4). We will request, as did our Lord, "Not my will, but Yours be done." Further, we will trust God in triumphs and trials, in darkness as well as in the light. We will walk by faith and not by sight (see 2 Corinthians 5:7), and we will rely on God with unquestioning confidence, resting in His love. The Spirit diminishes our inordinate affections for the bangles, baubles, and beads of this evil world system and causes us to set our "affections on things above, not on things on the earth" (see Colossians 3:2, KJV). "He [the Spirit] will guide you [us] into all truth" (John 16:13).

The baptism of the Spirit

The Person of the Holy Spirit enters our lives when we are converted, "born again." At that precise moment we are "baptized" in the Holy Spirit. At the same time we are adopted into God's family. When we answer yes to Jesus, the Holy Spirit empowers us with the capacity to speak with God from our inner self with our spirit and the Holy Spirit who indwells us. In the Upper Room, the Lord explained that the Spirit would not speak of Himself but from the Father, and that He would honor the Son (John 16:13-14). Thus, His ministry also includes setting before us the personal righteousness and holiness of the Lord Jesus. As God the Holy Spirit, He, of course, knows the thoughts of Deity and reveals them to us.

Is it better for Jesus to be away?

"I tell you the truth, it is to your advantage that I go away," Jesus declared in John 16:7. His disciples must have sat there, nonplussed, asking themselves, *How could it possibly be better for our Lord to go away?*" But Jesus pointed out, "If I do not go away, the Helper shall not come to you; but if I go, I will send Him to you" (John 16:7, NASB). If you project that statement a bit, maybe you can better understand it, for Jesus could, in His incarnate body, be in only one place at one time. When He was with the disciples on a mountain, He couldn't be in the marketplace or the Temple. But the Holy Comforter the Father was sending would have the capacity to indwell every believer, anywhere in the world. That, Jesus inferred, would be advantageous after His ascension to the Father.

What will the Holy Spirit do?

"And He, when He comes, will convict the world concerning sin, and righteousness, and judgment; concerning sin, because they do not believe in Me; and concerning righteousness, because I go to the Father, and you no longer behold Me; and concerning judgment, because the ruler of this world has been judged [stands condemned, NIV]" (John 16:8-11, NASB).

Concerning sin: The Holy Spirit makes us aware that sin is our major problem and that Jesus has dealt with it. One facet of the Spirit's ministry is to convict (reprove or make us feel guilty) us enough that we will confess our sins, trust in Jesus' sacrifice for them, and accept His grace to have our sins forgiven.

Concerning righteousness: "And righteousness . . ." When Jesus was here on earth and people could identify Him with their eyes and hear Him with their ears, they sensed in Him a quality and degree of righteousness they had never seen before. The Law assumed an entirely new dimension because He was living it out, fulfilling it (Matthew 5:17-18).

On the Day of Pentecost, fifty days after the Passover, Jesus' disciples were gathered and praying in an upper room. The Holy Spirit came as never before and never since. Flames of fire fell on them as the Spirit descended. They were filled with the Spirit's power *(dunamis)* and began speaking in languages that the various nationalities could understand. In fact, seventeen different tongues are listed (see Acts 2:8-11).

Since Pentecost, the Holy Spirit has kept Jesus' personal righteousness and holiness in the forefront of our thinking, so we are never compromised into settling for less than the perfect righteousness of God. This is the righteousness of our justification; the model of our sanctification; that which we shall gain completely in our glorification.

Concerning judgment: One work of the Spirit is to convince and convict mankind of the fact that God has already judged sin—to the extent that whoever has faith in Christ will never come into condemnatory judgment. "Therefore, there is now no condemnation [judgment, ASV] for those who are in Christ Jesus" (Romans 8:1). Through the Spirit mankind may recognize that dealing with sin is an inescapable responsibility from which even death does not remove us. Whoever does not accept the judgment God made for his sin at Calvary will sorrowfully appear before God to give an account at the "great white throne." Those without the imputed righteousness of God will be consigned to the lake of fire that burns forever. But this is the staggering truth: No one need ever be brought into condemnation because Jesus bore the judgment of God upon sin!

"He shall glorify Me" (John 16:14a, NASB). A continuing operation of the Spirit is to magnify and uplift Christ before mankind. If a preacher or teacher does not honor the Savior, it proves that the Spirit is not pleased with their ministry. Though Phillips Brooks of a previous generation defined preaching as "communication of the gospel through personality," if that personality does not lift up Christ, it is a personality lacking the Spirit's anointing. Preaching and witnessing without the Spirit's power will fall flat as a concrete flapjack. The work of the Holy Spirit is to glorify Christ by making us aware of Him and by unveiling Him to human personality. G. Curtis Jones observed, "If we accept Jesus Christ as the portrait of the Father, the Holy Spirit has the power which enables the likeness to come out of the frame of the Gospel story."

In the life of the believer, he continues to exalt the Lord Jesus. He sets before us the manifold aspects of His wisdom, holiness, grace, beauty, and love until long before we reach heaven—where we shall see Him face to face—we already have His image in our hearts. Who paints that on the canvas of our understanding? The hallowed Holy Spirit!

Equal with the Father and the Son

There are two formulas in the Scriptures that associate the Holy

Spirit equally with the Father and the Son: the *baptismal formula* and the *formula of benediction.* The baptismal formula is found in Matthew 28:19 in connection with the Great Commission: "Go therefore and make disciples of all the nations, baptizing them in the name of the Father and the Son and the Holy Spirit." Here Jesus put the Father, Himself, and the Holy Spirit together. From Pentecost to this day, Christians have used that formula in water baptism. Jesus, then, asserted the equality of the three Persons of the Godhead. The Spirit is not only a Person but also Deity.

The benedictory formula is in 2 Corinthians 13:14. Again the Holy Spirit is viewed in connection with the Father and the Son—"The grace of the Lord Jesus Christ, and the love of God and the fellowship of the Holy Spirit." Here Paul associates grace with the Lord Jesus; with God, love; and with the Spirit, fellowship. So, while the Persons are equal, the functions are here spelled out: 1. God is love. That is His essential nature. 2.The Lord Jesus Christ is the vehicle, the major expression of sovereign grace. This is because grace has to do with how God dealt with our sins in order to secure our salvation. 3. When it comes to putting believers together with God and with one another in a living, dynamic fellowship—the Church—that is the work of the Spirit. The administration of concerns within the Church, the giving of gifts, and the producing of God-desired outcomes are all the work of the Holy Spirit.

Do not tempt the Holy Spirit!

Because the Holy Spirit is a Person and is in a relationship with humans on earth, He is susceptible to treatment by them. In Acts 5:9, Peter asked dishonest Ananias, "Why is it that you have agreed together to put the Spirit of the Lord to the test?" You remember how wily Satan wanted Jesus to tempt or test God by carrying Him to the pinnacle of the Temple and suggesting, "Throw Yourself down . . . it is written, 'He will give His angels charge concerning You . . .'" Jesus shot right back: "You do not put God to a foolish test." We must exercise cautious reverence in our understanding of the Holy Spirit. God forbid that we would ever insult God who indwells us. "Do not put out the Spirit's fire [quench, KJV]" (1 Thess. 5:19).

Stephen, shortly before his martyrdom, lowered the boom on the council (the Sanhedrin): "You men . . . are always resisting the Holy Spirit'

(Acts 7:51a). When the Spirit would move us toward God's will, and we respond sinfully, that is rebellion and resistance. No doubt all the members of the council were doomed. How tragic it is if and when redeemed believers frustrate the Spirit's loving guidance!

God within us

Paul in Ephesians warned against lying, stealing, wrong kinds of speech, and bad attitudes toward one another. Then he laid this on them: "And do not grieve the Holy Spirit of God, with whom you were sealed for the day of redemption" (Ephesians 4:30). That word grieve means to make sad, cause grief and pain, burden down, and render sorrowful. How could a conscientious Christian do that to the Spirit? Probably the worst response simply is to ignore Him! He is God of very God living inside of believers. He is with us in all we face as our Helper, our Teacher, and our Friend to keep us from falling. And, if we ignore Him, living as though He were not within us, we are treating Him as an outsider. No wonder it grieves Him.

Charismatic/Pentecostal Movements

It seems that multiplied thousands of "mainline" believers are leaving their churches and seeking those who call themselves either "charismatic" or Pentecostal Christians. What has given impetus to this movement is the lack of power in many traditional churches, where oftentimes the Holy Spirit is virtually bypassed. Certain churches actually feel that the Spirit is more of an influence than a Person, a serious error. All too many professing Christians are fearful of becoming emotional and associate emphasis on the Spirit with so-called "holy-rollerism." Thus, there are two extremes concerning the Spirit: one that de-emphasizes Him and the other one that overemphasizes the Spirit almost to the exclusion of the Father and the Son.

The church at Corinth was in a dither similar to certain churches today. There were extremes in which members, who claimed to have a corner on the gifts of the Spirit, lorded it over others whom they considered inferior in *charismata* (the Greek for gifts). Actually, every born-again person is a "charismatic," for He has at least one gift of the Spirit—and all the fruit of the Spirit. Even as certain folks today, there were Corinthians who thought of the Holy Spirit as a drug trip, an exciting, tingling source of sensation. Yes, there are emotions with the Spirit's working. John Wesley, the founder of Methodism, testified that, upon meeting the Lord at Aldersgate Chapel, he felt "strangely warmed." But the manifestation of the Holy Spirit is far more than an ecstatic, warm feeling. He moves in every nook and cranny of our lives—heart, soul, spirit, mind, body. So, we must cultivate an attitude of reverence and awe toward Him, for He is God.

What follows is crucial, so I pray you will read with an open heart and mind.

The difference between the baptism of the Holy Spirit and being filled with the Spirit

The baptism of the Spirit occurs at the split second when we believe in and accept Jesus Christ as our Savior (see 1 Corinthians 12:13). ". . . Baptism in the Spirit' : . . is used by John in telling what Jesus would do (Matthew 3:11-12; John 1:33). . . . These predictions of Jesus and of John were evidently fulfilled on the day of Pentecost, although, in describing that event, Luke does not use that term."[1]

Being filled with the Spirit is to surrender the control of one's life and will, without restrictions, to God's will. The key is obedience (see Ephesians 5:18). ". . . Another expression is that of being filled with the Spirit.' This is a common expression in the New Testament (Luke 1:41,67; 4:1; Acts 4:8; 6:3; 7:55; 9:17; 13:9; Ephesians 5:18; et al). This expression calls attention to the inner work of the Spirit and possibly also to the more personal characteristics produced by the Spirit."[2]

After the Spirit miraculously "baptized" and empowered the disciples at Pentecost (Acts 2), only a few days later they were running low on power as they were threatened about preaching Jesus. Peter and John and a group of other believers, all who had been "baptized" in the Spirit, gathered. "After they prayed, the place where they were meeting was shaken.

---

[1]Carver, *Ibid.*, 114.

[2]*Ibid.*

And they were all filled with the Holy Spirit and spoke the word of God boldly" (Acts 4:31).

At Pentecost the Spirit came to indwell Jesus' followers "unto the consummation of the age." Before that time He would temporarily come on a person for a specific purpose, then leave, and then perhaps return later. There is one baptism in the Spirit but numerous fillings. When one is "filled" it means that one has allowed the Spirit to control and direct one's life. It implies that we have given up our "self control" and given God full sway. We must yield our lives to God and make God the Holy Spirit the president and not merely a resident. God's purpose is that we become "mature Christians," attaining completeness in Christ (Ephesians 4:13).

The Spirit is the commander in our spiritual warfare

Spirit-filled Christians are not perfect, but they "press toward the mark for the prize of the high calling of God in Christ Jesus" (Philippians 3:14, KJV). They still have the flesh to contend with, for the old sin nature wants us to live for self, but the new spiritual nature wants us to live for God. The Holy Spirit is the efficient agent of our cleansing, sanctification, and righteousness. The Holy Spirit develops us and helps us to mature and become Christlike. He fulfills the role of Sanctifier in the process that begins the moment we are saved and continues until death when the believer is made fully righteous and glorified in Christ.

Sanctification: Becoming more like the Master

The process of sanctification (becoming holy and pure in Christ) is lifelong (see 1 Peter 1:3; 2 Peter 3:18). Too many professing Christians recoil from the words "holiness," "purity," "righteousness," and "sanctification." Yet, without those qualities one gives evidence that one is not born again. Essentially, it means we are to become more like our Savior—and, of course, more like His Father, who is also ours. The apostle John summed up the end result of our sanctification: "Dear friends, now we are children of God, and what we will be has not yet been made known. *But we know that when he appears,* ***we shall be like him,*** for we shall see him as he is" (1 John 3:2, italics and underline mine). There it is. Even as our Lord is like the Father, so we will be like the Father, the Son, and the Holy Spirit! We will not be God, but we will have His traits.

In sanctification the believer is guided to maturity by the Holy Spirit (Galatians 5:13). *The Living Bible* paraphrase of Romans 12:2 goes: "Don't copy the behavior and customs of this world, but be a new and different person with a fresh newness in all you do and think. Then you will learn from your own experience how his ways will really satisfy you." Because of all Christ has done, believers are new persons (see 2 Corinthians 5:17). In this pilgrimage, join your heart and arms with multiplied millions of fellow believers from every race and background, because He has made you one in Him.

The Scriptures explain that sanctification is progressive. In conversion the sinner finds peace with God through Christ's shed blood . . . but then the Christ-life is only begun. The believer is to move on toward "unity in the faith and in the knowledge of the Son of God and become mature, attaining to the whole measure of the fullness of Christ" (Ephesians 4:13). Like Paul we should testify: "This one thing I do, forgetting those things which are behind, and reaching forth unto those things which are before, I press toward the mark for the prize of the high calling of God in Christ Jesus" (Philippians 3:13-14, KJV). Peter laid before us the steps of biblical sanctification:

> And beside this, giving all diligence, add to your faith virtue; and to virtue knowledge; And to knowledge temperance; and to temperance patience; and to patience godliness; and to godliness brotherly kindness; and to brotherly kindness charity. For if these things be in you, and abound, they make you that ye shall neither be barren nor unfruitful in the knowledge of our Lord Jesus Christ. But he that lacketh these things is blind, and cannot see afar off, and hath forgotten that he was purged from his old sins. Wherefore the rather, brethren, give diligence to make your calling and election sure: for if ye do these things, ye shall never fall (2 Peter 1:5-10).

Those who experience the sanctification of the Bible will manifest a spirit of humility. Like Moses at the burning bush (Exodus 2:2ff.) and Isaiah in the Temple (Isaiah 6:1ff.), they have had a view of the awesome majesty of holiness, and they see their own unworthiness in contrast with the purity and exalted perfection of the Infinite One.

Being filled with the Holy Spirit requires . . .

Understanding: We must recognize that God has given us the Holy Spirit to live within, and we must let Christ rule our lives.

Submission: The way to be filled with the Spirit (controlled and motivated) is to place Christ at the center of our lives. Yielding ourselves to God and His will involves putting ourselves totally and completely at His disposal.

Walking daily in faith: We must surrender ourselves to Christ daily.

The Spirit-filled life begins once we are thoroughly convinced that we can do nothing apart from the strength of the Spirit. Paul admonished us to let Christ's teachings live in our hearts, making us rich in wisdom. The Holy Spirit employs the Bible, the written Word of God, to teach, to rebuke, and to train us in righteousness (2 Timothy 3:16-17). To the extent that we listen to the Word and obey it, we are filled with the Spirit. At conversion, the Spirit enters our inmost being; at our surrender to God, the Spirit, already entered, assumes full possession.

Supporting Scriptures:

- **Spiritual baptism**

Only five verses in the Epistles refer to the baptism of the Holy Spirit—Romans 6:3; 1 Corinthians 12:13; Galatians 3:27; Ephesians 4:5; and Colossians 2:12. These references (especially 1 Corinthians 12:13) make it clear that spiritual baptism places us into the body of Christ. Romans 6:3 and Galatians 3:27 state it places us "into Christ." Colossians 2:12 declares that we are buried with Him. First Corinthians 12:13 emphasizes, "For by one spirit are we all baptized into one body. . . ." By being baptized into the body of Christ, we are permanently united to Christ and to one another.

- **Filled with the Spirit**

"Walk with the Spirit, and ye shall not fulfill the lust of the flesh" (Galatians 5:16).

"As the Spirit of the Lord works with us, we become more and more like Him" (2 Corinthians 3:18, TLB).

We arrive at maturity, that measure of development which is meant by "the fullness of Christ" (Ephesians 4:13-15).

"He shall glorify me; for he shall receive of Mine, and shall show it unto you" (John 16:14). The Holy Spirit is the personal representative of Christ upon the earth.

Outworkings of the Spirit

The same power of the Spirit, that enabled the apostles to preach the Gospel, is available to us today. Never before had the full impact of sin's repulsiveness been brought to bear on hearts and consciences as when the Spirit's power was upon the apostles.

Not to believe in Jesus Christ—and to willfully reject Him—constitutes the rotten essence of sin. The sin of sins is to reject Him who is the Light and Life, God's only provision for our eternal salvation. The Holy Spirit convicts people with respect to sin. Many reject the truth of Jesus' Godhood and Saviorhood. They refuse to humble themselves and to admit that they are sinners in need of the Savior. **Finally, to deny the Holy Spirit's work and power is to commit the unpardonable sin. For this there is no provision for escape from judgment.** The Son of God prays for us from His throne in heaven. The Holy Spirit prays for us from the throne of our heart.

The power of the Holy Spirit is manifested in a believer's life through two channels: the gifts of the spirit and the fruits of the spirit. The gifts of the Spirit are for building up the Body (Ephesians 4:12). The fruit of the Spirit constitute the fragrance that invites non-believers to become members of the Body.

The Holy Spirit . . .

- Prays (Romans 8:26);
- Convicts (John 16:8-11);
- Illuminates (John 16:12-15);
- Teaches (John 16:12-15; 2 Corinthians 2:13);
- Guides (Romans 8:14);
- Assures (Romans 8:16);
- Intercedes (Romans 8:26);
- Directs (Acts 20:22);

- Warns (Acts 20:23);
- Talks/Speaks (1 Timothy 4:1).

The Holy Spirit understands the thoughts of God and imparts knowledge to believers (see Romans 8:9; 11:1; 2 Corinthians 3:16; 2 Timothy 1:14).

Believers' bodies are the temple of God

When Christ was crucified, the Temple was no longer necessary, for God would reside in the hearts of those who love Him. Through Christ, the barrier of sin had been removed, and mankind's relationship could be restored. To symbolize the change, God tore the veil of the Temple (the curtain that separated the Outer Court from The Holy of Holies) from top to bottom (Mark 15:38). As God looks at the Christian, He sees the Holy Spirit within you. When the Holy Spirit moved in, He moved in to stay. "Or do you not know that your body is a temple of the Holy Spirit who is in you, whom you have from God and that you are not your own" (1 Corinthians 6:19).

The Holy Spirit is God's mouthpiece to believers

To walk by the Spirit is to live with moment-by-moment dependence on and sensitivity to the promptings of the Spirit. It is to become your lifestyle. Ask the Holy Spirit to increase your sensitivity about thoughts not in harmony with love, purity, and truth. If you are "walking the walk," you won't have difficulty admitting you are wrong and confessing your faults to one another, in addition to confession before God (see James 5:16a; 1 John 1:9).

The Holy Spirit does not speak on His own. Like Christ when He was on earth, this Person of the Trinity has willingly submitted to the Father's authority. All that He communicates to us is directly from the Father. "Howbeit when he, the Spirit of truth, is come, he will guide you into all truth: for he shall not speak of himself; but whatsoever he shall hear, that shall he speak: and he will show you things to come" (John 16:13). In other words, He will not speak on His own initiative.

The Bible is the Holy Spirit's most objective means of communicating with His people. Want to know what the Holy Spirit thinks about something? Then consult the Scriptures. Remember that the Spirit always moves in concert with God's revealed truth. One extreme to avoid is depending as much, or more, on certain preachers' and teachers' prophecies and "words of knowledge" than the written Word acted on by the Spirit. The Paraclete (from the Greek *parakletos*, usually translated Comforter, which means "one who goes alongside") will never lead you where the Word of God forbids you to go.

His role in prayer is to assist us in praying adequately to the Father. As Jesus intercedes for us as our High Priest, so the Holy Spirit joins Christ in interceding for us in prayer. When we hardly speak or even think, ". . . the Spirit helps us in our weakness. We do not know what we ought to pray for, but the Spirit himself intercedes for us with groans that words cannot express" (Romans 8:26). So, God the Son and God the Holy Spirit help us carry our petitions "boldly to the throne of grace" (see Hebrews 4:16).

Though the Scriptures themselves are light for us, there is still a necessity for additional illumination so we can clearly perceive the light. The same Holy Spirit who inspired the Scriptures throws light on the Word for our benefit, so we can hear, receive, properly understand, and assimilate God's message.

The Holy Spirit as teacher (John 16:12-15)

Jesus promised, "He will teach you all things" (see John 14:26). Jesus Christ was the Greatest Teacher the world has ever known, but when He was ready to depart, He briefed His apostles about the soon coming of a Teacher who would "guide you [them] into all truth" (John 16:13, KJV). Considering all that the incarnate Jesus taught, that is absolutely amazing. All truth!

Lord of our lives

I cannot overemphasize: for those who have accepted Christ as Lord of their lives, Christ dwells in them through the Holy Spirit. The King of Kings has received all authority, and the indwelling Spirit is infinitely more powerful than Satan and his demons. "Dear young friends, you belong to God and have already won your fight with those who are against Christ, because there is someone in your hearts who is stronger than any evil teacher in this wicked world" (1 John 4:4). That Someone is none other than the Holy Spirit.

Recognizing the Lordship of Christ is the result of spiritual discernment. Paul emphasized that no person is sincerely able to call Jesus Lord except through the leading of the Spirit (1 Corinthians 12:3). Confessing His Lordship is a product of faith, for by faith we accept Him as the Lord, the Master, of our lives. W. T. Conner noted, "The act of faith is an act in which we trust Him as Savior and at the same time submit to Him as Lord."

Trust and obey

Those who would experience the fullness of the Spirit must assume the attitude of the old hymn, *Trust and Obey*. **If you are a child of God, accept the thrilling fact that the Spirit dwells in you—and if you are an obedient child, the Spirit manifests Himself in you.**

It is vastly important for the Christian to accept and appropriate God's power, which is real and available. It is also vital for the Christian to recognize that God breathes His power on people only when they have committed to Him. When God's power enters a person He asserts it. Bishop Thomas Coke, one founder of Methodism in America, had already crossed the Atlantic Ocean nine times to carry the Gospel. Yet, at sixty-seven he obeyed the Spirit's leading to establish Wesleyan missions in India. He testified, "I am now dead to Europe and alive for India. God has said to me: 'Go to Ceylon!' [now Sri Lanka] I would rather be set naked on its coast, and without a friend, than not to go."

Even as by faith we accept Christ as Savior, so by simple faith we receive the fullness of the Spirit. As we received the Lord Jesus as our Sin Bearer, so we welcomed the Holy Spirit as our Comforter, Teacher, and Guide.

Going deeper with the Spirit

As Jesus is our friend, so is the Holy Spirit whom we can intimately know as a person. The Holy Spirit is God in the receptive human heart. He has knowledge and power (1 Corinthians 2:11; Romans 15:13). When we center our lives in Christ and surrender our egos, we permit the Holy Spirit to shape our lives and cultivate His fruit (singular in Galatians 2:22). The Holy Spirit wants to be our personal companion if we will let Him.

A prayer of obedience and commitment

Our Father, in the Name of Jesus Christ, I give You my body from my head to my feet, It is Yours entirely. I give You all my limbs, my eyes and lips, my brain—all that I am inside and outside. I hand all over to You, so your Holy Spirit may live in me the life that You please. In Your Name and in that of The Son and The Holy Spirit. Amen.

> Therefore, I urge you, brothers, in view of God's mercy, to offer your bodies as living sacrifices, holy and pleasing to God—this is your spiritual act of worship. Do not conform any longer to the pattern of this world, but be transformed by the renewing of your mind. Then you will be able to test and approve what God's will is—his good, pleasing and perfect will (Romans 12:1-2).

The giver of gifts

The Spirit-filled life is one of interdependency. We are to be dependent on the Holy Spirit, but we are to live interdependently with other believers. As the member's body parts work interdependently with one another to do the brain's bidding, so the members of Christ's body are to cooperate in accomplishing His will.

Spiritual gifts are the insignia of the Holy Spirit. The primary purpose of spiritual gifts is the building up of Christ's Body, the Church—not the personal gratification of the individual member. When we serve others through the use of our gifts, we are channels through which the grace and power of God are manifested. "Each one should use whatever gift he has received to serve others, faithfully administering God's grace in its various forms. If anyone speaks, he should do it as one speaking the very words of God. If anyone serves, he should do it with the strength God provides, so that in all things God may be praised through Jesus Christ. To him be the glory and the power for ever and ever. Amen" (1 Peter 4:10-11). The Holy Spirit distributes the gifts: "But one and the same spirit works all these things, distributing to each one individually just as He wills" (1 Corinthians 12:11, NASB).

A soul-searching question

Is there any unconfessed sin in your life that keeps you from a close walk with Christ? Do you have any broken relationships that require mending? Whatever it is, leave it with Christ as you confess and repent.

The fruit of the Spirit

Now let us review the fruit of the Spirit:

First Cluster—speaks of Godward relationship (love, joy, and peace).

Love—"By this all men will know that you are my disciples, if you have love for one another" (John 13:35). **True love is active, not passive.** God showed His love for us by taking the initiative in providing for our salvation (2 Corinthians 5:19). Jesus' love knows no bounds—from the lowest to highest, from the grungiest sinner to the purest saint. Only the Holy Spirit can produce such fruit.

Joy—Jesus said, "These things have I spoken to you, that my joy might remain in you, and that your joy might be full" (John 15:11; see also 16:24). Even as all the water in the world cannot quench the Spirit's fire, neither can all the troubles and tragedies of the world overwhelm the joy the Spirit kindles in human hearts. The basic enemies of joy are worry, guilt, and the fear of failure. When one rejoices in the Lord, worries are overcome, forgiveness is experienced, and one possesses the assurance that God's cause—and you personally—will triumph.

Peace—Peace carries with it the idea of unity, completeness, rest, ease, and security. "Thou will keep him in perfect peace whose mind is stayed on thee, because he trusteth in thee" (Isaiah 26:3). When one is wholly committed to do God's bidding, all the enemies of peace are overcome. Peace ensues because of the indwelling Spirit and in spite of any contingencies we are called on to confront. Peace is not the absence of conflict. Rather, it is the deep, abiding peace only Jesus can give. "Peace I leave with you; my peace I give to you; not as the world gives do I give to you" (John 14:25). Jesus makes this available through the Holy Spirit. "May the God of hope fill you with all joy and peace as you trust in him, so that you may overflow with hope by the power of the Holy Spirit" (Romans 15:13).

Second Cluster—speaks of interpersonal relations (patience, kindness, and goodness)

If we are short-tempered, unkind, and rude, we lack the second cluster of the fruit of the Spirit. When the Spirit controls us, He works to transform us so that the buds of patience, kindness, and goodness begin to blossom—and then **become fruitful.**

Patience—Patience is steadfastness ("hanging in there," not "losing one's cool") under provocation. If we are irritable, vengeful, or resentful, the Holy Spirit is not in charge. Patience is a trait of true Christlikeness, a quality we often like in others without demanding it of ourselves.

Kindness—Kindness and gentleness grow outward. Gentleness is love that endures. Jesus dealt tenderly and kindly with everyone, except self-righteous hypocrites like the scribes and Pharisees. He was justified in severely rebuking them. Even small children sensed His gentleness and approached Him eagerly without fear.

We must remember that the Holy Spirit is not a buffer against suffering. We may think of suffering as a sign that God does not love or has forgotten us, which is not the case. Every grief has a lesson to teach; every sorrow, a gift to give; every suffering, a reason.

Goodness—Seek to be like God because He alone is perfectly good. Goodness is love in action and is always accompanied by patience and kindness. By the power of the Holy Spirit, these traits of character become part of our lives that we might remind others of Him. "Let your light so shine before men, that they may see your good works, and glorify your Father which is in heaven" (Matthew 5:16, KJV).

Third Cluster—speaks of inward attitudes of one's self (faithfulness, gentleness, and self-control)

All of these mean putting God first, others second, and self third.

Faithfulness—In the New Testament "faithfulness" is closely akin to "faith," since faith telescopes into faithfulness or steadfastness. The Spirit works in us that He might work through us. "It is God who is at work in you, both to will and to work for His good pleasure" (Philippians 2:13, NASB). "He who began a good work in you will perfect it until the day of Christ Jesus" (Philippians 1:6). "You were faithful with a few things, I will put you in charge of many things" (Matthew 25:21). Lack of faithfulness is a mark of spiritual immaturity. One sign of emotional immaturity is the refusal to accept responsibility.

Someday all Christians will stand before Christ to give account of the works we have done since our conversion. He will judge us, not on the basis of how successful we were in the eyes of the world, but how faithful we were where He put us. Sometimes the greatest test of our faithfulness is how much time we spend reading the Scriptures, praying, and living in accord with the principles of righteousness.

Paul wrote to Timothy, "I have fought a good fight, I have kept the faith: Henceforth there is laid up for me a crown of righteousness, which the Lord, the righteous judge, shall give me at that day" (2 Timothy 4:7, KJV). The ultimate reward for faithfulness is highlighted in Revelation 2:16, "Be thou faithful unto death, and I will give thee a crown of life" (KJV).

Gentleness (Meekness)—Jesus said, "Blessed are the gentle ["meek," KJV] for they shall inherit the earth" (Matthew 5:5, NASB). Meekness is actually power and wildness under control. We might refer to this quality as love under discipline. *How can we be gentle and humble in heart as Jesus was?* (Matthew 11:29).

First, we do not rise up defensively when our feelings are ruffled, as Peter did when he cut off the high priest's servant's ear at the arrest of Jesus in Gethsemane (Matthew 26:53).

Second, we do not crave to have the preeminence (first place), as Diotrephes, "who loveth to have the preeminence," did (see 3 John 1:9, KJV). We must make sure that Christ has it in all we think, say, or do.

Third, we do not seek to be recognized and highly regarded or to be considered the voice of authority. God is not pleased with "church bosses" who must have the say so about every minute detail in the church. "Honor one another above yourselves" (Romans 12:10b).

Self-control (Temperance)—John Wesley's mother once wrote him while he was a student at Oxford that "anything which increases the authority of the body over the mind is an evil thing." Modern examples are alcohol, other drugs, and illicit sex. The highest mark of nobility is self-control. We usually think of temperance in terms of alcohol, but we should also include overeating (gluttony), use of tobacco, unkindness, gossip, pride, and jealously. The Word reminds us that "Those who live according to the sinful nature have their minds set on what that nature desires;

but those who live in accordance with the Spirit have their minds set on what the Spirit desires" (Romans 8:5). Temperance in regard to temper is self control.

Summary

The Holy Spirit wants to cultivate in us the nine fruit of the Spirit (love, joy, peace, patience, kindness, goodness, faithfulness, gentleness, and self-control). The Holy Spirit is already in every Christian's heart, and His intention is to produce the fruit in our spirits if we will let Him. It is essential that we allow the Spirit to eliminate the works of the flesh from our inner lives, so our "crop" of fruit is not stunted.

Above all else, to receive the fullness of the Holy Spirit is to be Christlike. Christ is The Light, but we are His little lights. We are also the salt of the earth that should season society for the Gospel (see Matthew 5:13-14).

Measurement of how well the fruit is growing in you

Do you exhibit . . .

Love—even for those who are unlovely or those who do not love us in return?

Joy—in the middle of painful circumstances?

Peace—when a blessing or goal you were counting on doesn't come through?

Patience—when things are not going fast enough for you?

Kindness—toward those who treat you unkindly?

Goodness—toward those who have been intentionally insensitive toward you?

Faithfulness—when friends have proved unfaithful?

Gentleness—toward those who have handled you roughly?

Self-Control—amid intense temptation?

If you as a businessman/woman were seeking an employee, and you had two applicants, with these qualities, which would you employ?

First employee	Second employee
Loving	Hateful
Joyful	Depressive
Peaceful	Stressed
Patient	Impatient
Kind	Rude
Good	Bad (insensitive)
Faithful	Back stabbing
Gentle	Rough
Self-controlled	Out of control

The gifts of the Spirit

God gives one or more spiritual gifts to every believer. Gifts are bestowed to edify one another, enabling us to serve and glorify Christ together. Each part of our human body (eyes, ears, feet, hands) is necessary to serve the whole. The Body of Christ requires members using their gifts for the upbuilding of the Church. "As every man [woman] has received the gift, even so minister the same one to another, as good stewards of the manifold grace of God" (1 Peter 4:18). The Holy Spirit has supplied sufficient gifts to meet every need of the Church. Our Divine Master wants all of the members to exercise all their gifts so His body may function smoothly and effectively.

The Bible lists approximately twenty-two gifts. I will touch on several.

Prophecy

The gift of prophecy is the Spirit-given ability to proclaim the Word of God with clarity and to apply it to a particular situation with a view toward correction and edification.

Evangelism *Ephesians 4:11*

Persons gifted in the area of evangelism have a strong desire to share the Gospel with non-believers in every situation and by all possible means. All believers are to witness, yet some have received special gifts for this ministry. "'Come, follow me,' Jesus said, 'and I will make you fishers of men'" (Mark 1:17).

Shepherding (Pastoring)

This entails watching out for the needs of the flock, counseling with members, guarding, guiding, and spiritually feeding with knowledge and understanding. Mature Christians being assigned to new Christians is another aspect of shepherding (1 Corinthians 12:29-30; 2 Corinthians 12:28; Romans 12:6-8).

Preaching/teaching Romans 4:11

The gift of teaching is the supernatural ability to explain clearly and apply effectively the truth of God's Word.

Exhortation (Encouragement) Romans 2:6-8

The gift of exhortation involves the supernatural ability to come alongside to help, to strengthen the weak, reassure the wavering, steady the faltering, console the troubled, and to encourage the believers.

Knowledge and Wisdom 1 Corinthians 12:8-10

It is not enough to be able to grasp and systemize the deep truths of God's Word. Also called for is the ability to relate those truths to the needs and problems of life. Wisdom involves the gift of putting knowledge to work in daily experience.

Gift of Helps 1 Corinthians 12:28; 1 Peter 4:11

The gift of helps carries the meaning of assistance or lending a hand. The gift of helps is the Spirit-given ability to serve the church in any supporting role, usually temporal, though sometimes spiritual. The gift enables one to serve joyfully and diligently wherever and whenever required. The ultimate end of helps is the building up of others. Christian workers like ministers, released from temporal tasks, can concentrate more on spiritual priorities. Although they ended up preaching and teaching the Word, The Seven in Acts 6 were originally set apart for their gifts of helps.

The gift of hospitality Romans 12:6-8

Peter urged the believers to use hospitality one to another without grudging (1 Peter 4:9). "Do not forget to entertain strangers, for by so doing some people have entertained angels without knowing it" [for instance, Abraham and Sarah] (Hebrews. 13:2). Open your home to help further God's work. "I was a stranger, and ye took me in" (Matthew 25:35).

The Gift of Giving *2 Corinthians 8:1-5*

This gift involves giving without pretense, without drudgery, and with love. Persons gifted in the area of giving have the ability to give material goods and financial resources with joy so the needs of the Lord's work are met. They have the capacity to recognize financial needs others may overlook. "Each man [or woman] should give what he has decided in his heart to give, not reluctantly or under compulsion, for God loves a cheerful [actually "hilarious" in the Greek] giver" (2 Corinthians 9:7).

The Gift of Administration/Government *1 Corinthians 12:28*

The gift of government is the Spirit-given expertise to preside, govern, plan, organize, and administer with wisdom, fairness, humility, service, confidence, ease, and efficiency. Persons gifted in area of administration are goal- and objective-oriented.

The Gift of Showing Mercy *Romans 12:6-8*

The gift of mercy means expressing compassion, especially in aiding the needy, whether physically and/or spiritually and emotionally. Persons gifted in the area of mercy model the emotions of our Lord as He "was moved with compassion on them" (see Matthew 9:36). Their hearts immediately go out to those who are suffering and burdened with cares. These persons usually desire friendships in which there is deep communication and mutual commitment. They have a tendency to avoid confrontation and firmness and often close their spirits to those they feel are overly harsh or critical.

The Gift of Faith *1 Corinthians 12:8-10*

The gift of faith is the Spirit-given insight to single out what God wants done—then to sustain unwavering confidence that God will do it, regardless of seemingly insurmountable obstacles.

The Gift of Discernment *1 Corinthians 12:8-9*

To discern, one has the ability to determine the real from the unreal;

the genuine from the spurious. Discernment is the gift to distinguish between the spirit of truth and the spirit of error.

A person with this gift discriminates between that which is raised up by God and that which pretends to be. They have the Spirit-endowed ability to unmask Satan's trickery, to detect unbiblical teachings, and to ferret out false teachers. They have the enablement to spot a phony before others see through such Satan-led phoniness.

The Gift of Miracles *1 Corinthians 12:8-10 and 12:28-30*

A miracle is an event of supernatural power. God chooses certain persons to communicate, and at times to serve as instruments of, His miracle-working power.

The Gift of Healing *1 Corinthians 12:8-10,28-30*

Certain Bible scholars feel there are four basic kinds of healing:

Healing of Sin

Bitterness, resentment, and hatred are serious sins. **One of the worst sins is the lack of forgiveness.** God is willing to forgive us of our sins if we forgive others. Christ said in Matthew 5:23, "Therefore, if you are offering your gift at the altar and there remember that your brother has something against you, leave your gift there in front of the altar. First go and be reconciled to your brother; then come and offer your gift" (Matthew 5:23-24). Often, when Jesus would heal a person physically He would add, "Your sins are forgiven." Though physical illness goes back to sin in the Garden of Eden, it is certainly not always directly linked to a person's sin. Yet, sometimes it is, as in the case of the Corinthians who defiled the Lord's Supper (see 1 Corinthians 11:30).

Inner Healing

If a child has a drunken father who is angry when he comes home, or has a mother who doesn't really want the child, that child is going to suffer in the soul. When we are loved, we begin to blossom like lovely flowers. When we ask the Lord to heal those things that have hurt us in the past, and continue to pull us down, He will do it. This type of suffering prevents us from receiving the freedom that Jesus Christ wants to give us as children of His Father. All of us have certain fears that hold us back. Psychologists have had a field day with phobias (fears from the Greek *phobos)*. Many fret and strain over things that will never happen. So many are afraid they will never have enough money. Others fear the loss of a mate, either through divorce or death. One of the deepest fears is that we won't be loved and accepted. Many people feel that God can't possibly love them, but they have failed to become acquainted with the truth of John 3:16.

Physical Healing

Jesus came to save people, thus to re-create fellowship between God and mankind. If a man were a leper, Jesus would cure his leprosy. Whatever the ailment, He would reach out to heal. "Jesus Christ is the same yesterday and today and forever" (Hebrews 13:8). He does not change. If we call upon the Lord with faith, and if it is God's will, He will still heal us today.

The Healing of Demonic Illness

Though our secular age discounts Satan and his demons, the truth is that he and his devils or demons will continue their malfeasance until they are cast into the lake of fire for eternity. As during Bible days, today some illnesses are caused by demonic spirits. People with special experience in healing those illnesses should be called in, and the healing should be done in private. If you have a Bible-believing, Gospel-preaching pastor, talk with him. If not find one! We must remember God is all-powerful and all-loving, so He desires our healing.

All healing is from God. Only He can heal, and we should ask for healing in the "Name above every name," that of Jesus Christ (see Philippians 2:9).

The Gift of Leadership Romans 12:6-8

Persons gifted in this area are enabled to lead others toward spiritual growth. They often are considered visionary and have the knack of setting goals and motivating others toward accomplishing the goals. They usually can communicate effectively to large groups of people.

The Gift of Tongues 1 Corinthians 12:10

According to Paul tongues was a lesser gift. "But in the church I would rather speak five intelligible words to instruct others than ten thousand words in a tongue" (1 Corinthians 14:19). There is no doubt that this gift has continued through the centuries, yet Paul felt that the gifts of teaching and prophecy were far more vital. It is definitely one of God's gifts, but should never become divisive. On the Day of Pentecost the gift of speaking in foreign languages was given to spread the Gospel. Those tongues were known. It appears that in Corinth some spoke in tongues that were unknown, except to the Holy Spirit. Perhaps those were "prayer" tongues basically to edify the tongues speaker. Tongues are neither the initial evidence of the Holy Spirit, as some contend, nor essential to salvation nor spiritual power.

Living in Christ

The vine is Christ; I am the branch. As it were, the Holy Spirit is the life-giving juice that runs through the vine into the branch. The branch lives, grows, and bears fruit, not by struggles and effort, but by simply **abiding** (being there)

By faith I have accepted the relationship of abiding. I am abiding in Christ, and His Spirit is filling my heart with the fruit of the Spirit. All of these are living in me (John 15:1-5). I understood that upon receiving the Holy Spirit, I was endowed with a source of power that will align my character with God's righteous standard.

Characteristics of the Holy Spirit

Comforter; Counselor; Teacher; Spirit of Jesus Christ; Spirit of Power; Spirit of the Living God; Spirit of Truth; Spirit of Sonship (Adoption); Spirit of Wisdom and Understanding; Giver of Gifts; Giver of the Fruit of Spirit; The Promised Holy Spirit; Voice of the Almighty; Voice of the Lord; The Sealer of Faith

Pray with me

Dear Father, in the Name of the Lord Jesus Christ, I come abiding in You, asking for the forgiveness of every sin and praying for the Holy Spirit to manifest His fruit in my life. Through the Spirit, may my life, without question, reflect Jesus Christ. In the Name that is above every name. Amen.

Holy Spirit, breathe on me, Until my heart is clean; Let sunshine fill its inmost part, With not a cloud between. Breathe on me, breathe on me, Holy Spirit, breathe on me; Take thou my heart, cleanse ev'ry part, Holy Spirit, breathe on me.—Edwin Hatch

For thought and discussion

1. Read Galatians 2:20 and Titus 3:5. What do they teach?
2. Scan John chapters 14—16. Outline Jesus' teachings about the ministry of the Spirit.
3. Review the fruit of the Spirit.
4. Also review the gifts of the Spirit.
5. Contrast the baptism of the Spirit and the filling of the Spirit.
6. If you are a Christian pray that the Spirit will keep you filled. If you are not born again ask Jesus Christ to save you, and you will be baptized into the Spirit.
7. In what areas do you need to grow spiritually?
8. To help you grow spiritually, what are you permitting God to do in your life?

Part V

God's Created Beings

- **God's holy angels**
- **Lucifer — the fallen angel**
- **Adam and Eve**

So God created man in his own image, in the image of God created he him; male and female created he them. And God blessed them, and God said unto them, Be fruitful, and multiply, and replenish the earth, and subdue it: and have dominion over the fish of the sea, and over the fowl of the air, and over every living thing that moveth upon the earth (Genesis 1:27-28, KJV).

'I will put enmity between thee [Lucifer] and the woman, and between thy seed and her seed; it shall bruise thy head, and thou shalt bruise his heel' (Genesis 3:15, KJV). So he drove out the man; and he placed at the east of the garden of Eden Cherubims, and a flaming sword which turned every way, to keep the way of the tree of life (Genesis 3:24, KJV).

14
God's Holy Angels

The angel of the Lord encamps around those who fear Him, and rescues them (Psalm 34:7).

And suddenly there was with the angel a multitude of the heavenly host praising God, and saying, Glory to God in the highest, and on earth peace, good will toward men (Luke 2:13-14, KJV).

Do I believe in angels? Assuredly I do. Angels have served as God's messengers down through the ages. Angels are spirits, but are able to assume human form.

Angel experiences I have known

May I share the experiences of my mother-in-law and my mother? **My mother-in-law,** Nannie, loved the Lord and was exceedingly active in church. She sang in the choir and taught a Sunday School class past the age of eighty. She died in 1995 at the age of eighty-eight. She drove to church both Sunday morning and evening—but died the following Tuesday. She had undergone an operation that was not supposed to be serious. My wife's brother suggested she wait until after her surgery to visit their home in Grenada, Mississippi. On Tuesday evening about 8:30 the doctor told Pate Brown, Nannie's son, not to stay up because Nannie was doing well and would be OK in ICU. She was being kept there only because of a shortage of nurses on the floor.

About 9 p.m. Pate was called to hear an unexpected message, "Nannie has just passed away." We later learned about a series of events that happened. Pate's daughter, Neecie, lived in Memphis, 120 miles from Grenada. She heads a Visiting Nurse Program and had a beeper. A few minutes before 9 her beeper signal sounded, and it listed Grenada Hospital's number. Neecie called the hospital to check on Nannie and was informed, "She's fine," but no one from there had called Neecie. Neecie then spoke to another ICU nurse and received the same report, yet Neecie told the nurse about her beeper and her concern.

After Neecie hung up, the nurse decided to check on Nannie. She found Nannie awake, and they talked. Then Nannie reached up, caught the nurse's arm with her hands, suddenly turned her head, and, with a glow on her face, asked, ***"Do you see those Angels? Aren't they beautiful?"*** Nannie then laid her head on the pillow, and her soul was absent from the body and in the presence of the Lord. An unusual footnote is that Neecie's beeper will receive signals only within a radius of 35 miles. Grenada is 120 miles away . . . but with God anything is possible!

My mother loved the Lord, praying and reading her Bible several times daily. Her gifts from God were faith and being a prayer warrior and an encourager! At the time of my mother's death, she had been in a wheelchair for fourteen years. As the result of a stroke and falling out of bed, she had to have one leg amputated. Mom was a delight to be around, even after a stroke. Always smiling and encouraging, she kept house, raised six children, cooked, sewed, and did what a normal farm homemaker wife would do.

I firmly believe she had an angel assigned to watch over her, even as I feel all believers do. On one occasion my brother was having an emergency appendectomy in Fort Worth, Texas. Mom woke up my father to tell him that one of their young sons was having surgery. My family at that time had no phone. A couple of years later, I had a dreadfully bad wreck, and my car landed in a bar-pit. Mom again woke my father to inform him that one of their sons was hurt and needed immediate medical attention. She immediately began praying, and I survived a broken neck.

People drove many miles to visit my mother, and have mentioned to me, "I just had to go because she blessed me and cheered me up." At one time the local church pastor was new. One of the first requests he received was to visit Mrs. Lane. He confessed to putting it off for weeks, but one Sunday afternoon he was visiting and was chewed out by a couple of members. So, he thought, *Well, it can't get worse so I'll visit my shut-in.* Later he shared with me, "When I left your mother's home, my spirit was lifted and I had a song in my heart."

A lady in the community remarked to me last year that my mother was "the finest lady I've ever known," and that a number of young people would go to Mom for advice and encouragement. Mom died thirty years ago, but people in the community still talk about her. She was not well-educated, didn't have much money, and was broken in body as the result of a stroke. Yet, she kept house, raised two teenagers after the stroke, and made time to help other people. She obviously was filled with the Spirit, and God endued her with special powers to help carry out His will. She was an inspiration to her children and grandchildren. When we had troubles, we could always think of Mom, whose Christlike spirit always pointed us to Him.

Angels

Angels were created by God and were made higher than man. In addition, they have greater intelligence and more power than humans. *Angels rejoice in heaven and constantly praise and worship the Godhead.* When God created the universe, these spirit beings shouted for joy at the demonstration of God's tremendous power. Jesus explained that, "Likewise joy shall be in heaven over one sinner that repenteth, more than over ninety and nine just persons, which need no repentance" (Luke 15:7, KJV; see also 15:10). *Angels provide protection for God's people.* "The angel of the Lord encampeth round about them that fear him, and delivereth them" (Psalm 34:7, KJV).

The Scriptures teach the existence of angels, both good and evil, and present proof that these are not disembodied spirits of dead persons. Angels were in existence before God laid the foundations of the earth. After the fall of Adam and Eve, angels were dispatched to guard the tree of life, and thus were present before human beings had died. Angels are in nature superior to man, for the psalmist sang that man was made "a little lower than the angels" (Psalm 8:5, KJV).

What angels are like

First, they are spiritual, God-created beings (Hebrews 1:14);

Angels are celestial beings intermediate between God and humans (Hebrews 2:7);

- Angels can be only at one place at a time;
- Angels are limited in power, but they have supernatural abilities;
- Angels are like wind and move quickly from place to place;
- They never marry nor are given in marriage (Matthew 22:30);
- They differ in rank and dignity (1 Thessalonians 4:16; Jude 9);
- They are referred to as "holy ones" (Job 5:1; Psalm 89:5).

Gabriel and Michael

The two angels mentioned most often are Gabriel and Michael, the archangels. Gabriel means "mighty one of God"—"God's Messenger." Gabriel interpreted a vision for Daniel (Daniel 8:16-27) and foretold the restoration of Jerusalem after "seventy weeks" (Daniel 9:16-27). He predicted to Zacharias the birth of John the Baptist (Luke 1:11-22). At Nazareth he gave the annunciation to Mary that she would be the mother of the Messiah (Luke 1:26-38).

Michael's name means "who is like God." While Gabriel is more of an announcing and preaching angel, Michael is more involved in protecting and fighting. Michael was assigned by God to throw Lucifer and his angels out of heaven and contended with Lucifer—Satan, the devil—over the body of Moses (see Jude 9; Daniel 10:13,21; 12:1; Revelation 12:7).

Special gifts, assignments, and responsibilities of angels

Angels as warriors: In a single night, an angel killed 185,000 Assyrian troops (2 Kings 19:35). Angels have been, and are, awesome fighters for God and also agents of His wrath and power. Angels have appeared clothed in garments that shine as lightning—also in human form to persons of faith. They have accepted the hospitality of human homes and have acted as guides to stranded travelers. Most of the time they have appeared in human form as men. However, it is possible they may have shown up as children or women. Many people have felt God is too awesome and too powerful for face-to-face meetings and feel more comfortable with an angel messenger. We should give heed to this note: we can pray for angelic help to be sent by God, but God should always receive the glory. Paul warns us against adoring and worshiping angels.

"Do not let anyone who delights in false humility and the worship of angels disqualify you for the prize. Such a person goes into great detail about what he has seen, and his unspiritual mind puffs him up with idle notions" (Colossians 2:18).

Angels have four basic functions: They worship God, act as liaisons between heaven and earth, guard believers, and serve as God's army.

Angel organization

The Scriptures suggest that angels are organized in an orderly fashion. Our evidence for angel organization includes a handful of terms in the New Testament referring to thrones, dominions, powers, rulers, and authorities. This terminology seems to imply different groupings or levels of angelic beings. God's Word underscores the fact that our warfare is "not against flesh and blood, but against the rulers, against the authorities, against the powers of this dark world and against the spiritual forces of evil in the heavenly realms" (Ephesians 6:12). Angels that excel in strength are sent from heaven to protect us when we ask God for help. The wicked cannot break through the guard that God will station about His people.

I firmly believe a guardian angel is assigned to believers in Christ and watches over us until death—then guides us from the confines of this world into the glory of Heaven. Angels are probably used by the Holy Spirit to help us grow in wisdom and understanding and to help us learn more about love.

Angels as messengers and warriors of God

• Angels were constantly watching out for Jesus when He was on earth.

• An angel of the Lord appeared to Joseph in a dream and announced, "Joseph, son of David, do not be afraid to take Mary as your wife because what she has conceived in her is from the Holy Spirit. She will give birth to a son, and you are to give him the name of Jesus, because He will save His people from their sins" (Matthew 1:20-21).

• Angels are one-way messengers from God to man. We should pray directly to God.

• An angel (*cherub*) guarded the gate of Eden.

• An angel appeared to Moses "in flames of fire from a burning bush" (Exodus 3:2).

• Angels can swiftly carry God's message to earth when He commands them, and they are not limited by gravity or other natural forces.

• The angel at Jesus' tomb had clothes that gleamed like lightning (Luke 24:4).

• Angels bring messages to you from God on high.

• Angels desire nothing else than to fulfill God's will.

• Angels were at Christ's birth, death, tomb, resurrection, and ascension.

• Angels were sent to Abraham with promises of blessings.

• Angels were sent to:
Elijah to feed him,
Elijah and Elisha with chariots and horses of fire,
Peter in prison,
Daniel in the lion's den.

There are special angels around God's throne who never, ever, stop praising God's name.

The heavenly beings sing together and shout for joy in recognition of God's work. The Bible describes angels as "ministering spirits" sent to those who will inherit salvation (Hebrews 1:14).

God is the Great Communicator speaking to us through the Son and the Spirit, through whom the angels are sent to serve us.

How can women/men be messengers of God like God uses angels?

• Minister to those who are sick, lonely, and afraid.

• Since angels are bearers of good news, especially relating to the coming of the Messiah, let us bear the good news of salvation provided by Christ.

• "Be not forgetful to entertain strangers: for thereby some have entertained angels unawares" (Hebrews 13:2).

The unholy angels, especially at the end of time

Satan, the Prince of Darkness

The fallen angels are "evil spirits" united with Satan in his rebellion The vast, highly organized army of demons behind the evil world system is to be reckoned with in the future. Satan is not God's equal but is powerful and a sworn enemy of God.

Satan is known as "the prince of this world" (John 12:31; 14:30; 16:11, KJV); "Beelzebub ["the lord of the flies"] the prince of the devils" (Matthew 9:34; 12:24; Mark 3:22, KJV); "the prince of the power of the air" (Ephesians 2:2, KJV). Satan stands condemned but continues to do his dastardly damage only to the extremity of the chain with which God has restrained him.

His frantic operations in these end times

In Revelation we read that one-third of the angels under Lucifer's control were cast out of heaven for refusal to obey God. There is a constant battle between the forces of good and evil. When persons consciously choose evil instead of good, they are making a determination not to follow God. Satan desires to have us. When he mobilizes his forces against us, God will grant us extra-special protection.

As we approach the end of time, Satan will work with his most hellish fury to deceive and destroy. He spreads everywhere the belief that he does not exist. His policy is to conceal himself and his modus operandi. None are in worse danger from the influence of evil spirits than those who ignore the ample testimony of the Bible and deny the existence and agency of the devil and his angels. Bible-believing Christians agree that demonic activity will increase as we near the last days. It is a viewpoint grounded not only in simple observations of world cataclysms, but, most importantly, from God's Word.

Paul reminded us " . . . that in later times some will abandon the faith and follow deceiving spirits and things taught by demons" (1 Timothy 4:1). The coming of the Lord will be preceded by "the working of Satan with all power and signs and lying wonders, and with deception and unrighteousness" (see 2 Thessalonians 2:9-10). **All whose faith is not**

firmly established on the Word of God will fall prey to the devil and his demons and will be overcome.

Martin Luther, the founder of the Reformation, was oppressed by the devil and his angels, even as we will be. One day, while writing in his study, he even threw an inkwell at the old deceiver. Many times while writing this book, I have experienced a dark power so strong that I have had to stop and pray, "In the name of Jesus Christ you are commanded to leave me alone." Then the peace of God would envelope me. No wonder Luther wrote *A Mighty Fortress Is Our God.* The third verse goes:

> And tho this world, with devils filled,
> Should threaten to undo us; We will not fear,
> for God hath willed His truth to triumph thro' us;
> The Prince of Darkness grim, We tremble not for him;
> His rage we can endure, For lo, his doom is sure,
> One little word shall fell him.

Three mighty angels announce the end of time

Revelation 14:6-12 reveals:

"And I saw another angel fly in the midst of heaven, having the everlasting gospel to preach unto them that dwell on the earth, and to every nation, and kindred, and tongue, and people. Saying with a loud voice, 'Fear God, and give glory to him'; for the hour of his judgment is come: and worship him that made heaven, and earth, and the sea, and the fountains of waters. And there followed another angel, saying, Babylon is fallen, is fallen, that great city, because she made all nations drink of the wine of the wrath of her fornication.'

"And the third angel followed them, saying with a loud voice, 'If any man worship the beast and his image, and receive his mark in his forehead, or in his hand. The same shall drink of the wine of the wrath of God, which is poured out without mixture into the cup of his indignation; and he shall be tormented with fire and brimstone in the presence of the holy angels, and in the presence of the Lamb.' And the smoke of their torment ascendeth up for ever and ever, and they have no rest day nor night, who worship the beast and his image, and whosoever receiveth the mark of his name. Here is the patience of the saints: here are they that keep the commandments of God, and the faith of Jesus."

Satan and his demons take advantage of human nature

Satan studies every indication of human nature's frailty. He marks our "besetting sins" and then makes sure that opportunities are available to gratify one's tendency to evil. Satan is making the world believe that the Bible is mere fiction, even though he himself believes its truth, to no avail (see James 2:19). Evil spirits, during the time of Christ on earth, manifested their power in the most striking manner. The Devil controlled earth because of Adam's sin.

Nearly every day there are evidences of Satanism or devil worship across our once-Christian nation. As I write this, teenagers in my home state, Mississippi, are under indictment for murder and criminal activity, which was part of their worshiping the devil. Sadly, though, a person may not consciously do obeisance to Satan. But if that person is unsaved, his/her "father" is the devil! Loving, merciful Jesus said that, not I. God has forbidden all forms of religion or "religious" practices except the acceptance and worship of Him. Further, He has forbidden all demonic practices and communication with departed spirits (Numbers 25:1-13; Psalm 106:28; 1 Corinthians 10:28; Revelation 16:14).

Jesus as the avenger

Jesus is Commander of the armies of heaven. John beheld a double-edged sword coming from the mouth of Christ—doubled-edged because it offers salvation for the believer and destruction for the unbeliever. In John's description of the time he was in the Spirit and was called up into heaven, he saw that Jesus' eyes were like blazing fire. John recognized Jesus as the avenger of His people. Jude foretold: "See, the Lord is coming with thousands upon thousands of his holy ones to judge everyone, and to convict all the ungodly of all the ungodly acts they have done in the ungodly way, and of all the harsh words ungodly sinners have spoken against him (Jude 14b-15; see also Revelation 19:7-9;11-14). "Then the end will come, when he hands over the kingdom to God the Father after he has destroyed all dominion, authority and power" (1 Corinthians 15:24).

Final cautions about angels

Pray to God, not angels;

Scripture discourages dealing with fortune tellers (Ecclessiates 9:5);

The evil spirits still try to place themselves on the level of God;

Satan knows your sins and will tempt you by giving you ample opportunities for sinning.

For thought and discussion

1. Name God's two holy archangels. Who was the archangel that was evicted from heaven?
2. What is the literal meaning of angel in both the Old and New Testaments? In what sense are Christians similar to them?
3. Relate how angels were involved in events surrounding Jesus' incarnation.
4. Read Colossians 2:8. How does such misguided activity occur today?
5. Where did demons (devils, evil spirits) come from, and who are they?
6. How do angels rank in relationship to God? To us?

15

Lucifer and the Fallen Angels

Jesus said, "I saw Satan (Lucifer) falling from heaven as a flash of lightning" (Luke 10:18).

It all began with a super-talented angel, Lucifer, who concluded that God the Father should recognize his abilities and reward him with a greater position. When that didn't happen, millions of fellow angels, agreeing that God was unjust, joined Lucifer's rebellion. The great war between Christ and Lucifer—now called Satan—had begun.

God first brought into existence the highest creature Deity could conceive, namely the anointed cherub. The highest and most powerful angel that God ever created was originally called "the anointed cherub" in Ezekiel 28 and the "day star" or "Lucifer" in Isaiah 14:12. He was perfect from every standpoint from the day he was created—until unrighteousness was found in him, and he fell, becoming Satan, the prideful adversary of God and man. He had enjoyed a station of authority and power in God's government for an unknown period. It seems that this creature, whose exquisite music beautified heaven, was the leader of a gigantic choir of angelic beings (Isaiah 14:11; Ezekiel 28:13d; Job 38:7). God endowed him with vast wisdom and prominence in heaven's government.

Rebellion in heaven

With our finite minds we cannot understand why God allowed Lucifer to have free will and autonomy, but He, in His providence, did. The contents of the head angel's rebellious thoughts, that led to the first sin, are recorded in Isaiah 14:12-14.

> How art thou fallen from heaven, O Lucifer, son of the morning! how art thou cut down to the ground, who didst weaken the nations! For thou hast said in thine heart, I will ascend into heaven, I will exalt my throne above the stars of God: I will sit also upon the mount of the congregation, in the sides of the north, I will ascend above the heights of the clouds, I will be like the Most High (Isaiah 14:12-14).

In heaven itself the law was broken. Sin originated in self-seeking Lucifer, the covering cherub, who desired supremacy not only in heaven but in the universe. He sought to gain control of heavenly beings, the ranks of angels and the cherubim and seraphim. He wanted to lure them away from their Creator and win their homage to himself. So, he misrepresented God, attributing to Him the desire for self-exaltation. With his own evil characteristics, he sought to invest the loving Creator. Thus, he deceived angels and caused them to doubt God's authority and word and to distrust His goodness.

God's love tempered with His justice

God had to break Satan's crafty, cunning power, but how? Since He is omnipotent, surely He could have put down Satan by force. The Holy One would not do it, because the exercise of strong-armed tactics is contrary to the principles of God's government. He desires only the service of love, and love can neither be commanded nor achieved by a show of force. On earth all the court orders, rulings, and civil rights laws cannot make people love one another. Only by love is love awakened. To know God intimately is to love Him. His character must be manifested in contrast to Satan's. For that Godly demonstration, only one Being in all the universe would suffice. Only He who fathomed the immeasurable dimensions of

God's love could make it visible. Upon the world's dark night "the **Sun** [none other than The Son] of righteousness shall rise with healing in his wings" (Malachi 4:2, KJV).

Swaggering Lucifer had asserted, "I will exalt my throne above the stars of God; . . . I will be like the Most High." But Christ, "being in the form of God, counted it not a thing to be grasped to be on an equality with God, but emptied Himself, taking the form of a servant, being made in the likeness of men" (Philippians 2:6-7).

Lucifer's twisted scheme

How far can you stretch your imagination? Far enough to imagine yourself as the angel once named Lucifer ("Light bearer"), now cast out of heaven and known as Satan ("Adversary")?

You're furious, depressed, fearful, uncertain. You shook your fist at The God who created you—and lost. Your position as the chief angel in heaven is gone forever. You still control a multitude of evil angels who followed you in rebellion against God, but you and they long ago were thrown out of God's presence. What would you do? You have no chance to regain your former position and residence either by force or pleading. Besides, you're committed to the course you have chosen. Your one all-consuming goal is to continue your rebellion against God and to make life miserable for Him, and all his creatures, as you possibly can.

How would you go about it? If you're a parent, you've already easily figured it out. Go after God's children! The old deceiver could no longer attack God directly, but he could hit Him through the men and women God had created and placed on a brand-new Earth. And if successful in exporting to Eden the rebellion he had begun in heaven, he might yet overthrow God's authority throughout the universe. His capricious mind began formulating strategy. Innuendo and subtle deception—the devious methods that afforded him a degree of success among the angels—surely ought to work with humans as well.

Jesus Christ the Son stood as an equal with God the Father and God the Holy Spirit. Lucifer, realizing that God is fair and truthful, doubtlessly concluded that God the Father would soon recognize his personal growth and qualifications and would promote him to a position equal with that of Jesus. "Your heart became proud on account of your beauty, and you corrupted your wisdom because of your splendor" (Ezekiel 28:17). "You corrupted your wisdom." In other words, Lucifer wasn't thinking straight. His judgment had become distorted by a false picture of himself that he had chosen to believe. Because of his wisdom, though faulty, and beauty, Lucifer had begun to view himself as more important in heaven's scheme of things than he actually was. He had become proud.

Pride—an exaggerated sense of one's importance—sets one up for a fall. "Pride goes before destruction, a haughty spirit before a fall" (Proverbs 16:18). And fall Lucifer eventually did. After his fall, God would speak of him:

> You were blameless in your ways from the day you were created till wickedness was found in you. How have you fallen from heaven, O morning star, son of the dawn! You have been cast down to the Earth, you who once laid low the nations! You said in your heart, "I will ascend to heaven; I will raise my throne above the stars of God; I will sit enthroned on the mount of assembly, on the utmost heights of the sacred mountain. I will ascend above the tops of the clouds; I will make myself like the Most High (Isaiah 14:12-14, NIV).

Satan's plot thickened

The angels had no conception of what evil or sin might constitute. All created beings in eternity lived—and always had lived—in a sinless environment. Sin was an unknown. When rebellion insinuated its first tentacle into Lucifer's mind, it came gently as a mere suggestion of discontent, a vague feeling that perhaps God did not fully appreciate his proficiencies. Lucifer himself did not understand all that was happening, but he rather enjoyed the strange notion. He toyed with it until it ripened into an idea, a conviction, an obsession . . . and then outright rebellion.

At first, as Lucifer spread his sin, other angels listened with puzzlement to intimations that God might have ulterior motives in His governing of heaven. As he became more settled in his opposition, he realized he could play dirty, using tricks that God couldn't. He could twist facts ever so slightly and input a totally different complexion on matters. God by nature, on the other hand, stuck to strict truthfulness. The very disposition of sin gave rebellion certain unfair advantages. Lucifer accused God of being selfish, arbitrary, unfair, and of using His power oppressively.

Why didn't God smash Lucifer then and there?

What if God had "let the hammer down" on Lucifer as many have suggested He should have? He would simply have proved that Lucifer was right! Every puzzled angel in heaven would have thought, *Lucifer has a point. God is dictatorial and arbitrary.* Look how He reacted the first time an angel questioned His authority. God would have been justified had He squashed Lucifer and sin before they could contaminate His universe—except that He was aware that stomping Lucifer was precisely how to make sure that the rebellion continued.

Since love truly is the basis of His government—and He values only voluntary obedience—God was limited in the response He could make to Lucifer's challenge. He had to operate in a manner consistent with His character. Yes, He could have whipped the rebellious angel back into line, or He could have destroyed him. But not if He remained true to Himself. The only real cure for the malady of sin lay in allowing it to run its course and demonstrate fully to the entire universe its deadly, horrible effects.

So God allowed Lucifer to spread his perverted half-truths. Lucifer took advantage of God's patience and love, interpreting it as weakness. Sin always has these momentary edges in its struggle against righteousness. But God had one immense advantage that Lucifer could not match—the power of truth and right. God was right, and Lucifer was wrong. For all its apparent edges, a lie can never win against the truth. Lucifer's rebellion is doomed to eventual failure. Victory may be long in coming, but it is sure!

God intervenes amid the rebellion

It is mind-boggling, but God decided to intervene and prove Satan's accusations false. How? By becoming a human being and living in complete obedience to His own law. How He personally entered the human arena shows God's penchant for doing things quietly and unobtrusively. "When the fullness of the time was come, God sent forth his Son, made of a woman, made under the law" (Galatians 4:4). **By the Holy Spirit, an**

obscure virgin conceived a child and gave birth in the humblest refuge the planet afforded—a stable for animals. The kings and potentates at first paid no attention to the obscure birth.

Christ's Deity did not in the least dilute His full humanity. His name was to be **"Emmanuel, which being interpreted is, God with us"** (Matthew 1:23, KJV). **So complete was His identity "with us" that He "was in all points tempted like as we are, but without sin."** (Hebrews 4:15).

The trial was on. Day by day the two protagonists met in hand-to-hand combat. Satan plied all his devilish skill in trying to trap Jesus into submission to the universal reality of sin. If Jesus had succumbed to temptation even once, Lucifer would have won his case at the bar of the universe. You and I know who won.

Christ showed up Lucifer

One of Christ's missions was to prove Satan wrong on every count of his devilish accusations against God. He must prove that men and women, connected with heaven through faith, do not have to sin. He must prove that sin is not necessary, not valid. Satan had invented sin. He flaunted it as a challenge to God, as a deplorable condition that even He could not conquer. But the Son of God must "condemn sin" by demonstrating that Satan's charge was false.

If Jesus were to enjoy any advantage that we can't also have, or if He were to be shielded from the full impact of temptation as we know it, Satan would have shouted "Foul!" to highest heaven. *Jesus would have no resources not available to us by faith.*

According to Scripture, God's personal intervention in this massive conflict was carried out in full view of the universe. Sinless angels and other beings understood the legal drama as it unfolded scene by scene. From His infancy in the rude stable, through childhood conflicts, through early youth and young manhood, through the arduous strain of His ministry, Jesus constantly faced and withstood the fiercest temptations Satan could hurl at Him.

On the cross Jesus endured the most severe, soul-wrenching trial any human has ever known—not merely excruciating physical suffering, but the torture of sin and the feeling of being abandoned by His Father.

Though sinless in His humanity, Jesus died the death of a sinner for us. But by faith, He shouted "It is finished!" The contest was done; He had won His battle and proved Satan wrong. He had sacrificed Himself to offer humanity freedom from the slavery of sin.

The Bible recognizes that Lucifer looks upon himself as "the god of this world" (see 2 Corinthians 4:4), and that millions worship him and the entrapments of his wicked world system. Ephesians 6:12-13 explains:

> For we wrestle not against flesh and blood, but against principalities, against powers, against the rulers of the darkness of this world, against spiritual wickedness in high places. Wherefore take unto you the whole armor of God, that ye may be able to withstand in the evil day, and having done all, to stand (Ephesians 6:12-13, KJV).

Our fight is not over mankind but rather with demonic powers from the kingdom of darkness.

The supremacy of Christ

In order for Jesus to become our Redeemer, He was born of woman and was made lower than angels. But in His resurrection, He ascended above the prince of the power of the air, above the god of this world, Lucifer, the devil. The triumphant Christ ascended far above all kingdoms, powers, principalities, and the rulers of darkness of this world (see Ephesians 1:20-21). And once again He is above the angels. Ephesians 2:6 says: "And God raised us up with Christ and seated us with Him." By following Christ we who were made lower than the angels—even the fallen angels—are lifted far above any angel because we sit with Christ! John exulted, "Ye are of God, little children, and have overcome them: because greater is he that is in you, than he that is in the world" (1 John 4:4).

Through Christ's redeeming work, the government of God stands justified. The Omnipotent One is made known as the God of love. Satan's charges are refuted, and his character unveiled. By love's self-sacrifice, the inhabitants of earth and heaven are bound to their Creator in bonds of indissoluble union. The work of redemption will be completed. In the place where sin abounded, God's grace much more abounds. The earth itself, the very field that Satan claims as his, is to be not only ransomed but exalted.

> After this I heard what sounded like the roar of a great multitude in heaven shouting: "Hallelujah! Salvation and glory and power belong to our God, . . ." The twenty-four elders and the four living creatures fell down and worshiped God, who was seated on the throne. And they cried: "Amen, Hallelujah!" . . . Then I heard what sounded like a great multitude, like the roar of rushing waters and like loud peals of thunder, shouting: "Hallelujah! For our Lord God Almighty reigns" (Revelation 19:1,4,6).

For thought and discussion

1. What was Lucifer's overriding sin in heaven? Relate his evil ambition to what he offered Eve and Adam in the Garden of Eden.
2. As a serpent was Lucifer originally a loathsome, ugly creature?
3. The New Testament has several titles for Satan (Lucifer, the devil, the serpent). Point out three of them.
4. Although God is omnipotent, why was He limited in His response to Satan?
5. Is the devil able to *make* anyone sin?
6. Presently we human beings are "a little lower than the angels." Will that always be the case?

16

Adam and Eve

Then God said, "Let us make man in our image, in our likeness, and let them rule over the fish of the sea and the birds of the air, over livestock, over all the earth and over all the creatures that move along the ground" (Genesis 1:26).

So God created man in His own image in the image of God He created him. Male and female, He created them (Genesis 1:26-27, NASB).

Creation

"In the beginning God created the heavens and the earth" (Genesis 1:1). Theologians have often called the opening verse of the Bible "the sublimest statement in human history." "In the beginning God . . ." There He was, the one and only God, the uncreated Creator, the unmade Maker, the Designer of the universe. How do we know that? By faith. Every rational human being will make a decision whether or not to believe in the true God in Christ, a false god, or no God at all. In the case of the second and third alternatives, the "god" is none other than Satan.

A matter of faith

The author of Hebrews clarified it: "By faith we understand that the universe was formed at God's command, so that what is seen was not made out of what was visible. . . ." (Hebrews 11:3). "And without faith it is impossible to please God, because anyone who comes to him must believe that he exists and that he rewards those who earnestly seek him" (Hebrews 11:6, KJV). It was *creatio ex nihilo* (creation out of nothing)—God created the universe out of nothing that was viable before He decided to create it. After a person believes in the existence of God and recognizes that He is revealed in Jesus Christ, then the Bible becomes the objective standard by which to seek spiritual truth. The Book of Books unquestionably assumes that God was and is and always was there. Further, it postulates the fact that God *created* the universe and the world, and all of their functions. And the crowning of His earthly creation is . . . mankind. Peter referred to those who reject the knowledge of God and His creation. "But they deliberately forget that long ago by God's word the heavens existed and the earth was formed out of water and by water" (2 Peter 3:5).

Evolutionary theory has become a "religion"

I never cease being amazed and appalled at the so-called scholars and scientists whose "religion" is evolution, the never-substantiated concept that this intricate and orderly world and human beings happened by accident. Evolution is only a theory, yet the evolutionists have turned it into dogma of religious proportions, though many of them do not believe in the Creator. With a single tooth, a piece of a jawbone, a fragment of rock supposedly from outer space, or an exploration of Mars, they exclaim, "We are coming closer to the truth about man's origin." In his day Paul cautioned Timothy to be "avoiding profane and vain babblings, and oppositions of science falsely so called" (1 Timothy 6:20b, KJV).

God's Creation

The Bible plainly teaches that the earth, plant and animal life, and mankind were directly created by God's acts of *special creation.* The earth was empty, a formless mass cloaked in darkness, and the Spirit of God was hovering over its surface. Then He began speaking things into existence. "Let there be light," He commanded, "and there was light," and that was "good." God then created day and night on the first day (Genesis 1:2-5).

And God declared, "Let there be an expanse in the midst of the waters, and let it separate the waters from the waters. . . ." (Genesis 1:6, NASB). The heavy moisture-laden mist that had been close to the ocean began to rise, forming the atmosphere. The firmament between the atmosphere and the waters was fresh air. The air divided the clouds from the waters. This happened on the second day. Then God created a firmament He called heaven, as He divided the waters from above and below. Thus ended the second day.

Swiftly, continents, islands, and mountains were shaped. It was beautiful land with lakes, rivers, and waterfalls. God named the dry ground "land," and the water, "seas." God once again pronounced it as good. Then God created *flora*, plant life—grass, herb-yielding seed, and fruit trees. The seeds would then produce the kinds of plants and trees from which they came. God did all of that on the third day (see Genesis 1:9-13).

On the fourth day God commanded, "Let bright lights appear in the sky to separate the day from the night. They will be signs to mark off the seasons, the days, and the years. Let the light shine down upon the earth"—so the sun and the moon were placed in the heavens. He flung stars out into the solar system He produced. Though light had existed since the first day, now Yahweh had refined the light that had brightened the previous chaos. It, too, was good! (see Genesis 1:14-19).

Then, on the fifth day the Lord began His work of creating *fauna*, sea creatures, fish and water mammals (whales and dolphins, namely). He had now populated the waters and moved to fill the sky with birds. It was good! Today we might use the word "excellent" (see Genesis 1:20-23).

God continued His crafting of living creatures on the sixth day. He ordered: "Let the land produce living creatures according to their kinds: livestock, creatures that move along the ground, and wild animals, each according to its kind. . . . God made the wild animals according to their kinds, the livestock according to their kinds, and all the creatures that move along the ground according to their kinds. And God saw that it was good" (Genesis 1:24-25). But He was not through.

A creature in God's image

God saved the best for last, yet the best would become the worst were it not for Divine intervention.

> Then God said, "Let us make man in our image, in our likeness, and let them rule over the fish of the sea and the birds of the air, over the livestock, over all the earth, and over all the creatures that move along the ground." So God created man in his own image, in the image of God he created him; male and female he created them (Genesis 1:26-27).

In the short time of six days God had:

- Created the Earth out of nothing;
- Divided land from sea;
- Covered all of the land with plants, trees, and flowers;
- Made birds and fish;
- Made small and large animals;
- Made man in His own image—man, His masterpiece and supreme object of His love, for whom He had provided a paradise on Earth; and,
- Made a woman (called Eve by Adam) from Adam's rib, wishing him to have a helpmeet (see Genesis 2:18-24).

Even though the omnipotent God was not tired, He "rested" on the seventh day. No doubt He left this as a lesson for subsequent generations to set aside at least one day a week for rest from activity. So, the Sabbath was incorporated in The Ten Commandments (Exodus 20:11). Most Christians changed the Hebrew Sabbath, Saturday, to Sunday, "the Lord's Day" (Acts 20:7), since Jesus rose from the dead early Sunday morning (Matthew 28:1).

Imago Dei—*the image of God*

"The image of God" is brimming with meaning. According to Genesis 1:27-28 God created man and woman "in His own image" and gave them charge over all the plants, animals, and inanimate objects on Earth. The original Hebrew word translated "image" probably means a shadow or reflection. What, then, does God's "image" signify?

Human beings are more than "animals"or "mammals." And the Lord God formed man of the dust of the ground, and breathed into his nostrils the breath of life; and man became a living soul" (Genesis 2:7). This image is exhibited by man's walking upright, but far beyond that—man is a spiritual personality. He has an intelligence not possessed by animals who react and respond instinctively. He has the power of will, the ability to choose that makes him a responsible moral agent; the capacity for rational affection; and a moral nature. A person with the slightest mental capability has a conscience implanted by God. Theologian J. M. Pendleton expressed it well:

> There is no reference to a bodily image, for God is a Spirit. Man, unlike all other creatures . . . was made a rational being, and in this sense he was created in the image of God. The possession of rationality does not, however, by any means exhaust the import of the words "in our image." They are in the highest sense expressive of holiness. We therefore read that "God hath made man upright" (Ecclesiastes 7:29). We learn, too, that regeneration restores fallen man to the image of God, which image consists " in righteousness and true holiness" (Ephesians 4:24; Colossians 3:10).

Chapter 2 of Genesis expands on the initial account, detailing names and places. God formed man "from the dust of the earth," named him Adam—which possibly means "of dirt" or "red clay"—and assigned him to become the gardener and husbandman in the Garden of Eden (remember that God created Adam from dust that He Himself had originally created). God in His creation filled the world with treasures of gold, silver, precious stones, nuts, fruits, grains, trees, ferns, flowers, birds, fish, and animals of every kind. He was preparing those presents for . . . Adam and Eve.

Adam and Eve in the Garden of Eden

There was a wide variety of fruit trees in the Garden, but God instructed Adam and Eve that they were not to eat of "the tree of the knowledge of good and evil." God warned them that, if and when they ate from it, they would certainly die. **The lesson here is to listen and obey God's will.** Failure to do so transferred Adam and Eve from a life of paradise to one of toil and heartache. God's creation was complete and His creative work, accomplished. God beheld all He had made and pronounced it as "very, very good" (Genesis 1:31).

The first Adam

After forming man's body out of the dust of the earth, God gave him an immortal spirit, a fact that differentiates man from animals. Adam, as he was created, was innocent of any evil. He and Eve were in full fellowship with God, who gave the highest honor and authority to them.

Through the centuries mankind has inquired, "Why did God create us?"His purpose is crystal-clear from the written Word: "For you created all things, and by your will ["for thy pleasure," KJV] they were created and have their being" (Revelation 4:11). It is His predetermined will that we exist for the glory and honor of His Name. He made us immortal like the angels, and we were never to experience sin, but Adam and Eve precipitated the blight of sin into human experience. Adam was the federal head of the human race. "Therefore, just as sin entered the world through one man [Adam], and death through sin, and in this way death came to all men, because all sinned" (Romans 5:12; see also 15,17,19).

The anatomy of Sins

Surely the majority of Christians—and even numerous non-Christians—are familiar with how sin entered into a once-sinless, pristine paradise. God issued only one prohibition to the first couple: "But you must not eat from the tree of the knowledge of good and evil, for when you eat of it you will surely die" (Genesis 2:17b). The Garden was prolific with delectable fruit trees, from which they could eat freely. The "tree of life" was available. Wondering what was meant by "good and evil," Eve was curious. Her curiosity did not "kill the cat"—but rather the human race.

The nature of the enemy

She had heard the voice of God and Adam, but now there was a new, intriguing one. The serpent, or snake, appeared. He doubtlessly was not repugnant as snakes have been since God cursed him with the fate of crawling on his belly and eating dust (Genesis 3:14). In fact, he was probably attractive and beautiful to Eve. The Bible warns that he may appear as "an angel of light" (2 Corinthians 11:14, KJV). Most conservative commentators believe Isaiah referred to his beauty and splendor (Isaiah 14:13-19). Although he was not called Satan or the devil in Genesis, the serpent's identity is subsequently revealed in God's Word. "But I fear, lest by any means, as the serpent beguiled Eve through his subtlety, so your minds should be corrupted from the simplicity that is in Christ" (2 Corinthians 11:3, KJV). "The great dragon was hurled down—that ancient serpent called the devil, or Satan, who leads the whole world astray. He was hurled to the earth, and his angels with him" (Revelation 12:9; also see vv. 14-15). "And he laid hold on the dragon, that old serpent, which is the Devil, and Satan, and bound him a thousand years" (Revelation 20:2, KJV).

The serpent was the shrewdest of all the creatures. Whether or not literally Satan, he was the instrument of that fallen angel as he tempted Eve. He had the audacity to question God and His plan "no no," subtly taunting: "Did God really say that you must not eat fruit from any tree in the garden?" (Genesis 3:1c, ICB).

> The woman answered the snake, "We may eat fruit from the trees in the garden. But God told us, 'You must not eat fruit from the tree that is in the middle of the garden. You must not even touch it, or you will die' (Genesis 3:2-3, ICB).
>
> But the snake said to the woman, "You will not die. God knows that if you eat the fruit from that tree, you will learn about good and evil. Then you will be like God!" (Genesis 3:4-5, ICB).
>
> The woman saw that the tree was beautiful. She saw that its fruit was good to eat and that it would make her wise. So she took some of its fruit and ate it. She also gave some of the fruit to her husband, and he ate it. Then, it was as if the man's and the woman's eyes were opened. They realized they were naked. So they sewed fig leaves together and made something to cover themselves"(Genesis 3:6-7, ICB).

Why have I used the *International Children's Bible* for the above passage? Because the origin of sin is that elementary in God's Word. The story of the Fall is not a fable or myth. It happened, and real personalities were involved: Eve, Adam, and the serpent (Satan, the devil, Lucifer, the prince of devils, Beelzebub).

The floodgates of sin

People have complained, "It's not fair to have sin and its consequences passed down to us because of Adam and Eve's sin."Actually, in a sense all of us are Adams and Eves. In our young lives we reach a moment when we must choose between good and evil, and invariably we opt for the latter. "Wherefore, as by one man sin entered into the world, and death by sin; and so death passed upon all men, for that all have sinned" (Romans 5:12, KJV). Read Romans 3:10,23; 6:23. Satan wanted mankind to transgress as he had—by willfully disobeying God and lusting to become like God or "be as gods" (KJV), attempting to usurp His authority. Sin is variously described as disobedience to or violation of God's directives; moral perversity; iniquity; transgression; prideful arrogance; unbelief; lack of faith; and rebellion against God (see Jeremiah 17:9; Romans 7:7,13; Ephesians 2:1-2; Hebrews 3:13; 1 John 3:4,6,8-9; 5:17).

Unresisted temptation: The door to degradation

It is uncanny how the process of Adam and Eve's yielding to temptation is borne out by John in his First Epistle: "For all that is in the world, the lust of the flesh and the lust of the eyes and the boastful pride of life, is not from the Father, but is from the world" (1 John 2:14, NASB).

"The lust of the flesh"—carnal desire for that which is forbidden by God—was operative as Eve, and then Adam, toyed with the seeming attractiveness of the appealing fruit. **"The lust of the eyes"** played its heinous role. To this day sin at first seems attractive and appealing. However, when the "fruit" of unrighteousness insinuates itself, the end result is disaster. **"The boastful pride of life"** sums up the attitude of the stubborn, rebellious sinner. The sinner's "trinity" is me, myself, and I. All of these bitter ingredients were involved in their sin—and in all of their descendants' transgressions, including yours and mine.

> When tempted, no one should say, "God is tempting me." For God cannot be tempted by evil, nor does he tempt anyone; but each one is tempted when, by his own evil desire, he is dragged away and enticed. Then, after desire has conceived, it gives birth to sin; and sin, when it is full-grown, gives birth to death. Don't be deceived, my dear brothers (James. 1:13-16).

Comedian Flip Wilson's "Geraldine" had a favorite alibi: "The devil made me do it."It is human nature to "pass the buck"and to blame another person for one's own sins. After their sin Adam and Eve immediately felt the twinge of guilty consciences, as represented by their shame over being naked. They covered their sex organs with loincloths of fig leaves. Like every admitted sinner since, they attempted to hide from God, but no one can. God called out, "Adam, where are you?" He knew where he was—but He wanted *Adam to know where Adam was!* Adam began to fess up. He was not really afraid because of his nudity, but because of his sin. God pressed the issue by asking, "Who told you that you were naked? Did you eat of the forbidden tree?"

The buckpassing began. Adam then rationalized—indirectly blaming God Himself and also Eve—"The woman You gave me fed me the fruit, and I ate it." When God asked her, "What have you done?" the first woman must have stammered, "Uh, the serpent enticed me—and, er—I did eat" (see Genesis 3:8-13).

The result: Retribution for the serpent; redemption for mankind

God placed an irrevocable curse on the serpent. He would grovel in the dust on his belly and be despised more than all other animal creatures. **Even as condemnation entered the world through Adam, so justification comes through the man Christ Jesus.** After Adam and Eve had sinned, and before they had a child, God declared that the seed of the woman would bruise the serpent's head. Genesis 3:15 is called "The Protoevangelium," the first prophecy of the Savior. "And I will put enmity between you and the woman, and between your offspring and hers; he will crush your head, and you will strike his heel." Through the Gospel, Christ is stomping on the serpent's head and will ultimately banish him into the lake of fire. Many scholars believe "strike" [bruise, KJV] refers to what happened when the nails were driven through Jesus' feet and exited through His heels when affixed to the Cross.

"You will bear children with intense pain and suffering," God pointed out to the woman. Giving birth without sedatives is considered possibly the severest pain, rivaled only by acute angina pectoris. Then, He turned to the man. "Because you listened to your wife and ate the fruit I told you not to eat, I have placed a curse on the ground. All your life you will struggle to scratch a living from it. It will grow thorns and thistles for you" (see Genesis 3:16-19). And we humans struggle to this day.

Satan is alive—but not well—on planet Earth . . .

Satan wielded his perverse influence on religious and government leaders to kill Christ on the Cross. But in so doing, he actually placed Christ in the exact position to atone for the sins of all mankind and to re-establish fellowship of man with God. Satan thought he had killed Christ as he had planned, but Christ didn't stay dead! Through Christ's resurrection, Satan became a defeated foe! After His resurrection, Jesus snatched the keys of death and hell from Satan and re-established God's full control of the earth. However, God allows Satan to tempt mankind in every conceivable manner until Christ returns to Earth as King of Kings and Lord of Lords.

The drama continues

The penalty of Adam's transgression was death—separation spiritually from God. The death against which God warned Adam was both physical and spiritual—that is, physical death but inestimably worse, spiritual death involving final and eternal separation from God . . . unless God could counteract the evil, oppressive effects of sin and death. To overthrow Satan's dominion, Jesus Christ entered the human realm. Adam was created to live forever in fellowship with his loving Creator, yet, as soon as Adam and Eve sinned, they began to die.

Like Adam before he sinned, Christ had a perfect physical body. Adam, however, transgressed, and sin entered his entire nature and corrupted him. But the Lord Jesus refused to yield to sin. Christ gave up His physical life as a ransom for the human race, so all those who trust Him are recipients of eternal life *which starts the moment one accepts Him.* "And this is the testimony: God *has given us eternal life,* and this life is in his Son. He who has the Son has life; he who does not have the Son of God does not have life" (1 John 5:11-12, italics mine).

Adam and Eve's covenant

When Adam and Eve were created, they stood in a moral relationship with their Creator. They possessed a duty of obedience to Him without any inherent claim to reward or blessing for that obedience. In His love, mercy, and grace, however, God voluntarily entered into a covenant with His creatures by which He added a promise of blessing to His Law. The covenant of grace fulfills the covenant of works because God graciously applies the merits of Christ to our account. So, by grace we may meet the terms set forth in the covenant of works.

When the fellowship between God and man was broken by man's deliberate sin, man was cut off from the light and life of the eternal One. His condition would result in his being alienated and estranged from God eternally. God does nothing accidentally, so He had a perfect reason for placing the tree of the knowledge of good and evil in the Garden. Understand it we do not, but its purpose was a test of the first couple's love for Him. The Creator had inundated them with the most luscious fruits ever and set them up in a "heaven on earth." **There is one never-failing test of love—obedience.** If Adam and Eve had completely loved God, and obeyed Him accordingly, He would have given them a life of paradise eternally.

The First Adam = Sin and Death
The Second Adam = Righteousness and Life

The first Adam failed to do the will of God, and mankind has suffered for innumerable generations. The second Adam (Christ) carried out God's will and offered redemption to fallen mankind. Throughout this book I have presented how to receive this redemption and have eternal life: trust Christ to save you (Acts 16:31); repent—turn away from—your sins (Acts 20:21); ask for forgiveness (Luke 18:13); confess Him as your Lord and Savior (Romans 10:9-10); and then follow the instructions of

God's Word through the leadership of the Holy Spirit (Psalm 119:105; John 14:26).

The restoration of peace

When man was created, he was at peace with God. When he rebelled his relationship with God was shattered. Man was no longer at peace with himself. Can these dimensions of peace be restored? Absolutely! Jesus Christ, the Prince of Peace (Isaiah 9:6), is a Peacemaker. God is "the God of peace" (Hebrews 13:20, KJV). Through the second Adam salvation—the cessation of strife between God and man—is offered. "Therefore being justified by faith, we have peace with God through our Lord Jesus Christ" (Romans 5:1, KJV). The Gospel is one of peace (Romans 10:15). The New Testament is packed with salutations of peace—*shalom* in the Hebrew Old Testament, *eirené* in the Greek New Testament.

> Now the God of hope fill you with all joy and peace in believing, that ye may abound in hope, through the power of the Holy Ghost. Now the God of peace be with you all. Amen (Romans 15:13,33, KJV).

Genuine believers are persons of peace and reconciliation, for one fruit of the Spirit is peace (see Galatians 5:22). From the media we are painfully aware that there is diminishing peace in our society."Why?" the social scientists inquire, "can we not have peace and reconciliation between various cultures?" It is because civilization at large will not call on "our peace [Christ] who hath made both one, and hath broken down the middle wall of partition between us" (Ephesians 2:14, KJV; see also Ephesians 2:15,17; 4:3; 6:15,23). Paul referred first to vertical reconciliation (between God and man) and then to horizontal (between man and man). Through His sacrifice our Lord has "made peace through the blood of the cross, by him to reconcile all things unto himself . . . whether they be things in earth or things in heaven" (Colossians 1:20, KJV). When we are reconciled it means the barriers between us are removed. By mutual consent we are drawn back together, and the grievances of the past are laid aside. There is nothing to compare with having "the peace of God, which transcends all understanding" (see Philippians 4:7). Only through the

Prince of Peace will we be at peace with God, with ourselves, and with one another.

One seldom-used verse of Charles Wesley's *Hark! The Herald Angels Sing* goes:

> Second Adam from above,
> Reinstate us in Thy love,
> Hark! the herald angels sing,
> Glory to the newborn King

For thought and discussion

1. Think on it. Why did God allow Adam and Eve to have free moral agency?
2. Since mankind was created in the image of God, what does that imply? Though we are not God or gods, how are we like Him?
3. What all was involved in God's curse on Adam and Eve and on the serpent?
4. Contrast "the first Adam" with the "the second Adam."
5. What is the never-failing test in our relationship with God?
6. Satan can appear even as "an —— of ——."

Part VI

Christ's Victory

But thanks be to God, which giveth us the victory through our Lord Jesus Christ (1 Corinthians 15:57, KJV).

In a loud voice they sang: "Worthy is the Lamb, who was slain, to receive power and wealth and wisdom and strength and honor and glory and praise!" Then I heard every creature in heaven and on earth and under the earth and on the sea, and all that is in them, singing: "To him who sits on the throne and to the Lamb be praise and honor and glory and power, for ever and ever!" (Revelation 5:12-13).

On his robe and on his thigh he has this name written: KING OF KINGS AND LORD OF LORDS (Revelation 19:16).

Wherefore God also hath highly exalted him, and given him a name which is above every name: That at the name of Jesus every knee should bow, of things in heaven, and things in earth, and things under the earth; And that every tongue should confess that Jesus Christ is Lord, to the glory of God the Father (Philippians 2:9-11, KJV).

17
Satan's Road to Disaster

When Satan lies, he speaks his native language, for he is a liar and the Father of lies (John 8:44).

Throughout this book I have prayed that the Holy Spirit would motivate me to withhold nothing of urgency from you. In Chapter 3, I dealt with "Heaven or Hell—Your Eternal Home." In 16 the subject was "Lucifer and Fallen Angels." Satan and his habitats, hell and the lake of fire, are not pleasant, popular subjects. Yet, they are essential if we are to reach people for Christ and heaven. Many will respond to the preaching of God's love, whereas multitudes of others will ignore the Gospel unless they are confronted with the horror of hell and the deception of the devil.

Jude challenged: "And of some have compassion, making a difference: And others save with fear, pulling them out of the fire; hating even the garment spotted by the flesh (Jude 1:22-23). Some translations say "snatching them from the burning" or "snatching them from the very fires of hell" (NASB).

The devil's had his day

Since his expulsion from heaven, along with one-third of the angels, Lucifer (Satan, the devil, the serpent, the "dragon") has had a field day deceiving multiplied billions to follow him on the broad road that leads to destruction. As I have already pointed out, in heaven he "had it made." He was the superior angel who was in charge of the angelic hosts. But, through prideful arrogance, he changed from the beautiful "morning star, son of the dawn" to a deceitful, ugly viper (see Isaiah 14:12-14). He exported his rebellion from heaven to earth. The fallen angels, now called demons, who sinned in the full light of God's presence, did so irrevocably and without possibility of reconciliation. Reread Chapter 16, "Adam and Eve," about his wiles in luring the first couple into sin, that afterwards has infected the entire human race.

He's mad as . . .

I firmly believe that Adam and Eve regretted their rebellion, repented, and were forgiven. But Earth had become a rebellious planet with Satan as its ruler. God judged the crimes of Lucifer and changed his name to Satan, the devil, and evil one. The name devil means "the accuser" and "slanderer." Ousting him from his position of authority in heaven's government, God sentenced Satan to eternal banishment. After his fall Satan became wholly possessed with unholy wrath toward God, hating with venom all that is divine and holy. Jesus taught that Hell (Hades) was created for the devil and his angels (Matthew 25:41).

Innumerable demons, who fell with their master, Lucifer, are operative in the world. They have followed their prince of darkness throughout untold centuries. Peter cautioned the scattered believers: "Be self-controlled and alert. Your enemy the devil prowls around like a roaring lion looking for someone to devour" (1 Pet. 5:8). So, the devil walks the earth unseen day and night. Satan is no atheist. He wants a religious world but one which rejects God's offer of a personal relationship with him through Jesus Christ. In fact, James wrote: "You believe that there is one God. Good! *Even the demons believe that--and shudder*" (James 2:19, italics mine).

His titles describe his sleazy work

First, he is the ruler of this earth. He is constantly busy through every conceivable venue, including human government and its political systems. Satan is capable of manipulating all forms of government for his purposes. The vast, highly organized army of demons behind the world system is clearly revealed in Ephesians 6:12: "For our struggle is not against flesh and blood, but against the rulers, against the authorities, against the powers of this dark world and against the spiritual forces of evil in the heavenly realms."

Second, Satan's second title is "prince of the power of the air." Before a person becomes a Christian, he/she is spiritually dead and is ruled by this prince. "And you were dead in your trespasses and sins in which you formerly walked according to the course of this world, according to the prince of the power of the air, of the spirit that is now working in the sons of disobedience" (Ephesians 2:1-2). As prince of the air, Satan rules over the thoughts of the world system. He originated the concept of brainwashing long before human rulers used it to manipulate prisoners of war.

With our hearts focused on Jesus, we are constantly having our minds renewed with God's view of life which is alien to the humanistic viewpoint of the world system. The *Moffat* translation renders Romans 12:2: "Don't let the world around you squeeze you into its own mold, but let God remold your minds from within."

Third, Satan's third title is "the god of this age." As already explained in these pages, he is the god of all those who do not follow Jesus Christ. Those who worship in any religious form apart from Christ are ultimately being deceived by Satan. All human beings are under Satan's rule until they open themselves up to God's deliverance through Christ. Then the god of this age can no longer control them. "For sin shall not have dominion over you: for ye are not under the law, but under grace" (Romans 6:14). He can tempt but no longer dominate us because we have placed our trust in Christ.

Satan is inferior

From the Word of God we learn that Satan is a powerful, sinister being, who has a kingdom of servile malignant spirits under him. These he has organized into a well-ordered government. Satan is a personal, powerful, and wise being who is diametrically opposed to God and mankind. He is against every decent, good characteristic in God and people who have trusted God. Believe it or not, he is subservient to the Almighty and must ask permission from Him before he can ever touch any believers. Job affords an apropos example of this arrangement.

Satan is subtle, beguiling, and crafty. He speaks with eloquence, and his appearance is stunning. Satan is a higher order of being than humans. He is a fallen angel, but he has more power than earthly creatures—but infinitely less power than Almighty God. Believers may be harassed, tempted, and accused by demons but never ever controlled by them. Every Christian is indwelt by the Holy Spirit, and His presence guarantees liberty from demon possession. The Holy Spirit is stronger than the devil and all of his malevolent demons.

Waging spiritual warfare until Jesus comes back

In Genesis, sentence was pronounced upon Satan, and in Revelation the sentence is prophetically shown as being executed. "Submit yourselves to God: Resist the devil, and he will flee from you" (James 4:7). Overcoming Satan and avoiding pitfalls he prepares for us is a matter of submitting ourselves to God and resisting the devil. Read Ephesians 6:10-18, which presents a modus operandi on preparation for resisting and overcoming Satan.

Would you believe that, since sin in the Garden of Eden, nothing in mankind has essentially changed? People are sinners, like their original parents. They have picked up on Cain, one of Adam and Eve's sons who murdered his brother, Abel; Cain's kinfolks are still killing all around us with a vengeance. So, after thousands of years the battle between good and evil is still raging. Every man, woman and child is caught in the crossfire.

• The first step in overcoming the deceiver is to acknowledge that he exists. The devil is ambivalent. He wants the avowed Satanist to worship and to believe in him. Yet, he would rather that believers ignore or make light of him, so he can then sneak up on their blind side.

• The second step is to recognize that he works through deception. Satan desperately desires to keep people in darkness about the teachings of Christ. Satan knows too well that all who he can induce to neglect prayer and searching the Scriptures will be overcome by his attacks. The great deceiver has his "agents" all over the world ready to present any and every kind of error to ensnare souls. The devil wants people to believe that any religion is OK, even though God's Word emphatically declares that the only way to God is Jesus Christ, The Way (see John 14:6). "Salvation is found in no one else, for there is no other name under heaven given to men by which we must be saved" (Acts 4:12).

The Bible was designed to guide all who wish to become acquainted with the one and only God of the universe. God gave to men the sure word of prophecy. That Book opens up to all who study it with a prayerful heart. "Light is sown for the righteous" (Psalm 97:11).

Power restricted—anointing retained

Though stripped of his authority and shorn of certain powers, Satan appears not to have suffered the deprivation of his anointing. For a complete demonstration of his diabolical nature and his aberrations of God's endowed gifts, he was allowed to become "the prince of the world" (John 14:30; 16:11), "the prince of the power of the air" (Ephesians 2:2), and "the god of this world" (2 Corinthians 4:4), invested with the power of death (Hebrews 2:14).

Commensurate punishment

Down through the millennia God has tolerated Satan and the repulsive forces of his kingdom of darkness. Ah, but at Christ's second coming, God will deal with him in a manner commensurate with his intolerable deeds. During the Millennium he will be incarcerated in "the pit of the abyss" for a thousand years:

> And I saw an angel coming down out of heaven, having the key of the abyss and a great chain in his hand. And he laid hold on the dragon, the old serpent, which is the Devil and Satan, and bound him for a thousand years, and cast him into the abyss . . . After this he must be loosed for a little time (Revelation 20:1-3, KJV).

At the close of the Millennial period Satan will be released for "a little (short) time" to carry out his last escapade. Totally defeated in his last-gasp attempt to conquer the Lord Jesus Christ, he will be cast into the lake of fire for eternal punishment.

> And when the thousand years are finished, Satan shall be loosed out of his prison . . . to deceive the nations which are in the four corners of the earth. . . . And the devil that deceived them was cast into the lake of fire and brimstone . . . tormented day and night for ever and ever (Rev. 20:7-10).

For thought and discussion

1. Satan prowls the earth like what kind of ravenous beast?
2. Write down several of Satan's characteristics.
3. Why is Satan thrilled if people fail to take him seriously—or even to laugh about him or not believe he exists?
4. Turn to John 8:44. Jesus exposed the evil one as a l—— and a m———.
5. What is his final, eternal destination?
6. Besides the beast and the false prophet, who else will accompany him there?

18
Sin and Redemption

For all have sinned and fallen short of the glory of God (Romans 3:23).

Man was created by a special act of God, in His own image. Human beings are the crowning work of His creation. Adam and Eve were innocent of sin in the beginning and were endowed by their Creator with freedom of choice. By their free choice they doubted God's word to them and disobeyed, thus introducing sin into the human race. Through the temptation of Satan, they transgressed the command of God and fell from their original innocence.

What is death?

God had warned them that if they ate of the tree of the knowledge of good and evil, they would die, meaning that the forces of death would begin to prey on their bodies. Eventually their spirit would be released from it and become separated. Death is separation. I believe that death came in the moment that Adam and Eve partook of that tree, but it required about 900 years for the physical decay of death to overcome them.

But there is another phase, **spiritual death.** After they sinned, Adam and Eve were driven out of God's presence. They no longer had the privilege of fellowship with Him. So on that very day, they not only began to die physically **but also die spiritually.** As a result, the human race fell from its sinless glory, ushering in death and despair in its wake.

Two civilizations

When Cain was born, Eve probably thought the promise of "the seed of woman" was being fulfilled, and that her first child, Cain, was God incarnate. Instead he turned out to be a murderer. Because "sin in the flesh" had entered the human family, mankind's whole mental and spiritual being was thrown off balance. In the process of time, Cain and Abel presented offerings to the Lord; Cain presented fruit from the ground, and Abel, a lamb. God was pleased with Abel's offering but not with Cain's. Cain then became violently jealous and killed his brother. "Sin in the flesh"—the spiritual "gravity" that pulls downward upon the spirit of man—results in "sins in the life."

Abel's offering, made in faith, evidently was the beginning of sacrifices, all of which were typical of the "Lamb of God, that taketh away the sin of the world" (John 1:29, KJV), the Messiah who was to come (see Hebrews 9:6-16).

The descendants of Cain sponsored a godless civilization, though developing the finer arts of music and poetry and the fundamentals of industrial activity. Eve bore another son, Seth, and his descendants became the godly branch of the human family. However, by the time of Noah, the tenth from Adam, evil had so permeated the entire Earth that God was forced to wipe man from the face of it, with the exception of Noah and his family.

Sin's putrid flower flourished and has ever since. "Wherefore, as by one man sin entered into the world, and death by sin; and so death passed upon all men, for that all have sinned" (Romans 5:12, KJV). "For as in Adam all die, even so in Christ shall all be made alive" (1 Corinthians 15:22, KJV).

Three dimensions of sin

(You might want to review Chapter 4 on "Salvation" and Chapter 16 on "Adam and Eve.")

First, sin is a lack or want of conformity to the law of God. **A sin of omission** is a failure to do what God commands. If God commands us to love our neighbor, and we fail to do so, that is sin. James describes a sin of omission to a tee: "Anyone, then, who knows the good he ought to do and doesn't do it, sins" (James 4:17).

Second, sin is defined as a transgression of the law. Here I speak about **sins of commission** whereby we commit actions, think thoughts, or speak words prohibited by God.

Third, sin is an action performed by reasonable creatures made in the image of God and who perform as free moral agents.

The devastating effects of sin

With each sin we commit, we add to our guilt and exposure to the wrath of God. Nevertheless, the grace of God is greater than all our guilt combined. As a result of our first parents' listening to Satan instead of God, human beings enter existence in a state of sinfulness. First of all, we all sin because we are sinners by nature. Paul told the Ephesians that before being saved they were by nature the children of wrath, even as others (Ephesians 2:3b). The true meaning of that is blood-curdling. "The children of wrath" means an unsaved person is targeted for God's indignation that is being built up toward their day of judgment . . . unless they "flee from the wrath to come" (Matthew 3:7, KJV) by receiving God's freely offered grace.

People have often opined, "Well, just let your conscience be your guide." That sounds good if one's conscience is informed and cultivated by the Holy Spirit and God's Word. However, if one's conscience is ignorant of Scripture or has become hardened by repeated sin, then that conscience cannot be a proper guide. Paul spoke of the reprobates who have sinned against the Holy Ghost as "Speaking lies in hypocrisy; having their conscience seared with a hot iron" (1 Timothy 4:2, KJV).That is an unspeakably horrible condition.

Unfortunately, some no longer have a conscience or either one that is warped by depravity. The New Testament (KJV) refers to the conscience thirty-one times. A few instances of good consciences are found in Acts 23:1; 24:16; Romans 9:1; 1 Timothy 1:5,19; 3:9; 2 Timothy 1:3; Hebrews 13:18; and 1 Peter 3:16,21.

Two references to flawed consciences are 1 Corinthians 8:12 and Titus 1:5.

A life of sin

A continued and willful rejection of God by the sinner has a disastrous effect on him. Such an attitude most frequently hardens the heart and renders the sinner incapable of genuine repentance and faith. On the other hand, every heart that genuinely turns to Christ will be saved, for Jesus promised: "For him that cometh unto me, I will in no wise cast out" (John 6:37, KJV).

Man's two natures

You might want to read pages 43-44 once again, since they touch on our two natures.

The old self (or "old man") is the sinful, fallen nature we possess as descendants of Adam. **The new self** is the nature we receive from God when we trust Christ as our Savior. I cannot emphasize enough how deceitful sin is. It promises pleasure—it gives pain. It offers life—it gives death. It opens up as bright as the morning—it closes as dark as the night.

The destructiveness of sin

Satan has effectively blinded humankind to the painful, damaging consequences of sin. Admittedly, certain aspects of sin are enjoyable for a fleeting moment. Paul wrote of Moses' "Choosing rather to suffer affliction with the people of God, than to enjoy the pleasures of sin for a season" (Hebrews 11:25, KJV). Sooner or later, sin will result in a form of destruction. In its wake, sin produces hurt, illness, remorse, shame, and at last, death. Sin may result in loss of property, freedom, family, and even life itself. Even as believers, we can grieve the Holy Spirit, lose our testimony, and break our fellowship with God.

Our Father's discipline

Our loving Father has gifted us with the Holy Spirit to convict us of sin. If we are unresponsive to the Spirit, our Heavenly Father will discipline us in love."For whom the Lord loveth he chasteneth, and scourgeth every son whom he receiveth" (Hebrews 12:6, KJV). It is important that

He disciplines believers to prepare them for their eternal home in heaven. Begin every day with a commitment to walk in the Spirit and keep your eyes on Jesus and the Cross. The Holy Spirit will become as important to you as you allow Him to be. He is polite and longsuffering. He won't force Himself on you but will sit back quietly, waiting for you to surrender and give Him absolute control.

A few of Satan's favorite lies

- If you obey God, you'll be miserable.
- The abundant life is trouble-free.
- Unbelievers don't want to hear the Gospel.
- You couldn't help yourself because the temptation was too great.
- If you fail, you're a failure.
- You are what others think of you.
- God can't use you.
- You can't obey God.

It is interesting that Satan lies to unbelievers to convince them they are not guilty, while he lies to believers to convince them they are guilty!

The unpardonable sin

Jesus taught that is a person speaks against Him, he can be forgiven . . . but if he speaks against the Holy Spirit, he will not be forgiven in this age or the age to come. To deny the Holy Spirit, along with His word and power, is to commit the unpardonable sin (see Matthew 12:31-32; Mark 3:29; Luke 12:10; Leviticus 17: 11-14). Blasphemy against the Holy Spirit is to reject and resist the wooing of the Spirit to the extent that one is so morally barren he attributes Satan with what is plainly God's work. The scribes and Pharisees had accused Jesus of performing miracles in the name of Beelzebub ("lord of the flies," a god), actually another name for Satan. There is tremendous confusion over what constitutes this pernicious sin. It is not murder, lying, stealing, suicide, adultery, or taking the Lord's name in vain. If you are worried about committing it, that proves *you have not for your conscience is still active*.

Jim Henry in the *Holman Bible Dictionary* has noted: "To blaspheme means to speak an insult against someone as to defame the person's reputation and character. The unpardonable sin is a persistent and deliberate sin against light, maintained in the face of the positive work of the Holy Spirit. This can happen to people today . . . The unpardonable sin is committed today when one sets mind and will and spirit against the Holy Spirit. This is telling the Spirit that He is trying to do something evil in the person's life by pointing one to Jesus. When do people reach that point? No one knows for sure, but each time people reject the movement of the Holy Spirit and Jesus' claim upon their lives, the sense of urgency and conviction gets weaker until, finally, it is too late."

If you have not accepted Christ, I pray you will today, for "Now is the accepted time; behold, now is the day of salvation" (2 Corinthians 6:2b, KJV). Putting it off is dangerous and deadly.

Redemption through Jesus, the 'second Adam'

God promised not only a Messiah, a Redeemer for mankind, but also a restoration to the wholeness with which He created mankind. God promises it through God the Son, who would become a man, "the second Adam" who would face the same kind of temptation that all human beings face, yet without ever sinning. He would be fully human, so human it would be as though He were not God; and yet so much God it would be as though He were not man.

Jesus could have answered no to the Cross, but He willed to do God's will, praying to the Father, "Not my will, but thine be done" (Luke 22:42). Jesus turned down all the subtle suggestions of Satan and his seemingly logical arguments. Yet, Jesus trusted His Heavenly Father rather than the deceiver. Thus, Jesus became the second Adam, the whole man, the Savior of man, through whom you and I can be made whole human beings now.

Defended by the Holy Spirit, as was the second Adam

Our Lord and Savior did not sin. Yet, all the rest of us have and will. The Holy Spirit assures us that after we receive Christ, we may sometimes become confused because the old temptations resurface. We are subject to the sins of the flesh and the spirit—lust, greed, covetousness, impatience, losing our temper, becoming prideful, and exhibiting jealousy. This is distressing and may lead to spiritual depression. The moment we received Christ and were regenerated by the Holy Spirit, we were given a new nature. However, when our old sin nature begins to assert itself, a new believer may begin to doubt the reality of his salvation. This is the devil at work.

The Holy Spirit gives us assurance that we are redeemed. "The Spirit himself testifies with our spirit that we are God's children" (Romans 8:16). Pray each day for forgiveness of sins (see 1 John 1:9). Trust in and keep your eyes on Jesus (see Hebrews 12:1-2). In addition to His role in converting persons, the Spirit cultivates Christians' character, comforts them, and bestows spiritual gifts by which we serve God through the church. His presence in the Christian is the assurance of God to nurture the believer toward fullness in Christ. He enlightens and empowers individual believers and the corporate fellowship of the Church in worship, evangelism, and service.

No wonder John Newton called grace "Amazing"

Only God's grace can incorporate us into His holy fellowship and enable us to fulfill His creative purposes. The sacredness of human personality is evident in that God created humans in His own image, and that Christ died for mankind, Therefore, every person possesses dignity and is worthy of respect and Christian love.

Through grace God canceled our sins by nailing them to Christ's Cross. In that demonstration of divine love, God wrested away Satan's power to condemn us for our sin. The believer's unconditional acceptance by Christ is a profound, life-changing truth. Salvation is not simply a ticket to heaven. It is the beginning of a dynamic, new relationship with God. We are united with Him in an eternal, inseparable bond.

> For I am convinced that neither death nor life, neither angels nor demons, neither the present nor the future, nor any powers, neither height nor depth, nor anything else in all creation, will be able to separate us from the love of God that is in Christ Jesus our Lord (Romans 8:38-39).

We are bound in an indissoluble union with Him, as fellow heirs in Christ. The Holy Spirit has sealed us into that relationship, and we are consummately secure with Christ (Ephesians 1:13-15).

Receiving God's redemption

"Yet all who received Him, to those who believed in his name, he gave the right to become children of God (John 1:12).

We are to **believe** that He died on the cross for us and rose again from the dead so we can be saved.

We are to **receive** Him personally into our hearts. God has done all that is necessary to make our salvation possible, but, like any other gift, we must receive it.

I invite you this moment to pray, asking Christ to forgive you of your sins and inviting Him to enter your life as your personal Lord and Savior.

"God has given us eternal life, and this life is in his Son. He who has the Son has life; he who does not have the Son of God does not have life. I write these things to you who believe in the name of the Son of God so that you may know that you have eternal life" (1 John 5:11-13).

May God bless you as you commit your life to Christ and follow Him throughout this life and the life to come. And as you face that day in the future when He will call you to spend eternity with Him in heaven, may you boldly testify with the apostle Paul, "I know whom I have believed, and am convinced that he is able to guard what I have entrusted to him for that day" (2 Timothy 1:12).

For thought and discussion

1. There are two kinds of death. What are they? What is the difference between the first death and the second?
2. What was the difference between Abel's and Cain's offerings?
3. List the three dimensions of sin. Give examples from your own experience or the lives of others.
4. What does the unpardonable sin constitute? If one is worried about committing it, has she/he? Explain your answer.
5. What are some of Satan's favorite lies? Have you ever been duped into believing any of them?
6. How did Christ cancel our sins?

PART VII

Bible Prophecies for the End of Time

Watch therefore, because you do not know on what day your Lord comes. This know, that if the master of the house had known in what watch the thief would come he would have watched and would not have permitted his house to be robbed. Wherefore you also be prepared, because in the hour when you are not thinking the Son of man comes (Matthew 24:42-44).

19

The Rapture and Second Coming

At an undesignated time in the future, our triumphant Lord will lead a spectacular procession into heaven. Those in that innumerable company will be His Body, the Church, His Bride. He will descend to the air, first calling out those who are dead. Then He will snatch up all believers still living on Earth to meet Him!

But I would not have you to be ignorant, brethren, concerning them which are asleep, that ye sorrow not, even as others which have no hope. For if we believe that Jesus died and rose again, even so them also which sleep in Jesus will God bring with him. For this we say unto you by the word of the Lord, that we which are alive and remain unto the coming of the Lord shall not prevent [precede] them which are asleep. For the Lord himself shall descend from heaven with a shout, with the voice of the archangel, and with the trumpet of God: and the dead in Christ shall rise first: then we which are alive and remain shall be caught up together with them in the clouds to meet the Lord in the air: and so shall we ever be with the Lord (1 Thessalonians 4:13-17, KJV).

When Christ left His disciples He promised, "And if I go and prepare a place for you, I will come again, and receive you unto myself; that where I am, there ye may be also" (John 14:3, KJV). Paul predicted in 1 Thessalonians 4 that the **Lord Himself** is coming back for His Church, comprised of every person who belongs to Him by the right of redemption. He will shout, along with the voice of the archangel, and the trumpet of God will reverberate around the world.

Resurrection and transformation at the rapture

Those believers whose bodies have died—whose spirits have been in heaven—will rise first, their decayed bodies being transformed and reuniting with their spirits to then constitute perfect spiritual bodies. Then Christ's disciples still alive on Earth will follow them, rising to meet the Lord in the air without undergoing physical death. In his memorable resurrection chapter, 1 Corinthians 15, Paul gloried:

> In a moment, in the twinkling of an eye, at the last trump: for the trumpet shall sound, and the dead shall be raised incorruptible, and we shall be changed. For this corruptible must put on incorruption, and this mortal must put on immortality (1 Corinthians 15:52-53, KJV).

They will exchange these corruptible, mortal bodies for incorruptible, immortal ones like the resurrection body of our risen Lord. Only born-again believers will meet Christ in the air.

The tribulation

Non-believers must remain and suffer through a seven-year period of tribulation.

> For then shall be great tribulation, such as was not since the beginning of the world to this time, no, nor ever shall be. . . . Immediately after the tribulation of those days shall the sun be darkened, and the moon shall not give her light, and the stars shall fall from heaven, and the powers

> of the heavens shall be shaken (Matthew 24:21,29, KJV; see also Mark 13:24).

Christ will descend with supernatural power and glory, accompanied by the hosts of heaven. "And he will send his angels with a loud trumpet call, and they will gather his elect from the four winds, from one end of the heavens to the other" (Matthew 24:31). First Thessalonians 4:13—5:1ff. present a description of the rapture. Jesus Christ will return at the rapture "like a thief in the night"—that is, suddenly and unexpectedly (see 2 Thessalonians 5:2).

His sudden return will surprise untold billions who have rejected Him. However, it will not befuddle those of us who have accepted Him in faith, thus anticipating, and even longing for, His second coming. The Scriptures give us ample signs that presage when His return is imminent. All who believe the Bible is the authentic Word of God recognize its indisputable teachings that the Head of the Church will return at an appointed time.

Two phases of His second coming

The rapture *(parousia)* of the Church—This is the redemption referred to by the Lord in His Olivet discourse (Luke 21:28). The saints of God will meet the Lord in the air and return to heaven with Him.

The coming to earth *(apokalupsis)*—At the end of the tribulation the Lord will split the skies and return with His heavenly host—including the believers of all eras—and will defeat the forces of evil headed up by Satan and his hellish cronies, the beast and the false prophet."And give relief to you who are troubled, and to us as well. This will happen when the Lord Jesus is revealed from heaven in blazing fire with his powerful angels. He will punish those who do not know God and do not obey the gospel of our Lord Jesus" (2 Thessalonians 1:7-8). The tribulation period will have lasted seven years, and the second phase of the Lord's return will occur at the end of that horrific time.

Who are the 144,000?

The rapture will occur, as Paul wrote, "in a moment, in the twinkling of an eye," and the Bridegroom, Christ, will rescue the Church, His Bride.

Then God will send His judgments on the earth. Though those judgments will be unspeakably appalling, they will also serve as a torrent of rain that will water the seed sown in the hearts of the Jews. One hundred and forty-four thousand Jews will embrace their Messiah and imperil themselves on behalf of Christ's truth and righteousness. God will supernaturally select and protect them—12,000 from each of the twelve tribes. These Jews will apparently turn to Christ soon after the rapture (see Revelation 7:3-8). God will sustain them while death and devastation rule around the world. "A thousand may fall at your side, and ten thousand at your right hand; but it shall not come near you" (Psalm 91:7). Their preservation will testify to God's power and grace.

Those Jewish evangelists will figure strongly in reaching multitudes (see Revelation 3:9)—although Paul warned: those who deliberately reject Christ may be blinded by Satan and remain in obstinate unbelief, even after they see the Church removed from the earth (2 Thessalonians 2:9-12). Revelation seems to indicate that more people will be saved during the tribulation than during any other brief period in history. God's Word will be proclaimed with authoritative power and conviction throughout the entire earth during the world's time of great sorrow and disparity in the future.

The rapture to precede the Great Tribulation

"Ye turned unto God from idols, to serve a living and true God, and to wait for his Son from heaven, whom He raised from the dead, even Jesus who **delivereth us from the wrath** [in this case, a reference to the tribulation] **to come**" (1 Thessalonians 1:9-10, KJV, bold face mine).

"The righteous perisheth, and no man layeth it to heart; and merciful men are taken away, none considering that **the righteous is taken away from the evil to come.** He entereth into peace" (Isaiah 7:1-2a, KJV, bold face mine).

"For **God appointed us not unto wrath,** but unto the obtaining of salvation through our Lord Jesus Christ, who died for us, that, whether we wake or sleep, we should live together with him" (1 Thessalonians 5:9-10, bold face mine).

Further facts about the rapture

The Church officially came into being on the Day of Pentecost when the Holy Spirit was sent to baptize believers into a bodily union (see 1 Corinthians 12:13) and will end with the Rapture. The Lord will continue adding to His Body until it is completed, at which time He will return to snatch out of this earth all who have received Him—from the day of Pentecost until that very moment.

The word "rapture" itself does not appear in the Bible. It is a Latin word, which means to carry or snatch away into ecstasy. The word in the Greek new Testament is *harpazo*, which has been translated "caught up" (1 Thessalonians 4:17). *The rapture is imminent.* The dictionary defines "imminent" as "likely to happen without delay" or "impending." Christ asked us to watch and wait: "So you also must be ready, because the Son of Man will come at an hour when you do not expect him" (Matthew 24:44). As believers living in the Church age, we must constantly remember our Lord's warning that His rapture could happen at any moment. In Revelation 3:11 Jesus advised, "I am coming soon. Hold on to what you have, so that no one will take your crown"(see also Revelation 22:7,12,20).

Timing of the rapture

As pointed out in the Word, only God knows the exact time (see Matthew 24:36). Admittedly, there are differences of opinion concerning the second coming and the events surrounding it. There are three ideas about the rapture and its relationship to the tribulation. Some place the rapture before the tribulation ("pre-trib"); others claim that the rapture will occur after the first three-and-a-half years and before what is sometimes referred to as "the time of Jacob's trouble," the last half of the tribulation ("mid-trib"); and still others contend, at the end of that period ("post-trib").

I am personally convicted that the rapture will come immediately before the tribulation—and for many reasons. One of the most tenable is Paul's statement that the Antichrist cannot appear until that which "restrains" him is "taken out of the way" (see 2 Thessalonians 2:7). I believe the restrainer of evil in the world today is the Holy Spirit's working through the Church. So, when the Church is removed, the Antichrist will rear his ugly head.

When the Rapture occurs most of Christ's Body will already be at home with Him, waiting for their resurrection bodies. "Even so them also which sleep in Jesus will God bring with him" (1 Thessalonians 4:14b; see also 2 Corinthians 5:1-9; 1 Corinthians 15:51-53). It is inconceivable that Christ would split His Body, leaving some behind. Our Lord will not return until His Body is complete. He will not leave part of it on earth to suffer through the tribulation (Acts 15:13-18; 1 Corinthians 12:12-27; Ephesians 2:19-22; 5:25-33).

The two comings

The "day of the Lord"—a time of vengeance, darkness, gloom, and judgment (Joel 1:15; 2:1; 3:14; and Acts 2:19-21) is obviously the tribulation. The "day of Christ" (foretold in 1 Corinthians 1:8; 2 Corinthians 1:14; and Philippians 1:6,10; 2:16)—is the day of the Bridegroom and relates wholly to rewards and blessings of the saints at His coming. The coming **for** His Church is associated with praise and reward; the coming **with** His Church is associated with judgment upon His enemies—hardly the "blessed hope" of Revelation 22:12 and Luke 14:14.

At the rapture, the Lord comes **for** his saints (1 Thessalonians 4:16), while at the second coming the Lord comes **with** His saints (1 Thessalonians 3:13). At the rapture, the Lord comes only for believers, but His return to the earth will impact *all people*. The rapture is a translation/resurrection event where the Lord transports believers "to the Father's house" in heaven (John 14:3), while at the second coming believers return from heaven to the earth (Matthew 24:30).

"One taken, another left": "Then shall two be in the field; the one shall be taken, and the other left. Two women shall be grinding at the mill; the one shall be taken, and the other left" (Matthew 24:40, KJV). While this quotation indicates that there will be a separation of the people living in the days immediately preceding the great tribulation, it does not imply that half of the world's people will be taken and the other half left. Rather, Christians will be taken, whereas unbelievers will be left to pass into the great tribulation. Jesus explained in the Sermon on the Mount that the way to eternal life is narrow, and that comparatively few walk therein, whereas the road to everlasting destruction is broad and wide. We must understand these verses in the light of our Lord's other positive teachings.

"Night and Day": Jesus spoke of the Rapture as being both at night and day. Two men will in bed at night; one will be taken and the other, left. Two women will be grinding at a mill; one will be taken and the other, left. When the rapture occurs, it will be night in certain portions of the globe, but day in others. In those statements Jesus gave evidence that He knew the world was round (see Luke 17:25-37).

Bogus Security: At the time of the rapture, the world's people will have a false feeling of security, for before the day of the Lord the doctrine of peace and safety will be preached. As I write this all of this is occurring. Numbers of the world's leaders think that mankind is solving the problems of human misery and misunderstanding. They are naïve enough to feel that civilization is being put on a firm, unshakable basis without recurrence of the various ills that have plagued the human family from its beginning.

Then sudden destruction will fall on an unsuspecting world. The great tribulation will envelop the Earth in a shroud of doom. But civilization will be on a low moral plane, as it was during the days of Noah. People will depend on the whirl of society, trade, and commerce, looking forward to a bright future without the slightest premonition of the darkness ahead. (As I write this the Stock Market, which millions seem to worship as a god, has plummeted more than 550 points in a day, a record decline. Our president is meeting with the leader of Communist China, one of the most repressive societies in the world. China, admittedly planning to conquer the world, is given "favored-trade" status while enslaving millions of people. To view the signs of the times, all one must do is keep up with the media.) Then suddenly the time will arrive for the Son of man to remove His servants from the world and leave those who have not received Him.

Why so long . . . and when???

Jesus and the New Testament writers urged that we watch for the signs of the end of the age and not be caught off guard. Innumerable Bible believers who have studied the Scriptures and the signs of our times believe that the rapture is not far away. In fact, it could occur while I am completing this manuscript! What counts most of all is that we recognize: God's patience with sin is not a sign of weakness. He has tolerated the evil of the ages not because He was powerless to do anything about it, but because of His plan, mercifully and patiently, to allow one generation after another the opportunity to repent.

To this day London's Hyde Park affords a venue for speakers of every sort, from the vilest to the holiest. Once a provocative atheist had gathered a crowd and was reviling God and all Christians. Looking up toward the sky he shouted, "If there's a God up there, strike me down right now. If you don't it'll prove You don't exist!" When nothing happened he chortled, "You see, there's no God, or He would've done me in." A gentle little woman raised her hand and answered, "Young man, He's there all right. The reason He didn't destroy you on the spot is because He loves you."

God speaks rather softly today through conscience, through the evidences of nature, through the witness of His people, and through the "still small voice" of His Holy Spirit (1 Kings 19:12, KJV). In the tumultuous days described in Revelation, though, He will thunder loudly through supernatural judgments described as trumpets. While God's people often seem like pawns in the hands of political power-brokers—while disease and death seem ultimately to prevail over our fragile existence—the God of Revelation would remind us that all who trust His Son will live with Him in the end. When God pulls down the final curtain on human history, every enemy will be forced to bow their knees and "confess that Jesus Christ is Lord, to the glory of God the Father (Philippians 2:11b, KJV).

Signs of the times

"Now," Jesus admonished, "from the fig tree learn her parable: when her branch is now become tender, and putteth forth its leaves, ye know that the summer is nigh; even so ye also, when ye see all these things, know ye that he is nigh, even at the doors. . . ." "All these things" mentioned refer to the global wars, pestilences, and tremendous earthquakes in all kinds of places. "But of that day and hour knoweth no one, not even the angels of heaven, neither the Son, but the Father only" (see Matthew 24:32,33,36, KJV). Christ knows the day and hour now, since He laid aside His earthly limitations at His ascension.

This benighted Earth has undergone two World Wars, the Korean War, the Vietnam War, and thousands of lesser conflicts. At this moment, according to historians, there are at least sixty-five trouble spots on this globe where there is bloodshed, warfare, and threat of conflagrations.

Revolutionary terrorism is a constant menace, even on Main Street U.S.A.

Nearly every day there are tremors of earthquakes around the world. Diseases we once thought virtually stamped out have had a resurgence—for instance, tuberculosis, anthrax, yellow fever, and the bubonic plague. Recently discovered pestilences like HIV-AIDS, Ebola, and Ecoli have surfaced, including virulent diseases not yet labeled. Millions of people are hungry or starving to death throughout the world. Jesus predicted a widespread persecution of Christians and Jews in the end times.

We have seen the Jews regroup and Israel established as a nation in 1948. Jerusalem was freed and attached to Israel during The June War of 1967. Scripture makes it plain: the generation that sees "all these things" ought to recognize that Christ's coming is near. As we rush toward the year 2000, we sense an air of apprehension and expectation about us. The events in the Middle East, the rash of natural disasters, and the moral decadence of our day arouse in Christians the expectation that Jesus Christ will soon descend from heaven with a shout.

No different from the days of Noah (Matthew 24:37-41)

Even though there are profuse signs of Christ's coming, the majority of people resemble those of Noah's day. Refusing to believe Noah's warnings, the populace was engaged in "business as usual," along with poking fun at the old man building a ship. They were marrying and giving in marriage, eating and drinking, and doing plenty of sinning before the Deluge drowned all the unsuspecting people of the world, except Noah and his immediate family. They were engaged in that activity until the very day Noah entered into the ark. "As it was in the days of Noah, so it will be at the coming of the Son of Man" (Matthew 24:37).

The call for being alert and prayerful

The parable of the two stewards (Matthew 24:45-51)

> Who then is the faithful and wise servant, whom the master has put in charge of the servants in his household to give them their food at the proper time? It will be good

for that servant whose master finds him doing so when he returns. I tell you the truth, he will put him in charge of all his possessions. But suppose that servant is wicked and says to himself, "My master is staying away a long time," and he then begins to beat his fellow servants and to eat and drink with drunkards. The master of that servant will come on a day when he does not expect him and at an hour he is not aware of. He will cut him to pieces and assign him a place with the hypocrites, where there will be weeping and gnashing of teeth.

The parable of the ten virgins (Matthew 25:1-13)

At that time the kingdom of heaven will be like ten virgins who took their lamps and went out to meet the bridegroom. Five of them were foolish and five were wise. The foolish ones took their lamps but did not take any oil with them. The wise, however, took oil in jars along with their lamps. The bridegroom was a long time in coming, and they all became drowsy and fell asleep.

At midnight the cry rang out: "Here's the bridegroom! Come out to meet him!"Then all the virgins woke up and trimmed their lamps. The foolish ones said to the wise, "Give us some of your oil; our lamps are going out." "No," they replied, "there may not be enough for both us and you. Instead, go to those who sell oil and buy some for yourselves." But while they were on their way to buy the oil, the bridegroom arrived. The virgins who were ready went in with him to the wedding banquet. And the door was shut. Later the others also came. "Sir! Sir!" they said. "Open the door for us!" But he replied, "I tell you the truth, I don't know you." Therefore keep watch, because you do not know the day or the hour.

Words of reward

The Lord of the Church promised to reward those who are faithful. He will personally evaluate the life of every believer and bestow the proper reward. During His earthly ministry, He did not hesitate to speak of rewards for His followers (Matthew 5:12; 6:1-6,18; 10:41-42). The apostle Paul also emphasized rewards for the faithful (1 Corinthians 3:8-14; Colossians 2:18; 2 Corinthians 5:10; 2 Tim. 4:8). **The Lord saves by grace and rewards for faithfulness.** Salvation is not a reward, for it is the free gift of grace. God will give rewards for our works done in His Name. And the day of reward, at His coming for us, may occur at any moment! (Revelation 22:12).

> His lord said unto him, Well done, thou good and faithful servant: thou hast been faithful over a few things, I will make thee ruler over many things: enter thou into the joy of thy lord (Matthew 25:21,23, KJV).
>
> And the Lord said, Who then is that faithful and wise steward, whom his lord shall make ruler over his household, to give them their portion of meat in due season? (Luke 12:42, KJV).
>
> Be thou faithful unto death, and I will give thee a crown of life (Revelation 2:10, KJV).

Rapture and second coming passages

Rapture Passages

John 14:1-3
Romans 8:19
1 Corinthians 1:7-8
1 Corinthians 15:51-53
1 Corinthians 16:22
Philippians 3:20-21
Philippians 4:5
Colossians 3:4
1 Thessalonians 1:10
1 Thessalonians 3:19
1 Thessalonians 4:13-18
1 Thessalonians 5:9
1 Thessalonians 5:23
2 Thessalonians 2:1
2 Thessalonians 2:3
2 Timothy 6:14
2 Timothy 4:1
2 Timothy 4:8
Titus 2:13
Hebrews 9:39
James 5:7-10
1 Peter 1:7,13
1 John 2:28-3:2
Jude 21
Revelation 2:25
Revelation 3:10

Second coming passages

Daniel 2:44-45
Daniel 7:9-14
Zechariah 2:10
Zechariah 14:1-15
Matthew 13:41
Matthew 24:1531
Matthew 26:64
Mark 3:14-27
Mark 14:62
Luke 21:25-28
Acts 1:9-11
2 Thessalonians 2:8
Acts 3:19-21
1 Thessalonians 3:13
2 Thessalonians 1:6-10
1 Peter 4:12-13
2 Peter 3:1
Revelation 22:7, 18-20
Jude 14-15
Revelation 1:7
Revelation 19:11—20:6

Rapture and second coming contrasts

Rapture/translation	**Second coming/ established kingdom**
1. Translation of all believers	1. No translation at all
2. Translated saints go to heaven	2. Translated saints return to earth.
3. Earth not judged	3. Earth is judged, and righteousness established.
4. Imminent, at any moment, signless	4. Follows predicted signs, including tribulation
5. New in the Old Testament	5. Predicted often in Old Testament
6. Believers only	6. Affects all mankind
7. Before the day of wrath	7. Concluding the day of wrath
8. No reference to Satan	8. Satan bound
9. Christ comes for His own.	9. Christ comes with His own.
10. He comes in the air.	10. He comes to earth.
11. He claims His bride.	11. He comes with His bride.
12. Only His own see Him.	12. Every eye shall see Him.
13. Tribulation begins.	13. Millennnial kingdom begins.

Christ's return to earth; order of events as I see them

• Rapture of the church before the tribulation period;

• A northern confederacy's (Russia and its allies) invasion of Israel shortly before or at the beginning of the tribulation . . .

When does the Russian invasion of Israel (described in Ezekiel 38—39) occur? Is it at the beginning of the tribulation? Is it part of the battle of Armageddon which is waged at the end of the tribulation? Or, is it the same as the battle of Gog and Magog which appears at the end of the millennium? I have placed the invasion at the beginning of the tribulation because Ezekiel 39:9 indicates that Israel will seize sufficient fuel from the defeated Russian forces to supply the nation's necessities for seven years. I can think of no reason for the mention of the seven years except to relate the time period to the lengths of the tribulation. God will supernaturally destroy these invading forces in league with other enemies of Christ and His followers.

The European nations, from all I can gather from the Word, will form a union of states; according to the Scriptures, will select a ruler of the union who will make war with other nations. He will fool the world and will sign a seven-year peace treaty with Israel, apparently giving this beleaguered nation a sense of security never enjoyed since its rebirth in 1948. He will eventually be revealed as the Antichrist. During the tribulation God will send to earth a series of judgments.

Certain Bible students place all of the judgments in the second half of the tribulation because Jesus referred to those three-and-a-half years as "the great tribulation" (Matthew 24:21). But Jesus was speaking of the Jews. The nation of Israel will experience peace during the first half of the tribulation while a sizable remainder of the world will be engulfed in nuclear war resulting from the conquests of the Antichrist. Once the Antichrist has consolidated his world empire, he will turn his attention to Israel. He will double-cross the Jews by violating their rebuilt Temple and declaring himself to be God (2 Thessalonians 2:4). Empowered by Satan, he will then pick up where Hitler left off by trying to exterminate the Jewish people as a race.

A tribulation emphasis: Judaism and the law

The church in our age is under grace, but the tribulation will be characterized by Law and Judaism with the proclamation of the Gospel of the Kingdom and Christ as the coming King (Matthew 24:13-14). The Antichrist will not be revealed until the Church, indwelt by the Holy Spirit, has gone (2 Thessalonians 2:7-9). This, however, does not rule out the working of the Spirit during the tribulation. This terrible period is referred to as the "time of Jacob's trouble" (Jeremiah 30:7), with its center in Jerusalem and the land of Israel (Daniel 12:1; Matthew 24:15-22).

At the end of the tribulation period, 200 million troops will attack Israel and will be destroyed by God and His angels (see Revelation 9:16). This massive army will consist of a confederacy of Antichrist forces, probably including Chinese, Russian, and Middle Eastern troops.

The nation of Israel will accept Christ as Messiah. As a result, God will respond by pouring out upon them the spirit of grace and supplication to spiritually revive them. Thus will the nation be born in a day. Two days later, the heavens will be rent asunder, and the Lord Jesus Christ, our Messiah, will return to earth. In that day He will stand upon the Mount of Olives and deliver His people. This program of events for the last three days of the tribulation is set forth in Hosea 5:15—6:2.

The millennial period of 1,000 years will begin.

Signs to watch

- The preaching of the Gospel to all nations;
- The European union coming together;
- Russia and her leadership;
- The Temple being rebuilt in Israel and resumption of animal sacrifices;
- Peace treaty between Israel and Islamic nations and particularly leadership by a leader outside of that area;
- The growth in consumption of oil as a result of China and other nations becoming industrialized;
- Watch for increased business activity and increased business leadership from Rome, which will become the center of world commerce in the tribulation.

If you are a Christian you should pray, even as John did, "Even so, come, Lord Jesus." In The Revelation, the last Book of the Bible, Jesus deliberately reminds us, "Behold, I come quickly" (Revelation 22:7,12, KJV). He graciously extends a final invitation to the effect that He is coming, so we must come to Him in order to "flee from the wrath to come" (see Matthew 3:7; Luke 3:7, KJV).

> And the Spirit and the bride say, Come. And let him that heareth say, Come. And let him that is athirst come. And whosoever will, let him take the water of life freely. For I testify unto every man that heareth the words of the prophecy of this book, If any man shall add unto these things, God shall add unto him the plagues that are written in this book:
>
> And if any man shall take away from the words of the book of this prophecy, God shall take away his part out of the book of life, and out of the holy city, and from the things which are written in this book. He which testifieth these things saith, Surely I come quickly. Amen (Revelation 22:17-21).

For thought and discussion

1. What are the two phases of Christ's second coming? Do you agree or disagree with this view—or are you simply undecided?
2. True or false. The exact terms "rapture" and "second coming" are in the Scriptures.
3. At the rapture who will be resurrected and transformed first?
4. Review the order of events during the end time.
5. Basically, what will transpire during the tribulation period?
6. Name several nations that will figure prominently in the end times.
7. Write down as many of the signs of the times as you can.

20
God's Judgments

For God shall bring every work into judgment with every secret thing whether it be good or whether it be evil (Ecclesiastes 12:14, KJV).

The habit in numerous churches today is either to play down this subject or ignore it altogether. In this day of "feel-good" religion—most people like to think of God as a God of love . . . and He is.

However, the Bible also reveals Him as a God of judgment and justice. He commanded the Deluge to destroy the wicked in Noah's day. He rained down fire and brimstone on the perverted cities of Sodom and Gomorrah. And throughout biblical and secular history, He has continued to exercise His righteous indignation. "Behold, the days come, saith the Lord, that I will raise unto David a righteous Branch, and a King shall reign and prosper, and shall execute judgment and justice in the earth" (Jeremiah 23:5, KJV).

God is going to judge every human being in history. The redeemed will stand before "the judgment seat of Christ" to receive rewards, but the unredeemed will appear before the overpowering "great white throne" I have previously mentioned. **If *you*** have not received Christ, ***you*** will regrettably be numbered with those who are condemned at that great white throne. Every chapter of this book has emphasized that Christ will save you from eternal disaster **if you will only trust Him as your Lord and Savior.** "The Lord is not slow in keeping his promise, as some understand slowness. He is patient with you, not wanting anyone to perish, but everyone to come to repentance" (2 Peter 3:9).

Contrast between His first and second comings

Jesus came the first time as a virgin-born child who grew into manhood. Though He was God incarnate, the Word made flesh, He voluntarily limited Himself so He could more completely identify with human beings. Years ago there was a child's prayer that went: "Blessed Jesus, meek and mild, have mercy on this little child." L. M. Maxwell wrote a classic about Him, Born Crucified. That was His "Mission Incarnate." John the Revelator combined the aspects of His first and second comings in one verse, Revelation 13:8: "And all that dwell upon the earth shall worship him, whose names are not written in the book of life of the *Lamb slain from the foundation of the world.*"

The **first time** He was "the Lamb of God, who takes away the sin of the world!" (John 1:29b). He was the Suffering Servant foretold by the prophet:

> He was despised and rejected by men, a man of sorrows, and familiar with suffering. Like one from whom men hide their faces he was despised, and we esteemed him not. Surely he took up our infirmities and carried our sorrows, yet we considered him stricken by God, smitten by him, and afflicted. But he was pierced for our transgressions, he was crushed for our iniquities; the punishment that brought us peace was upon him, and by his wounds we are healed. We all, like sheep, have gone astray, each of us has turned to his own way; and the Lord has laid on him the iniquity of us all (Isaiah 53:3-6).

The author of Hebrews also summed up facets of both comings: "Let us fix our eyes on Jesus, the author and perfecter of our faith, who for the joy set before him endured the cross, scorning its shame, and sat down at the right hand of the throne of God" (Hebrews 12:2). At His advent He ministered and served, obeying His Heavenly Father as an example for us. He referred to Himself as "gentle and humble in heart" ["meek and lowly in heart," KJV] (see Matthew 11:29). All the fruit of the Spirit were perfected in Him. He launched His ministry by reading from the scroll in the synagogue at Nazareth. The very chapter He read, Isaiah 42, was about Himself. Verse 3 prophesied of Him as being so caring and tender that He would not even break a "bruised reed" by stepping on it or snuff out "smoking flax," the wick of an oil lamp (see Matthew 12:20). What a poignant picture of our compassionate Savior! William Hunter lyricized about Jesus, "The Great Physician":

> The great Physician now is near, The sympathizing Jesus;
> He speaks the drooping heart to cheer, Oh! hear the voice of Jesus.
> Sweetest note in seraph song, Sweetest name on mortal tongue;
> Sweetest carol ever sung, Jesus, blessed Jesus.

If you have never settled on Jesus, that is why I urge you to embrace Him as your loving Lamb right now. For when He comes **the second time**, *it will be as the King of Kings and Lord of Lords and a conquering Lion.* One of the strangest references in the Bible is found in Revelation 6:16 concerning "the day of the Lord": "They called to the mountains and the rocks, Fall on us and hide us from the face of him who sits on the throne and from the wrath of the Lamb!'" This is the same meek, mild, tender Lamb who will unleash His just judgment as the "Lion of the tribe of Judah" (Revelation 5:5).

At the time of the Flood people were glorying in sin and loved it. That has not changed in all subsequent history. Every form of perversion recorded in human history is being practiced today on a far broader scale.

Aspects of God's judgment

Initially, God's judgment is corrective, intended to remind us that we must allow God to discipline us before more serious complications emerge. God can use trials and difficulties to shape us more into His image, helping us to grow in the faith. The writer of Hebrews advised, "My son, do not make light of the Lord's discipline, and do not lose heart when he rebukes you, because the Lord disciplines those he loves, and he punishes everyone he accepts as a son" (Hebrews 12:6; see also vv. 7-11).

Holiness and righteousness are among His perfect characteristics. "The Lord is righteous in all his ways, and holy in all his works" (Ps. 145:17, KJV). "Your [referring to God] eyes are too pure to look on evil; you cannot tolerate wrong"(Habakkuk 1:13).

Because of His nature, God will carry out justice and judgment. "Just as man is destined to die once, and after that to face judgment . . ." (Hebrews 9:27). You and I will die if Jesus tarries. That moment of passage is almost as unpredictable as the exact time of Christ's second coming, so it behooves us to prepare for both! The prophet Amos pled, "Prepare to meet thy God, O Israel" (Amos 4:12c, KJV). That includes us as well.

When we break the natural law, we pay a price; likewise when we abuse the environment. *But when we violate God's moral and spiritual laws, the most dreadful price of all is extracted.* "God hath appointed a day," the Scriptures assert, "in the which he will judge the world." Are you ready for that day?

Aspects of God's love

Yet, God is love. Is that incompatible with His disciplinary actions? Not at all. Parents who truly love their children exercise loving and firm direction and discipline when necessary—"tough love." *By His loving nature God would far rather cleanse and forgive you than apply punishment, whether "corporal" in this life or "the (spiritual) death penalty" in eternity.* God wants to enter your life and overflow it with His supernatural love, a love that can cause you to love the unlovely and even your avowed enemies.

His love is ceaseless. Though a believer may put Him to an open shame, though an unbeliever adamantly spurns His love . . . God still loves. Even loving earthly parents continue to love a rebellious, hateful son or daughter. Remember the story of "The Prodigal Son." The God of love "loves with an everlasting love" (see Jeremiah 33:3). He loves us in spite of our sinfulness and outright refusal to obey Him. If the Bible contained nothing but one verse, John 3:16, that would capsulate the unending, all-encompassing love of God toward us.

An urgent message for unbelievers

People have inquired, sometimes insincerely, "How could a good, loving God send anyone to hell?" He doesn't. By refusing God's gift of love, a person consigns himself to follow Satan to that terrible place (see 2 Peter 3:9). Yet, God does demand repentance (see Joel 2:12-13) and the acceptance of the grace expressed through Jesus Christ (see Romans 10:9-10). God is full of love, but God cannot countenance sin. Because of His love, He has provided mankind with a sin covering—the blood of His Son. Because of His righteousness, He must deal with those who reject that covering. That will occur when He sends His Son back to earth.

Jesus is returning in wrath, righteous indignation; He will pour out that wrath on those who have rejected His grace and mercy (see 1 Thessalonians 1:10). The Bible declares that every person is under either God's wrath or grace (see John 3:36). This is no in-between situation. What you do with Jesus will determine your eternal destiny. The late evangelist Angel Martinez noted that at the judgment, Jesus will say to God's children, "Come with me into your Father's house." To the children of the devil He will say, "You go along to your father's house, too."

Four main judgments

1. At the Cross of Calvary: There the stroke of judgment that was to fall upon all mankind fell upon Christ; accepting His finished work on Calvary, we are forever free, and our salvation never again will come into question (see John 3:14-19,36; 5-24; Galatians 2:20; 6:14-16; Colossians 2:20-23; 3:3).

2. The Judgment Seat of Christ: There each believer is to be judged and rewarded according to his deeds in the flesh. This judgment is of tremendous importance in that no believer should deliberately neglect his service under God; however, no one should serve God out of fear of punishment or for promise of reward. Love for God should be one's overriding motive. This judgment will come about following the rapture (see 2 Corinthians 5:5-10).

3. The Great White Throne Judgment: At the end of His millennial reign, Christ will call all the wicked, those who have rejected Him—

and only the wicked—before the great white throne. Upon them He will pronounce eternal doom (see Revelation 20:11-15).

4. The Judgment of Israel

The judgment at the Cross

The good news of the New Testament is that God is reconciling all unto himself and making peace through the blood of Christ's cross (see Colossians 1:19, 20). Our Lord, in speaking of His followers, stated that they who hear His Word and believe upon Him have eternal life: "Verily, verily, I say unto you, He that heareth my word, and believeth him that sent me, hath eternal life, and cometh not into judgment, but hath passed out of death into life" (John 5:24; see also Psalm 40; Hebrews 10:1-8). **The calamity that was due to strike us, was borne by Jesus, and those who accept Him are delivered (Isaiah 53:5, 6). Thus, the believer's judgment occurred at the Cross.**

Christ in His death satisfied the justice of God and paid the penalty for our sins. When we accept Him, His righteousness is imputed (credited, transferred) to us. "For by one offering he hath perfected for ever them that are sanctified" (Hebrews 10:14, KJV). The Cross, therefore, was the first judgment. Those who accept the Christ of the Cross will never come into judgment to be tried concerning their salvation.

The judgment seat of Christ

Since the judgment of the believer occurred at the Cross, there is no necessity for his coming into judgment. Yet, he will stand before the judgment seat of Christ to receive his rewards for service rendered. In 2 Corinthians 5:10 Paul wrote that the Lord will reward each person according to what he/she has done in the body: "For we must all appear before the judgment seat of Christ; that every one may receive the things done in his body, according to that he hath done, whether it be good or bad."

One must not confound this "judgment seat" of Christ with the judgment of the "great white throne," which is found in Revelation 20:11-15. The judgment of the great white throne follows the millennial age and is the tribunal before which the wicked are ushered for judgment and condemnation. That Christians will never appear before it is clear from John

5:24, which declares emphatically that those who believe on the Lord Jesus Christ shall not come into the judgment but have passed out of death into life: "I tell you the truth, whoever hears my word and believes him who sent me has eternal life and will not be condemned [judged]; he has crossed over from death to life."

Every person's work will pass in review before God and will be registered for faithfulness or unfaithfulness. Opposite each name in the books of heaven is entered with terrible exactness every wrong word, every selfish act, and every unfilled duty. According to 1 Corinthians 3:11-15, some will receive greater rewards than others, while others may garner little or no rewards. Salvation assures us of heaven, but rewards are given according to the works and deeds performed on earth. **Our faith insures us our salvation; our works, rewards.**

Characteristics of the judgment seat of Christ

First, *the judgment seat of Christ is not a judgment of unbelievers but of believers.* Paul described the person at the judgment seat of Christ as one who is saved and a brother. Second, *all believers will be there.* Paul noted that we "must" appear, a word denoting obligation and necessity. It is the same word Paul used in Acts 25:10: "I stand at Caesar's judgment seat, where I ought to be judged." Third, *although all believers will be present, this will not be a group evaluation.* It will be strictly a judgment of individual believers. Fourth, *the purpose of the occasion is to give an account of ourselves, but not of our sins.*

Because the Lord will appear a second time for salvation without reference to sin (see Hebrews 9:28), and because our sins and iniquities He remembers no more (see Hebrews 10:17), God will not bring up our past sins at the judgment seat of Christ. All of our sins were judged at the cross. The judgment seat of Christ is not a judgment to determine salvation. Rather, it is a time when as God's servants and stewards, we will stand before our Lord and give an account of what we did with what He entrusted to us.

The fifth characteristic of His judgment seat concerns the Judge, none other than the ***Lord Jesus Christ Himself.*** As the judge of both the living and the dead (see Acts 10:42), He alone has the last word at the final review. There will be no jury or deliberation. The ultimate verdict concerning our faithfulness will be His and His alone Because Jesus is "the righteous judge" (2

Timothy 4:8) who, with the authority of the Father, will judge "without respect of persons" (see 1 Peter 1:17; John 5:26-27), we will not have to worry whether we will have a fair trial.

*The **sixth** and final characteristic of the judgment seat of Christ is the timing.* Jesus said, "And, behold, I come quickly, and my reward is with me, to give every man according as his work shall be" (Revelation 22:12, KJV). Paul indicated in 1 Corinthians 4:5 that before the future time of judgment can commence, the Lord must first return. Hence, a Christian's appearance before the judgment seat will not happen immediately after he or she dies, but upon Jesus' return for the Church.

The Great White Throne Judgment

There is a sense in which this event, described in Revelation 20:11-15, is a concluding act. It will transpire 1,000 years after the resurrection of the redeemed. By that time, all of the judgments described here will have occurred. Even the devil himself will have been consigned to the "lake of fire and brimstone" (see Revelation 20:10). The Christ who suffered for our sins will sit on that throne. It will literally be a time when there will be no place for Christ's rejecters to hide. In this final resurrection—the resurrection of the unsaved dead—the sea, the grave, death, and Hades will deliver up their captives to face their eternal appointment.

It will be the climactic hour when "every knee shall bow." This bowing of the knee will not result in salvation but will be an acknowledgment that Jesus Christ is Lord and God. The day of grace, long mocked at and taken for granted, will have come to a screeching halt. In the words of the late pulpiteer, R. G. Lee, it will be "Payday Someday."

"And the books were opened, and another book was opened, which is the book of life. And the dead were judged out of those things which were written in the books, according to their works" (Revelation 20:12, KJV). The books will witness to the degree of guilt carried by the offenders. Perhaps a modern parallel is the use of video cameras against offenders in court. There is no point to argue for innocence when the act is on tape for the court to view. No one who stands before the Great White Throne will be exonerated.

"And whosoever was not found written in the book of life was cast into the late of fire" (Revelation 20:15, KJV). There it stands—a text laying bare the most solemn truth faced by men and women of all generations. No, it certainly doesn't provide "positive-thinking," good-feeling sermonic material. No smiley faces here. However, Jesus promised that when the Holy Spirit came He would "reprove the world of sin, and of righteousness, and of judgment" (John 16:8, KJV, italics mine). It is for us to believe and proclaim "all the counsel of God" (Acts 20:27).

Twofold purpose for the judgment of Israel

The majority of the world's people are oblivious to any impending judgment for their actions. Evolution and its twin, secular humanism, have convinced the masses that morality is a foundation of shifting sand. They have been brainwashed into thinking there are no absolutes and thus no ultimate authority to which they must answer for their deeds. But a day of reckoning is coming. The God who created this world and draws people to Himself through His Son will at last judge the world that rejects Him.

God has decreed a period in the future when He will judge all of the nations and people of the world. This seven-year period is referred to in the Bible by a number of terms. In the Church, it is generally spoken of as the tribulation period. Jeremiah referred to this period and captured God's purposes, for it is both for the Gentile nations and Israel: "For I am with thee, saith the Lord, to save thee; though I make a full end of all nations to which I have scattered thee, yet will I not make a full end of thee, but I will correct thee in measure, and will not leave thee altogether unpunished" (Jeremiah 30:11, KJV).

God's purpose for Israel in the tribulation is to save them from destruction during a time of intense anti-Semitism and to prepare them for their coming Messiah. He also will "correct thee [Israel] in measure" for the sins they have committed in their rebellion against Him. These two purposes are depicted in an analogy of the birth process.

Beginning of sorrows

The initial outbreak of the Tribulation is referred to as the "beginning of sorrows" (Matthew 24:8). As labor pains suddenly convulse a woman, so the judgment of God will shake Israel and the nations of the world suddenly and unexpectedly. The initial outpouring of God's judgment in the tribulation is described in the seal judgments of Revelation 6.

These judgments are devastating in themselves, but they are not nearly as intense or painful as the latter judgments of the tribulation. In these initial judgments, the rider of the white horse, the Antichrist, will begin to conquer (v. 2); a series of wars will start (vv. 3-4); famine will follow (v. 6); and 25 percent of the earth's inhabitants will die (v. 7-8). At that time believers will be martyred for their faith (vv. 9-11). Finally, natural disasters will occur (vv. 12-17) with a severity that people have never seen before.

The judgment will be excruciating. Yet, as with labor pains, the process will speed up and will intensify. This traumatic process will accomplish God's judgment on the earth. The armies of the nations will be destroyed at Armageddon. Well over half of the earth's inhabitants will die. God will make "a full end of all nations" (see Jeremiah 30:11). Israel will be judged, and two-thirds of its people will die during that time (see Zechariah 13:8-9).

Israel will be spared complete destruction, although all the armies of the earth will be marshaled against them. **Their only hope will be to call on the Messiah, and that is what they will do.** Zechariah 12:10 prophesies: "They shall look upon me [the Messiah] whom they have pierced." At that point, Israel will receive Jesus as Messiah.

The analogy of birth pangs

God uses the analogy of birth to illustrate His deliverance of Israel. Isaiah 66:7-9 predicts:

> A voice of noise from the city, a voice from the temple, a voice of the Lord that rendereth recompense to his enemies. Before she travailed, she brought forth; before her pain came, she was delivered of a man child. Who hath heard such a thing? who hath seen such things? Shall the earth be made to bring forth in one day? or shall a nation be born at once? for as soon as Zion travailed, she brought forth her children. Shall I bring to the birth, and not cause to bring forth? saith the Lord: shall I cause to bring forth, and shut the womb? saith thy God.

Notice: 1. *Israel will bring forth a man-child (the Messiah) before the time of travail (the tribulation).* Of course, this came about when Jesus was born in Bethlehem. 2. *As a result of the travail, the people of Israel will be ready to receive their Messiah.* 3. *God will not allow this to be a stillbirth.* The nation will not be destroyed during the period of labor pains. The process will be painful, but at the end the nation of Israel will be born—born spiritually (born again) as each individual Jewish person accepts Jesus' death on the Cross as payment for his or her sin and receives Him as Messiah. **For the first time in history an entire nation will accept Jesus Christ.** God's final judgment of Israel will be finished. He will deal with them for their sins, but with everlasting love He will use the circumstances to draw them to Himself.

God often works in the same manner with individuals. He allows, even thrusts troubles into our lives, to impress on us our need of Him. When matters seem the most desperate, He is ready to deliver us. As the psalmist said, "My help cometh from the Lord, who made heaven and earth" (Psalm 121:2, KJV). No trial is deeper than His grace.

No judgment without prophetic warning

God in the old days warned the prophets. How will He warn us today? The Scriptures describe many warning signs.

God warned of the flood

The people in Noah's day had drifted far from God. They were evil virtually to the extent people are today. They had reached a nadir where God had to destroy them because His holiness demanded it. The Lord revealed to Noah that He would, by means of a global flood, blot out the entire human family from the face of the globe. **All the people of the world, except Noah and his family, were destroyed. But the point is: God did not send the flood without first warning Noah, who in turn pleaded with the people to repent.**

The destruction of Sodom and Gomorrah

Lot, a worldly minded child of God, pitched his tent toward Sodom. It was not long until he moved into Sodom and became identified with the immoral people and the degenerate system of politics and social life. Today, a gross sexual sin is named after Sodom. The Sodomites were so exceedingly corrupt that Lot, though spiritually weak, became uncomfortable. His righteous soul was vexed by their ungodly deeds. No longer would the Lord tolerate this condition. Before moving into action, the Lord Jesus Christ, in His pre-incarnate state, left heaven to warn mankind of His impending action.

Because Abraham alone could be trusted, the Lord informed him that Sodom, Gomorrah, and all the cities of the Jordan plain would be destroyed. But why? Because of His beneficent nature and aware of the force and purpose of prophecy, Abraham began to intercede for his self-centered nephew, Lot. Because of this man's intercession judgment was deferred until Lot and his two daughters could be rescued. His materialistically minded wife would also have been delivered, but in disobedience she looked back and was overtaken by the judgment—turned into a pillar of salt. God patiently and carefully gave warning of impending judgment. In that instance Abraham was the prophet. That tragic story extends all the way from Genesis chapter 10 through chapter 18!

Countless volumes have appeared concerning the patriarchs, judges, good kings, and prophets who cried out for their people to repent and return to the true and living God, Yahweh.

God sent His prophets to warn all Israel—and then Israel and Judah after the kingdom was divided. Israel's history is a litany of rebellious sin, then repentance, then prosperity, then rebellion once again, then persecution and slavery, then deliverance . . . and then a repetition of spiritual declension once again.

Warnings before the tribulation

The Bible teaches that God will warn all the earth through an angel before He pours out His final bowls of wrath at the end of the tribulation (see Revelation 14:6-7). Since the entire seven-year tribulation will be a time of unprecedented wrath, God will alert Earth's people before the onset of the tribulation.

How can we recognize the season of the Lord?

In the Word of God we are given many signs of Christ's second coming (see also Chapter 19 of this book):

The signs of nature—earthquakes, famines, pestilence, and signs in the heavens, famines, violence, and wars. Like birth pangs that become more painful, Jesus predicted that the days right before His coming would have increased famines, violence, and ethnic wars, a clear picture of our planet (see Matthew 24:6-8). One of six people on earth suffer from hunger, and that will worsen. Violence is epidemic, and a study of wars since 500 B.C. shows a recent, dramatic increase of eighty-two world conflicts since 1990. All but three have been civil or ethnic.

Increase in earthquakes. From 1880 until Israel was reborn, there averaged only 2.3 earthquakes per decade worldwide above Richter 6.0. Also like increasing birth pangs, in the 1950s there were nine; in the 1960s, thirteen; in the 1970s, fifty-one; in the 1980s, eighty-six! The 1990s have already seen more than 100, with tens of thousands dead (see Matthew 24:7).

The signs of society—immorality, lawlessness, terrorism, atheistic humanism, materialism, and despair, explosion of technology, travel, and education Two key conditions described about 2,500 years ago for the second coming are that "travel and education shall be vastly increased" (Daniel 12:4, TLB). In all history, the vast increase in travel has come prior to mid-century with the skyrocketing of both ground and air transportation; in education, with the advance of science and computers.

Spiritual signs. There are negative signs like cults and Satanism. There are positive ones like the worldwide outreach of the Gospel, the pouring out of the Holy Spirit, and prophetic illumination—that is, the understanding of Bible prophecy.

The signs of technology. These include biblical prophecies that can only be explained by the development of lasers, computers, aircrafts, and nuclear weapons.

The sign of world politics. The emergence of Russia and China as major world powers; the consolidation of Europe into a loose confederation of states; the emergence of NAFTA and GATT, along with an effort at international control of the environment

The signs of Israel. The regathering of Israel as a nation in May 1948, the revival of the Hebrew language, the reclamation of land, and the occupation of the city of Jerusalem in 1967.

The two world wars—nation against nation. The First and Second World Wars in 1914-1918 and 1939-1945

The signs of Israel are more important than the others. The reason for this is that the Jewish people are God's prophetic time clock. What may we watch for?

- The Temple being rebuilt;
- Sacrificial system being reinstated;
- Israel signing a peace treaty where it is guaranteed peace by a group of nations representing the revitalized Roman Empire.

Our Lord prophesied about the latter-day re-establishment of Israel (symbolically the fig tree):

> Now learn the parable from the fig tree: when the branch has already become tender and put forth its leaves, you know that summer is near; even so you too, when you see all these things come to pass, recognize that He is near, right at the door. Truly, I say to you, this generation will not pass away until all these things take place (Matthew 24:32-34).

Many believe that the generation which was living during the re-establishment of Israel is the very generation that will see the end-of-time events materialize. That means: some of those living in 1948 will still be on earth when Christ returns. If we add four score and ten to 1948, we could be looking at twenty years hence. Yet, only God is aware of the date.

Conservative and Orthodox Jews are still watching for the first coming of the Messiah. They will not be surprised by His coming, but they will be astounded by the nail prints in His hands and the fact that it will not be His first, but His second, coming.

The end times

I, along with many evangelicals, believe that Daniel prophesied a revised Roman Empire out of which the Antichrist would arise (see Daniel 7). Ezekiel foretold that Israel would be living in peace when the land is invaded by Russia (see Ezekiel 38). Paul observed that at a time when the world would be shouting peace and safety, destruction would come suddenly (see 1 Thessalonians 5:3).

What about *you?*

Our Savior will also be our Judge at the day of judgment. Run from Him now, and you will meet Him as Judge then—and without hope. Run toward Him now, and you will have a mutual reception. He will receive you as you receive Him. The greatest thing you will ever do is give your heart and life to Christ. In the long run **every Christian is a winner and, in God's sight, a success!**

Perhaps you have heard this phrase: "Heaven is a holy place for a holy people; a prepared place for a prepared people." Are you holy and are you prepared? How will you meet Him? As a Lamb or a Lion? As a Judge or as a Justifier? God will punish unconfessed, unforgiven, unrepented-of sin. He will have the last word. "Dearly beloved, avenge not yourselves, but rather give place unto wrath: for it is written, Vengeance is mine; I will repay, saith the Lord" (Romans 12:19, KJV).

As Jesus' detractors scoffed at Him while He was on Earth, multiplied millions do today, but judgment is around the corner. Years ago there was a TV expression, "Here come de judge." That was funny in its context, but there is nothing comical for the unbeliever about the reality of . . . "Here comes The Judge, the Lion of Judah!"

For thought and discussion

1. After going back through this chapter, list at least ten signs of the times.
2. Contrast Christ's first and second comings.
3. Why are the signs of Israel extremely important? In what year was Israel re-established as a nation?
4. Jot down the signs of nature that will presage the season of the Lord.
5. Refer to biblical examples of warnings before God's judgments were exacted.
6. To what does "the beginning of sorrows" refer?

Appendix

Definitions of the Christian Faith

Accept Jesus Christ. When a person, by faith, receives Christ into his life, believing that Christ is the Son of God, that He died for one's sins, that He rose from the dead, and that He is still alive (see Chapters 4 and 5 of this book).

Angel. The literal meaning translated "angel" in both Old and New Testaments is "messenger." The good angels are spiritual beings who reside in heaven and also do God's bidding on Earth (see Matthew 1:20; 4:11; Luke 1:13,26,28; 2:9). They are superior to humans. The fallen angels were originally in heaven but were cast out when they followed Lucifer (Satan, the devil) in attempting a rebellion against God (see Chapters 14 and 15).

Baptism. The ordinance that initiates a convert into a local body or denomination of Christians. According to the denomination's policies it is performed either by sprinkling water on the head or being immersed. Baptism in the name of God the Father, God the Son, and God the Holy Spirit symbolizes the believer's faith in a crucified, buried, and resurrected Savior. It also stands for the believer's death to sin, the burial of his old life—and through Christ's resurrection—his new life (see Chapter 10).

Believer. A Christian, a disciple or follower of Jesus Christ, one who is born again into God's spiritual family (see Chapters 2,4,5, and 10),

Bible, The Holy. This sacred Book was "inspired" (God-breathed) by the Holy Spirit and is the objective revelation of God and His plan for mankind and the world. It is comprised of two main sections, the Old Testament and the New Testament. It was written, under God's direction, over a period of 1800 years (2 Timothy 3:16-17; see Chapter 9).

Born again. The act of regeneration when a person accepts Christ as Lord and Savior (see John 3:1ff., Titus 3:5; 1 Peter 1:23). The term, "born-again Christian," is often used to distinguish a mere "professing" Christian from one who is genuinely saved.

Communion, Holy (The Lord's Supper). The celebration of communion (or The Lord's Supper) is based on Jesus' Last Supper, a Passover meal, with His disciples, when He instructed them to institute it as an observance. The Supper represents the atonement of Christ as the only means of our justification (God's receiving us as righteous) and the mainstay of our new life in Christ. There is no magic in it. Observing it blesses us but it is not a saving observance. It is memorial in nature (see 1 Corinthians 11:23-26). It "shows forth" and dramatizes our Lord's broken body and shed blood on the Cross. When we partake of communion, it means we believe that Christ has made an all-sufficient substitutionary sacrifice for our sins (see Chapter 10).

Devil (Satan, Lucifer). He is referred to as the "prince of darkness," "of the power of the air," and "of the world." He is the archangel who, along with his angels (now known as devils, demons, or evil spirits), were ejected from heaven because they rebelled against God. He is the ultimate evil spirit. Only God has power over him. As Christians, who face almost ceaseless temptation by him, we must keep our faith strong through prayer, Bible study, worship, and witnessing.

Evangelical. A born-again believer, an evangelical accepts the Bible as the Holy Word of God and seeks to share his/her faith with others.

Faith. Belief in God, His Word, and His leadership. Faith is believing by receiving Christ, in spite of physical or seemingly tangible evidence. One is saved only through a combination of God's grace and faith (see John 20:29; Ephesians 2:8-9; Hebrews 11:1ff.; also Chapter 6 of this book).

Gentile. One who is not Jewish.

God. The all-knowing, all-powerful Being who created and continues to sustain the world and all living things in it. As Christians we believe in a living, loving, and merciful God, who also is holy, just, and righteous. There is only one God who is in three persons, The Father, The Son, and The Holy Spirit (see Chapters 11—13).

Grace. Grace is God operating in love toward all people. His extension of forgiveness of our sins (pardon and reconciliation) is an expression of His grace, which is often defined "as unmerited favor." Through all Christ did, God unconditionally bestows His grace on all who will accept His gift of salvation and eternal life.

Heaven (also called Paradise). The holy, perfect place, the eternal destination and home where all those who have trusted Christ will go.

Holy Spirit (Holy Ghost, KJV). The Third Person of the Trinity who, since Pentecost, has permanently resided in all believers. The baptism of the Spirit occurs when one accepts Jesus Christ as Lord and Savior. There is one baptism but many fillings in the life of a Christian (see Acts 2; Acts 4:31). The Holy Spirit is the efficient agent of our cleansing from sin and our sanctification. He is our Comforter, Counselor, Sanctifier, Guide, and Witness. Through the Spirit, Christ lives in the believer (see Galatians 2:20; also Chapter 13 of this book and Sanctification).

Justification. Justification is that judicial act of God by which He declares the sinner free from all guilt and sin, because Jesus died in his place on the Cross, and because of the sinner's faith in Christ. At conversion the believer is justified (made right with) God, and—because of the covering of Christ's blood—God then looks upon him as though he had never sinned.

Meditation. It is the activity of calling to mind, dwelling on, and applying to oneself various truths about God's works and ways learned through His Word under the tutelage of the Holy Spirit.

Omnipotence. The characteristic of God as almighty and all-powerful (see Chapter 11).

Omnipresence. The characteristic of God as being everywhere at once (see Chapter 11).

Omniscience. The characteristic of God as all-knowing (see Chapter 11).

Parable. Jesus told practical, simple stories, called parables (from the Greek, meaning that which is "thrown in" alongside), in order to convey basic truths about the human condition and God's compassion, love, judgment, and power. Jesus related over two dozen parables as recorded in the New Testament (see Chapter 1).

Prophet. One who is inspired by God to proclaim His message and also to foretell future events. An example from the Old Testament is Isaiah; one from the New, John the Baptist.

Propitiation. This is a term for Christ's substitutionary, vicarious atonement in which deserved wrath is repelled or tuned away by the satisfaction of justice

Sabbath. This is the seventh or last day of the week observed by Jews and some other bodies as a day of worship and rest. Most Christians now worship on the first day of the week because that celebrates His resurrection (see Acts 20:7).

Salvation. The divine act of being saved (converted, ransomed, redeemed) by God from sin and its punishment (here and hereafter in hell) if one accepts Christ's provisions by faith and repentance.

Sanctification. This is the process by which, according to the will of God, we are made partakers of His holiness and righteousness. It is a progressive work begun at the moment of conversion. It is carried on in the hearts of believers by the presence and power of the Holy Spirit, in the continual use of the means of prayer, reading the Word of God, fellowship with Christians, self-denial, and self-examination (see Chapters 2,4,5).

Saved. That is our condition when we have accepted Christ into our hearts. Other terms are converted, born again, ransomed, redeemed, reconciled, ransomed, and adopted into God's family.

Scripture. The books, passages, and verses of the Holy Bible, God's written Word.

Sin. Humans are sinners by nature (see Psalm 51:5; Romans 3:10,23). Sin is either by commission or omission. When we disobey God or go against His will through thoughts, attitudes, or deeds, we are sinning. Only through the grace of God may humans be freed from the payment, penalty, and punishment of sin.

Temptation. It is the enticement to do evil, to sin, that presents itself to all Christians. Our own Lord was tempted, yet without sin. Since we are imperfect, we may sin, but the Christian's new nature in Christ combats the domination of sin (see Chapters 1—2,4—5).

Trinity. Though this term is not used in the Bible, it means the perfect union of Three Persons in one God. God the Father, God the Son (Jesus Christ), and God the Holy Spirit are co-equal and co-eternal. The mystery of the Trinity is that it is humanly incomprehensible and thus difficult to express. Jesus Christ is God, and God is Jesus Christ, as well as the Holy Spirit. They are not three Gods but three Persons in the Godhead.

Virgin Birth. Jesus was born of a virgin, Mary, and was fathered by a divine act of the Holy Spirit. Jesus had no heavenly mother and no earthly father (Luke 1:37).

Word of God. This is a common term for the Scriptures, the Holy Bible—the written Word (see Chapter 9). It is also a designation for the Lord Jesus Christ, the living Word (see John 1:1-3,14; also Chapters 1,12).

INDEX

Index

About the Author

Ira M. Lane, Jr., has distinguished himself as an advocate for better health care but also as a churchman who is deeply concerned with the nation's spiritual health. He has written a number of books, pamphlets, and articles about the healthcare field. Two of his outstanding contributions in healthcare field have been securing improved indigent care funds for the poor and improvement of the quality of healthcare developmental programs. Now, from ardent study and deep conviction he prayerfully offers *The Gospel! A Layperson's Guide to Christ-centered Living for the End Times.*

From 1960 to 1993 he served as Chief Executive Officer of the Tennessee Hospital Association. An active member of the St. Paul Southern Methodist Church in Nashville, he is past Chairman of the Board of Stewards and presently continues as a member of the Board. Natives of Mississippi, he and his wife, Jan, have two grown children, a daughter and a son, and one grandchild.

He graduated from Mississippi State University and has done graduate studies at the University of Michigan and Cornell University. Prior to his notable service with the Tennessee Hospital Association, Lane was Assistant Administrator of the Greenwood-LeFlore Community Hospital in Greenwood, Mississippi. From there he accepted a position as the Director of Hospital, Physicians, and Public Relations for Louisiana Blue Cross in 1956, where he served until June 30, 1960, when he assumed his position as CEO for the Tennessee Hospital Association.

He was Chairman of the Operations Committee and a member of the Board of McKendree Village, Hermitage, TN, for twenty-five years. McKendree is a large, highly regarded healthcare and retirement facility for senior adults, operated by the United Methodist Church. Lane's professional memberships include: American Hospital Association, American Society of Association Executives, National State Hospital Association Executives Forum (was President of that organization twice), and American Management Association.

Honors received include: Meritorious Service Award from the Tennessee Licensed Practical Nurses Association; Distinguished Service Award of the Tennessee Hospital Association; Distinguished Service Award of the Memphis Hospital Council; Founders Medal of Honor from HFMA; Executive Forum Award from the National State Hospital Association Executives; Meritorious Service Award from the Tennessee Society of Nursing Service Administrators; Distinguished Service Award from the Southeastern Hospital Conference; Henry C. Hottum Award from HFMA; Outstanding Association Executive Award from the Tennessee Society of Association Executives; received the Ira M. Lane, Jr., Communicator of the Year Award from the Tennessee Society of Hospital Public Relations; received the Award of Honor from the American Hospital Association; and received the Ira M. Lane, Jr., Management Award from the Hospital Financial Management Association.

His books in the healthcare field include: *The Responsibilities of Hospital Trustees*, which was adopted by forty-two state hospital associations for distribution to their members; *The Value of Cost of Healthcare*; *The 1983 Environmental Assessment of the Hospital Industry in Tennessee; The Hospital Cost Equation*, distributed to 1800 hospitals in the Southeastern area of the nation; *Guide for Hospital Governance;* and the 1993 *Environmental Assessment of the Healhcare Industry in Tennessee.*